WRITING STUDIES RESEARCH IN PRACTICE

WRITING STUDIES
RESEARCH
IN PRACTICE

METHODS AND METHODOLOGIES

Edited by Lee Nickoson and
Mary P. Sheridan

WITH A FOREWORD BY GESA E. KIRSCH

SOUTHERN ILLINOIS UNIVERSITY PRESS
CARBONDALE AND EDWARDSVILLE

Library of Congress Cataloging-in-Publication Data
Writing studies research in practice : methods and
methodologies / edited by Lee Nickoson and Mary
P. Sheridan, with a foreword by Gesa E. Kirsch.
    p. cm.
Includes bibliographical references and index.
    ISBN-13: 978-0-8093-3114-7 (pbk. : alk. paper)
    ISBN-10: 0-8093-3114-4 (pbk. : alk. paper)
    ISBN-13: 978-0-8093-3115-4 (ebook)
    ISBN-10: 0-8093-3115-2 (ebook)
1. English language—Rhetoric—Study and teaching.
2. Report writing—Study and teaching. I. Nickoson, Lee, 1967– II. Sheridan, Mary P., 1966–
PE1404.W747 2012
808'.042072—dc23   2011052220

To our academic and personal role models:

the researchers represented in this collection, who whether in person or through their scholarship have inspired and guided our work for many years

and our children, Mary P.'s daughter, Mary Pauline, and sons, Luke and Aidan, and Lee's daughter, Olivia. Our children's playfulness and curiosity remind us that the world is an interesting place and our lives are full of wonder.

Contents

Foreword: New Methodological Challenges
for Writing Studies Researchers

Gesa E. Kirsch

Readers of this volume can expect to find exciting new work on research methods and methodologies. When Patricia Sullivan and I first published *Methods and Methodology in Composition Research*, the "social turn" was prominent in rhetoric and composition studies (see Journet, this volume, for more details). Since that time, a number of other "turns" have shaped research in the field. Among the most notable trends has been a focus on ethics and representation, on computers and composition, on visual literacy, on activist research, on globalization, and on archival research, to name a few. We now regularly study rhetorical activities in a much-wider range of contexts than twenty years ago: in after-school settings (e.g., Sheridan, this volume), in service-learning and community organizations (e.g., Goldblatt), in the many social networking sites unfolding on the web (Hawisher and Selfe; Haas, Takayoshi, and Carr; Palmquist, Mullin, and Blalock, this volume), in historical contexts (e.g., Rohan; Lamos, this volume), and among groups often considered to reside at the margins of society (e.g., Inoue, this volume; Canagarajah, this volume; Daniell; Mathieu; Royster; Sohn). Much of this new research is taking place within a U.S. context, but composition scholars are also beginning to cross borders and study rhetorical activities in international and transnational contexts (e.g., Lunsford, this volume; Daniell and Mortensen; Hesford and Schell). Clearly, these expanding contexts for writing studies challenge researchers to adapt and refine research methods and to develop new ones.

One particular challenge researchers now face is adapting different research methods to diverse settings and reporting this research in genres that best reflect these methods. Many scholars do this by creating hybrid genres. Take, for example, Charlotte Hogg's fascinating study *From the*

challenges   genre disruptions

Garden Club: Rural Women Writing Community. In her research, Hogg
uses a variety of research methods to study rural women's literacy, including historical research, interviews, participant-observation, oral history,
reflection, memoir, and autoethnography. Since Hogg has a personal connection to the rural women she studied (including her grandmother and
other women she knew as a child) and to the town, Paxton, Nebraska
(where she spent several years as a child), she includes family history, childhood memories, and description of town events in her research narrative.

Works like these raise many questions: How do we read and interpret
the author's "passionate attachment" to her subject (a term coined by
Jacqueline Jones Royster in *Traces of a Stream*)? How do we gain a critical
distance if the author is so central to the research narrative? Or is a critical distance not desirable? Where does research end and memoir begin?
How do we assess this kind of hybrid genre? As research? As memoir? As
a historical narrative? What are the qualities for excellence in any one of
these genres? Clearly, there is value to reflecting on cultural memory, to
researching a subject with a personal connection, and to using local history as a starting point. Yet, this new kind of work also poses challenges
for readers and writers alike: how to be respectful yet also critical, descriptive yet not excessively so, analytical while narrating a town history. These
challenges are not easy to meet, but they offer exciting opportunities for
new kinds of insights, writing, and knowledge. As Royster and I note
elsewhere, it is precisely "in this balancing act that we find the promise
and potential in much of the new work in our field" (662).

In her chapter in this volume, Liz Rohan argues for the value of this
kind of research—research that attends to the local, evolves over time, and
proceeds as a "lived process." Rohan argues that researchers who attend
to place, imagination, and intuition in their archival work often create
deeper connections with their subjects, which, in turn, can yield richer
findings. Importantly, this new understanding of archival work leads to
methodological changes that Rohan begins to sketch out in her chapter.
Furthermore, in *Beyond the Archives: Research as a Lived Process*, Rohan
and I document the power of this approach to research: how exploring a
personal connection, a chance discovery, or an intriguing fact can inspire
researchers, foster a commitment to the work, and bring passion into the
research process.

A second methodological challenge researchers face frequently these
days arises from the effort to foster interactive, collaborative, reciprocal,
mutually beneficial, nonhierarchical relations with research participants
and their communities. Researchers now regularly invite participants

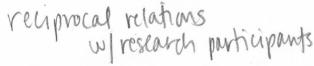

to become coresearchers, copresenters, and coauthors of their work. At times, researchers turn over control almost completely to research participants. For instance, Cynthia L. Selfe and Gail E. Hawisher, in their collaborative work with transnational graduate students, asked participants to document, video record, and reflect on their own literate practices as they communicate across different cultures, languages, and continents in settings of their choosing (e.g., home, office, library). Many of these students had moved from one region of the world to another for political, economic, or educational reasons and used different media to communicate with different audiences—e-mail, texting, phone calls, and traditional letters. In this particular study, Selfe and Hawisher asked participants to create self-representations of their literate lives: Participants could record literate activities they deemed important, at times that suited them, in locations they felt comfortable doing so. Participants were also invited to include commentary, reflection, and soundtracks in their video recordings. Researcher-participants collaboratively analyzed, interpreted, presented, and published their work in different venues, such as at conferences, in journals, online, and in video recordings. This study is an interesting, rich example of the new dimensions of collaborative work, challenging us to rethink traditional roles/boundaries between researchers and participants, the shape of research material (what's included, highlighted, and omitted, and who does the selecting), and the uses of different media to represent this work.

In the current volume, Christina Haas, Pamela Takayoshi, and Brandon Carr study one example of how the many interactive, searchable, and social networking sites now available on the web have radically transformed language use among the current generation of students—how they communicate, network, and share information. Specifically, they focus on the features and uses of instant messaging among undergraduate students and call for the development of methodologies that reflect these new forms of communication. They illustrate the importance of getting access to "insider" information, in this case, working collaboratively with research participants who may use technologies in ways that researchers might not know or imagine. Haas, Takayoshi, and Carr point to the rich literacy lives that students experience online—often outside the classroom and outside the domain of supervision—and suggests that these literate lives beg a host of new research questions.

A third methodological challenge arises directly from the increasingly collaborative nature of research: As writing studies has expanded its scope and breadth to include the rhetorical activities of those whose

collaborative.

voices have been neglected, silenced, or rarely heard, scholars are showing a renewed concern for representing participants with respect, care, and complexity. This challenge is equally important whether we write about contemporary or historical figures. In our collaborative work, Royster and I explore how to represent historical figures fairly, thoughtfully, and honestly. We ask, "When we study women of the past, especially those whose voices have rarely been heard or studied by rhetoricians, how do we render their work and lives meaningfully? How do we honor their traditions? How do we transport ourselves back to the time and context in which they lived, knowing full well that is not possible to see things from their vantage point?" (648). These questions are particularly challenging when researchers study historical figures whose values or worldviews they may not share. How do we represent these groups fairly, respectfully, and accurately? Researchers are more likely now to recognize the vulnerability of historical figures and their own responsibility to create comprehensive, multidimensional, and complex portraits of those who came before us. Questions of ethics and representation are of critical importance here.

The same kinds of ethical challenges are also faced by researchers investigating institutional histories: When they uncover the histories of programs, administrators, or policies that appear conservative, perhaps even bigoted, sexist, or racist from our perspective, how do they represent them fairly, thoughtfully, and critically at the same time? Steve Lamos offers some answers to these questions in his fascinating chapter "Institutional Critique in Composition Studies" (this volume). Lamos discusses the challenge of writing institutional histories with honesty, accuracy, and enough historical detail to capture the culture and politics of the time but without pointing a blaming finger at key administrators or policy makers who may have carried out the mission of their institutions even if they did not create or agree with those policies. Ethics and representation, then, play a key role when researchers study people, places, or programs whose beliefs, values, and worldviews they might find at odds with their own.

Similarly, and perhaps more obviously, living research participants and communities deserve careful, thoughtful, and ethical representations. In this volume, Heidi A. McKee and James E. Porter examine the vulnerabilities of web participants in social-networking groups. They argue that even though web users may post their writing on publicly accessible blogs or social-networking sites, researchers need to remain vigilant about participants' privacy, vulnerability, and consent. McKee and Porter offer a thoughtful analysis of distinct web forums and provide a matrix for thinking systematically about ethical issues when studying literacy, social networking, and rhetorical activities on the web—a rich, new territory of potential insights and quandaries.

The contributors to *Writing Studies Research in Practice* rise to the many new challenges contemporary writing researchers face. They chart important new directions for research and examine the enduring power of some research methods and the evolving nature of others. They also reflect on the field's dynamic changes and offer their visions for the future. What struck me in particular when reading the chapters in this book is that scholars in composition studies write with self-confidence and experience, reflecting on how research methods and methodologies have evolved over the last few decades. No longer do scholars apologize for using, adapting, or borrowing methods that originated in the social sciences; instead, these scholars offer critiques and insights on what methods have proven useful for what kinds of questions (Fishman), reflect on their own "proclivities" (Broad) and "research stance" (Grabill), explain how methods are changing to meet emerging questions (Selfe and Hawisher), articulate the historical and theoretical assumptions of different methodologies (Journet), and argue for approaches to research that can contribute to social change (Blair).

Writing Studies Research in Practice also offers welcome practical, hands-on advice from scholars working on a wide range of topics. Their pragmatic advice makes this book a valuable resource for scholars interested in research and methodology, in designing and conducting research, and in better understanding questions of ethics and representation. This inspiring collection shows that writing studies is now a mature and well-established discipline. Along with that growth and maturity comes the accompanying development of new journals, new web sites, new conferences, new resources, and new research methods—all of which shape much of the discussion in this volume. *Writing Studies Research in Practice* brings home that it is an exciting time to be in rhetoric and writing studies: The field invites, recognizes, and rewards innovative research and provides many forums for sharing, enhancing, and enriching our understanding of methods and methodologies.

Works Cited

Daniell, Beth. *A Communion of Friendship: Literacy, Spiritual Practice, and Women in Recovery.* Carbondale: Southern Illinois UP, 2003. Print.

Daniell, Beth, and Peter Mortensen. *Women and Literacy: Local and Global Inquiries for a New Century.* New York: Erlbaum/NCTE, 2007. Print.

Goldblatt, Eli. *Because We Live Here: Sponsoring Literacy beyond the College Cur-*

riculum. Cresskill: Hampton, 2007. Print.

Hesford, Wendy S., and Eileen E. Schell. "Configurations of Transnationality: Locating Feminist Rhetorics." *College English* 70.5 (2008): 461–70. Print.

Hogg, Charlotte. *From the Garden Club: Rural Women Writing Community*. Lincoln: U of Nebraska P, 2006. Print.

Kirsch, Gesa E., and Jacqueline Jones Royster. "Feminist Rhetorical Practices: In Search of Excellence." *College Composition and Communication* 61.4 (2010): 640–72. Print.

Kirsch, Gesa E., and Liz Rohan, eds. *Beyond the Archives: Research as a Lived Process*. Carbondale: Southern Illinois UP, 2008. Print.

Kirsch, Gesa E., and Patricia A. Sullivan, eds. *Methods and Methodology in Composition Research*. Carbondale: Southern Illinois UP, 1992. Print.

Mathieu, Paula. *Tactics of Hope: The Public Turn in English Composition*. Portsmouth: Boynton, 2005. Print.

Royster, Jacqueline Jones. *Traces of a Stream: Literacy and Social Change among African American Women*. Pittsburgh: U of Pittsburgh P, 2000. Print.

Selfe, Cindy, and Gail Hawisher, with Patrick Berry, Shafinaz Ahmed, Vanessa Rouillon, Gorjana Kisa, and Mirza Nurdic. "Transnational Literate Lives: An Emerging Research Methodology for a Globalized World." *Practicing Research in Writing Studies: Reflexive and Ethically Responsible Research*. Ed. Katrina Powell and Pamela Takayoshi. Cresskill: Hampton, forthcoming. Print.

Sohn, Katherine Kelleher. *Whistlin' and Crowin' Women of Appalachia: Literary Practices since College*. Carbondale: Southern Illinois UP, 2006. Print.

Acknowledgments

Several people helped us turn our idea for this collection into a reality. In particular, we thank Gesa E. Kirsch for her suggestion we take up this project; Karl Kageff and the Southern Illinois University Press editorial team, in particular Wayne Larsen and Mary Lou Kowaleski, for their encouragement and keen eyes; the contributors for being a pleasure to work with even during speedy turnarounds; the external reviewers, who offered helpful guidance; the students in Lee's fall 2009 research-methods class for their feedback on what graduate students want from such a collection; Kevin Roozen, Liz Rohan, and Karen J. Lunsford for being sounding boards about this collection; Caroline Cole for her close reads of our chapter drafts; and Jenny Venn for her fabulous cover art. This collection truly was a collaborative effort, and we will be forever grateful to each of the many people who helped us bring *Writing Studies Research in Practice* to publication.

WRITING STUDIES RESEARCH IN PRACTICE

Introduction: Current Conversations on Writing Research

Mary P. Sheridan and Lee Nickoson

Regardless of the field or discipline, conversations about methods and about the motivations for and possible implications of those methods (methodologies) have often focused on foundational questions, such as what are people doing? How are they doing it? And why are they doing it this way? Even as these questions endure, the specifics change. This has been the case in writing studies, where radical changes in what we consider writing and research on writing over the last twenty years have prompted a need to adapt traditional types of research. Dramatic changes in digital writing and research, for example, challenge traditional mono-modal assessments of what constitutes writing; a greater understanding of classrooms as nestled in complex networks calls for alternative approaches to these traditional sites of study; and the increasing recognition of extracurricular writing demands that we expand where we study.

Attending to the changing disciplinary landscape challenges scholars to pursue new ways of investigating what it means to study writing today. As we examine the practical, theoretical, and ethical issues facing contemporary writing researchers today, we need to ask: What questions about writing interest us now? What methods can help us address our field's questions? What do we gain, and lose, from adopting a particular methodology? Although *Writing Studies Research in Practice: Methods and Methodologies* explores these questions from a multitude of intra-disciplinary perspectives, the conversations contained here maintain a shared understanding of research as situated, systematic, and reflective investigation of literate activity with the goal of deepening our understanding of why, how, when, where, and what writers write. The following twenty chapters represent variously positioned arguments on how and

def of writing research

1

why research about writing is currently being conducted. Contributing authors offer practical advice as well as reflect upon their experiences with particular methods and methodologies, a perspective that all too often is absent from a study's final publication. In this way, *Writing Studies Research in Practice* invites readers to contemplate the many pragmatics and problematics involved in studying writing from researchers directly and, in so doing, invites readers to become versed in multiple practices of our field so that we might continue to develop the practices needed to identify and study today's pressing research questions.

Enduring Questions

Readers will find that many of the following chapters describe *what* the researchers do and *how* they do it—the methods or practices researchers engage in as they identify research topics, design strategies for collecting, managing, and interpreting the collected data, and determine how to represent their findings. These are important steps in any research project, and yet, such questions will make little sense without knowing the *whys* of research. Consequently, contributors also explain their methodologies, the epistemological and theoretical interests that drive researchers' understanding of their study and of themselves (their roles and responsibilities) within that study. Although readers may find the distinction between *methods* and *methodologies* to be hazy, such slippage exposes the complex ways researchers navigate this intertwining of practice and theory.

Readers will also find many current research approaches bound to past incarnations, though the contours of these approaches shift and blur in powerful ways. One place this blurring occurs is in what we consider literate activity. For example, Christina Haas, Pamela Takayoshi, and Brandon Carr illustrate that although emoticons play a central role in pervasive, everyday writing practices such as texting, these visuals also challenge our understanding of what counts as a content unit for analysis in our studies of writing. A second place this blurring occurs is in just how multilayered learning environments are. As Asao B. Inoue, Steve Lamos, and Karen J. Lunsford each argue, literacy is learned and practiced in complicated, seemingly invisible ways, yet we carry the values of complex activity networks with us as we learn and research, as we move from space to space. A third place we see this blurring of boundaries is in the overt overlap of methods: Richard Haswell and Bob Broad each argue for qualitative researchers to consider using quantitative methods, and vice versa, as the situation demands. The many discussions housed here illustrate that writing research is indeed a rich, dynamic, and multipositioned enterprise.

The following chapters describe the methods writing studies researchers use in order to capture the complexity of this enterprise.

Origins of This Collection

This collection is the result of a conversation that began in the spring of 2007, when Lee learned she would teach a graduate seminar on research methods the following fall semester. This was her first foray into teaching such a course, the sole methods course required of students enrolled in her home program. Lee understood her charge to include introducing graduate students to a contemporary landscape of writing research and helping them think about why this landscape may be a dominant one. As Lee set about determining what texts, discussions, and questions might best serve the needs of rising researchers, she reached out to Mary P., who had done similar investigative work for methods courses she had taught at her home institutions.

In the months that followed, we discussed both enduring questions and recent changes to the field in order to understand what, exactly, is included under the umbrella of writing research today. In the process, we examined the methodological extensions and innovations that coincided with research into contemporary practices, such as research that sought to reimagine how technology has contributed to our always-evolving understandings of what we consider writing, how we conduct our research, and where we publish our findings. We privileged work that speaks to diverse audiences and influences on our classroom practices and that represents the explosion of research into the extracurriculum. Yet, when we searched for collections to help us present these efforts to our students, we were surprised by the continued reliance on texts from twenty-plus years earlier and two in particular: Janice Lauer and J. William Asher's *Composition Research: Empirical Designs* (1988) and Gesa E. Kirsch and Patricia A. Sullivan's *Methods and Methodology in Composition Research* (1992) (see the chapter by Rickly in the current volume). These were foundational texts for our own understandings about researching writing, so we were pleased to be in familiar territory, but much has changed since these volumes were published. Where were the reflective, generalist, edited collections that captured the methodological innovations within the field of writing studies?

Now, there have been many important developments to the body of literature on writing research. In the last few years alone, the field has benefited from edited handbooks on and syntheses of research: Charles MacArthur, Steve Graham, and Jill Fitzgerald, *Handbook of Writing*

Research; Peter Smagorinsky, *Research on Composition: Multiple Perspectives on Two Decades of Change*; Charles Bazerman, *The Handbook of Research on Writing: History, Society, School, Individual, Text*; and Charles Bazerman and Paul Prior, *What Writing Does and How It Does It*. Similarly, several collections specialize in writing studies' subdisciplines: Heidi McKee and Dànielle DeVoss, *Digital Writing Research*; Heidi McKee and James Porter, *The Ethics of Internet Research: A Rhetorical, Case-Based Process*; Gesa E. Kirsch and Liz Rohan, *Beyond the Archives: Research as a Lived Process*; Alexis E. Ramsey, Wendy B. Sharer, Barbara L'Eplattenier and Lisa Mastrangelo, *Working in the Archives: Practical Research Methods for Rhetoric and Composition*. Additionally, a few book-length offerings continue the straightforward, "how-to" approach to conducting research found in Wendy Bishop's earlier work on ethnography, *Ethnographic Writing Research: Writing It Down, Writing It Up, and Reading It*, such as Ann M. Blakeslee and Cathy Fleisher's *Becoming a Writing Researcher*.

These texts illustrate that as much as things have changed over the last many years, the fundamental "hows" and "whys" of research have not; researchers continue to grapple with the practical, theoretical, and ethical problems involved in any study of writing, whether in traditional or emerging subdisciplines. And yet, these texts do not provide those new to particular methods or methodologies a survey of contemporary writing studies research as innovative practice today. Thus, we envisioned *Writing Studies Research in Practice* as a purposeful revisiting of Kirsch and Sullivan's *Methods and Methodology in Composition Research*. We, too, solicited chapters written in a purposefully reflective manner so as to expose the lived, often unruly way research actually happens, especially when researchers are self-consciously reworking previous methods and methodologies. Even as we approached *Writing Studies Research in Practice* as a revisiting of Kirsch and Sullivan's influential text, it is its own scholarly effort, reflecting how and why contemporary researchers are adapting and extending existing methods to better address the concerns of today's practitioners.

As we thought about who may be best poised to contribute to such a project, we knew we wanted a range of researchers, from state universities to private colleges and from experienced researchers pushing their own work in innovative ways to those new to the professorate who may be bringing fresh ideas about what, how, and why to research contemporary writing practices. We charged these researchers to address what they feel are the benefits, challenges, and considerations involved in enacting various forms of writing research. In particular, we asked authors to

[handwritten marginal note: re-envisioning of Kirsch + Sullivan]

consider four questions: How do they understand and come to writing research? What practical, theoretical, and ethical problematics confront writing researchers today? What does one gain and lose from adopting a particular methodology? And, finally, what might researchers be overlooking, excluding, silencing?

These questions, we believe, can be particularly useful for the two main audiences we seek to engage: new(er) writing studies researchers who may be embarking on their first long-term research project and more-experienced writing scholars who may appreciate learning about methods they may not have firsthand experience with, whether for themselves or for students they teach and advise. For newer researchers, the collection offers diverse methods and methodologies that while by no means exhaustive, might help people to consider and ultimately decide which ones to engage in their own research. For experienced scholars, the collection can help them locate themselves and their students in a greater range of conversations about what writing researchers do and why they do it. Both audiences will find a breadth of approaches writing studies scholars use, as well as varied reflections about why researchers use these approaches, from introspective discernings of unacknowledged stances (e.g., Grabill) to outward calls about how we should make our research practices more public to other researchers and to broader constituencies (e.g., Broad; Haswell; Palmquist, Mullin, and Blalock). In doing this, the chapters posit methods and methodologies as heuristics, fluid models that can help researchers best address their research needs.

Organization

The following chapters detail the practices and underlying beliefs of contemporary researchers within writing studies. To do that, each chapter situates contemporary research within historical traditions, describes key practices that distinguish particular methods, and reflects upon areas where these methods could be extended to meet the questions these researches are currently investigating. We divided this collection into three sections. The first situates research approaches that have been historically important to writing studies research. Extensions in these research traditions have had a strong impact on where writing researchers often work: academic and community settings. Consequently, the second and third sections of the collection focus on the diverse issues related to researching in these sites. The second section focuses on research within traditional composition settings. The third section focuses on, as the title indicates, reconceptualizing what we consider traditional methodologies and sites of inquiry.

The first section, "Reimagining Traditional Research Practices," builds upon, questions, and expands some of the more commonly used approaches to conducting writing research, such as narrative, historical, interview, content analysis, ethnography, and cognitive research. Debra Journet and Liz Rohan open this section by each analyzing how the stories we tell about ourselves powerfully shape our research, a conclusion that highlights how these stories themselves need to be examined. Cynthia L. Selfe and Gail E. Hawisher are also interested in narratives, but they advocate for more participatory analysis from those reading their research than has historically been an option, such as when they post their video-taped interviews online. Christina Haas, Pamela Takayoshi, and Brandon Carr as well as Kristine L. Blair are also interested in how technological affordances contribute to changing research practices. Overtly invoking the discourse analysis tradition, Haas, Takayoshi, and Carr examine how emerging talk and text, such as emoticons, call researchers to remix textual and visual methods and methodologies for content or discourse analysis. Blair translates a more traditional methodology of feminist writing research to digital environments. Sheridan continues the examination of how researchers are making methods their own in her account of how contemporary writing studies scholars are using ethnographic work. Kristie Fleckenstein rounds out this section in her reevaluation of how cognitive work can inform today's writing research. In particular, Fleckenstein uses ecological cognition research to examine the electronic writing and reading processes of students enrolled in an online class. As a group, the chapters in this section detail how researchers are reconceptualizing a variety of methods and methodologies in order to investigate how writing functions in people's lives today.

Chapters in the second section, "Revisioning Research in Composition," examine the historically privileged institutional site of university composition programs and classrooms, yet they extend this important tradition through various revisionings of what, who, and how we approach classroom, program, and institutional study. Some research in this section focuses on studies of writing that have pedagogical development as their primary goal. Nickoson offers readers an overview of the pragmatics, problematics, and possibilities surrounding teacher research in which teaching and research are understood as mutually informing and sustaining efforts. A. Suresh Canagarajah explores how he uses autoethnographic study to understand the composing processes of multilingual writers. Asao B. Inoue and Doug Hesse each forward compelling calls for renewed programmatic attention to classrooms through attention to writing assessment and writing-program assessment, respectively. Still other research examines cross-institutional or long-term institutional issues that affect the classroom. Steve Lamos discusses institutional critique as a means of better understanding institutional dynamics, while Jenn Fishman explores the value of longitudinal research in studying how "writing creates and is created" by communities of writers. By examining issues of race and power, responsibility and blind spots, the chapter discussions in this grouping show how research on the composition classroom remains a fertile site for study.

The chapters in the third and final section, "Reconceptualizing Methodologies and Sites of Inquiry," explore the decision-making processes involved with enacting quantitative and qualitative frameworks for writing research, whether in local, international, and/or digital communities. Uniting these conversations is a shared focus on contested, emerging, or shifting boundaries, both those surrounding methodological decision making and those surrounding sites of inquiry. Richard Haswell and Bob Broad define the historical anchor categories of quantitative and qualitative methods as well as applaud the increased acceptance of drawing on multiple methods from across these useful traditions to capture the richness and complexity of today's research questions. Their challenge to a quantitative-qualitative binary highlights how those researching community-based questions start from an orientation, as Jeff Grabill might say, as opposed from a particular method. For Grabill, such community-based research asks academics to expand our understanding of how we define our commitments to local communities. Karen J. Lunsford focuses on even-broader collaborations as she examines the complexities and possibilities involved in conducting international writing research. Mike Palmquist, Joan Mullin, and Glenn Blalock demonstrate through activity analysis the challenges and potential benefits they discovered from their efforts to create web-based communities for writing research. Lastly, Heidi A. McKee and James E. Porter discuss the ethical complexities surrounding Internet writing research. In examining these community sites, the researchers in this section once again extend traditional understandings of research, updating older frameworks to answer contemporary questions such as what drives our research with and/or about particular communities? How might we revise our approaches to researching and representing research of nontraditional sites of inquiry?

These diverse essays reflect not only a pushing against past research traditions but also an embracing of these traditions. One such example

is collaboration. Collaboration has been a long-standing writing studies research tradition, and these essays highlight how collaboration has
become accepted in ways that would have seemed unusual just a few
decades ago. Whereas twenty years ago, *Methods and Methodology* had
only one of the fourteen body chapters collaboratively authored, in this
collection multiple chapters are collaborative, whether in explicit authorship or in authors explicitly highlighting their collaborations with
the participants of the study, perhaps as a feminist practice (Blair; Selfe,
and Hawisher), as an ethical move (McKee and Porter), or as the engine
that drives the research project in the first place (Palmquist, Mullin, and
Blalock). A second example of embracing past traditions is a heightened
attention to activism and advocacy. Current understandings of composition studies emerged out of providing people with more access to the
university. This collection continues this activist project through calls
to reconceptualize writing assessment theory to better account for race
(Inoue) or through explicit discussions of scholars becoming agents of
social change, whether via community action (Grabill) or via conversations designed to affect educational policy on local (Hesse), national,
and international levels (Canagarajah; Lunsford). Similarly, attention to
issues of difference and diversity, multiplicity and absence pervade these
chapters (for example, Blair; Canagarajah; Inoue; Lamos) in ways that
highlight how fundamental such issues are to learning and writing, in
short, to contemporary writing studies research. Such building on past
work helps contemporary cohorts of researchers remain true to ongoing
concerns within our field as well as forge new methods and methodologies responsive to today's research contexts.

   Of course, we realize that no one collection can do or include everything. The collection before you is no exception. We are woefully aware
that some research traditions remain either absent (e.g., case-study research and surveys) or underrepresented (e.g., quantitative, rhetorical,
linguistic, and international research). Despite being unable to include an
exhaustive account of current research practices, we nonetheless imagine
that this collection can illustrate the diverse, overlapping, and evolving
possibilities for how contemporary writing studies inquiry is variously
identified, practiced, and represented.

   We hope readers find in this collection a resource on practical issues
and a heuristic for how researchers make sense of their research, in
part by making methods their own. By articulating under what conditions certain research works well and where it may not go as planned,
contributing authors provide important background information about

how to situate particular methods and methodologies. In the process, *Writing Studies Research in Practice* explores foundational and burgeoning research traditions that help researchers pursue what writing means in the lives of people today.

Works Cited

Bazerman, Charles. *The Handbook of Research on Writing: History, Society, School, Individual, Text*. Mahwah: Erlbaum, 2007. Print.

Bazerman, Charles, and Paul Prior. *What Writing Does and How It Does It*. Mahwah: Erlbaum, 2004. Print.

Bishop, Wendy. *Ethnographic Writing Research: Writing It Down, Writing It Up, and Reading It*. Portsmouth: Heinemann, 1999. Print.

Blakeslee, Ann, and Cathy Fleisher. *Becoming a Writing Researcher*. Mahwah: Erlbaum, 2007. Print.

DeVoss, Dànielle, and Heidi A. McKee. *Digital Writing Research: Technologies, Methodologies, and Ethical Issues*. Cresskill: Hampton, 2007. Print.

Kirsch, Gesa E., and Liz Rohan, eds. *Beyond the Archives: Research as a Lived Process*. Carbondale: Southern Illinois UP, 2008. Print.

Kirsch, Gesa E., and Patricia A. Sullivan, eds. *Methods and Methodology in Composition Research*. Carbondale: Southern Illinois UP, 1992. Print.

Lauer, Janice, and J. William Asher, eds. *Composition Research: Empirical Designs*. New York: Oxford UP, 1988. Print.

MacArthur, Charles A., Steve Graham, and Jill Fitzgerald, eds. *Handbook of Writing Research*. New York: Guilford, 2008. Print.

McKee, Heidi A., and James E. Porter. *The Ethics of Internet Research: A Rhetorical, Case-Based Process*. New York: Lang, 2009. Print.

Ramsey, Alexis, Wendy Sharer, Barbara L'Eplattenier, and Lisa Mastrangelo, eds. *Working in the Archives: Practical Research Methods for Rhetoric and Composition*. Carbondale: Southern Illinois UP, 2010. Print.

Rickly, Rebecca. "Messy Contexts: Research as a Rhetorical Situation." *Digital Writing Research: Technologies, Methodologies, and Ethical Issues*. Ed. Dànielle DeVoss and Heidi McKee. Cresskill: Hampton, 2007. 377–97. Print.

Schell, Eileen, and K. J. Rowson, eds. *Rhetorica in Motion: Feminist Rhetorical Methods and Methodologies*. Pittsburgh: U of Pittsburgh P, 2010. Print.

Smagorinsky, Peter, ed. *Research on Composition: Multiple Perspectives on Two Decades of Change*. New York: Teachers College P, 2006. Print.

PART ONE

Reimagining Traditional Research Practices

1.

Narrative Turns in Writing Studies Research

Debra Journet

"Narrative" is a powerful word and concept in composition studies. As a discipline, we generally use narrative as both a mode of student writing (e.g., literacy narrative or personal narrative) in which students construct stories of events or actions that are important to them, and as a research genre (e.g., case study or ethnography) in which the researcher represents her findings by telling a story. In each case, narrative is valorized as a way of paying attention to the local and specific characteristics of experience, particularly as they are situated within social and cultural contexts. Indeed, one might say that the history of composition research is, in part, the history of coming to terms with narrative.

This chapter outlines some of the ways narrative has been used in composition research. In particular, I examine what is at stake for researchers in the commonly assumed connection between narrative and personal experience. My argument is that the conflation of narrative and the personal is a product of how narrative research genres have been constructed and employed in the discipline. Though claims are often made that narratives of personal experience are inherently more authentic accounts, I argue instead that such narratives are, at least in part, conventionalized ways of representing disciplinary knowledge. As a research genre, they thus demonstrate tacit and explicit agreements—built communally and negotiated over time—about what constitutes a persuasive story.

To amplify this argument, I compare composition's use of research narratives to another set of disciplinary narratives that I have elsewhere analyzed: historical narratives produced by evolutionary biologists (Journet, "Ecological," "Synthesizing," "Limits"). Unlike composition narratives, these biological narratives are not based on personal experiences of the writer or his subject. However, like composition narratives, they deal with unique sets of events or individuals and are constructed with

narratives are conventionalized

the aim of convincing readers that they represent true accounts of what happened and what it meant.

Comparison of narratives written by scientists and compositionists raises several issues relevant to our research practices. Scientific research reminds us that not all narratives of real phenomena are first-person accounts in fact; many other genre conventions exist for persuading disciplinary readers that a narrative is adequate to the evidence. But whereas the conventions scientists use depend heavily on agreements about methods as well as rhetoric, composition research narratives frequently rely on what I call tropes of authenticity. My argument is that composition's research narratives of personal experience, rather than being inherently authentic, are also the product of genres: conventional stories we have learned to value as a discipline. We applaud these stories because they seem to provide a way to escape the restrictions of other academic genres. But I suggest this is not because personal narratives are inherently transgressive or revolutionary, but rather because, right now at least, they are still being written against the grain of academic discourse.

Narrative and Composition Research

In early composition research, narrative often had a "bad name" because it did not seem to be "rigorous" or "sciency" enough. Despite the fact that early process research described and documented a set of actions that could be understood as a kind of narrative (people engaged in the processes of composing in order to write a text), those actions were generally presented in the introduction-methods-results-discussion (IMRD) format of social science research that foregrounds "data" rather than "story." Beginning sometime in the 1980s, when compositionists began to make the famous "social turn," composition research started to emphasize the social contexts and personal histories out of which writing arises and concomitantly to incorporate narrative more explicitly into research genres. This new interest in narrative was often presented not only as a rhetorical shift to a different discursive format but also as access to different dimensions of what writing is and how it is produced. Much of this rhetoric concerning narrative modes was connected to new interests in ethnographic research and was marked by emphasis on narrative's libratory, even transgressive, potential to reveal aspects of writing hitherto unavailable to researchers who worked from more "distanced" or "objective" perspectives.

In an even more recent turn (roughly from the mid-1990s), composition research has continued to foreground narrative's capacity to render the complexities of individual and social experience but has also paid more

discuss IMRAD

attention to how particular stories are formed within genres and are thus constructed out of the shared theoretical, methodological, and rhetorical commitments held by researchers and the community of readers and writers in which this work occurs. Accompanying this new awareness of the constructed nature of narrative was a number of studies examining the specific rhetorical characteristics of narrative genres, as well as the kinds of knowledge claims that such narrative genres make possible. At the same time, there were important discussions in composition and related disciplines about narrative inquiry as a research methodology and in influential autobiographical narratives written by compositionists documenting their own literacy, educational, or professional histories.

In adopting these new positions, composition participates in what is sometimes called the "narrative turn" in the human sciences: a deepening understanding that narrative is fundamental to how people organize and make sense of their lives. For compositionists, this narrative turn came not only in empirical research (of the sort I am discussing here) but also in other endeavors I do not have space to consider—including a new sense of narrative theory as it has been defined in diverse disciplines, an expanded awareness of narrative historiography, and a greater interest in narrative as a form of student writing (Boehm and Journet; Journet, Boehm, and Britt). However, despite this growing awareness of narrative as a genre—as a way of constructing experience or discourse—composition still frequently defines narrative in contradistinction to the more "objective" or "rational" methods characteristic of those disciplines that produce "scientific" (often quantitative) knowledge. Arguments for narrative in composition have thus, from the start, often been proffered from a defensive position and articulated in terms of the experiential, contextual, and even ideological truths narrative makes possible. In particular, narrative has sometimes been presented as an almost direct way to represent qualities of personal experience—a kind of transparent window onto individual subjectivity.

Narrative and the Personal

Why does this move from "narrative" to "personal" appear so often in composition research? It is not that researchers do not recognize that there are other forms of narrative than personal stories: Narratives can be constructed from a range of impersonal points of view, just as personal accounts do not always take the form of narrative. Nor do all researchers subscribe to the idea that explicitly personal perspectives necessarily create more authentic or accurate representations than do other perspectives on teaching or research. Nevertheless, when we talk about narrative in rhetoric and composition and when we make claims for its power, it is almost always in terms of personal—often autobiographical—stories of individual teachers, students, and researchers. Two tacit and almost tautological assumptions seem to be operating. The first is that narratives are always (or most important) first-person stories of significant individual actions and changes. The second is that personal experiences and commitments are always (or most important) revealed in narratives. And although both of these assumptions may often be true, they are not, as I argue, necessarily or always the case. That is, there are narratives that are not based on personal experience. And there are ways other than personal narrative to render the specific details of unique people or events. It is thus worth asking, I believe, what is at stake in the almost inevitable conflation of "narrative" with "personal" in composition research.

In response to this question, I make three points. My first is fairly obvious but is also perhaps more complex and important than we often recognize: There is a range of narrative genres, not all of which involve personal experience and not all of which are narrated from the point of view of the writer. That is, stories can be narrated from a variety of different perspectives—perspectives that are both close to and distanced from the experiences being narrated. We readily understand this in fiction, as we differentiate between omniscient and limited narrators (Booth) or, to use more modern terms, between homodiegetic, heterodiegetic, or extradiegetic narration (Abbott). And it is equally true of other narrated genres. Clifford Geertz, for example, discusses how author-saturated ethnographic narratives differ from author-evacuated narratives in anthropology, and Greg Myers describes differences between narratives of nature and narratives of science in evolutionary biology.

My second point is that disciplinary narratives, of the sort produced by composition researchers, are the product of genre commitments: shared assumptions about theory, method, and rhetoric that let disciplinary communities understand, negotiate, and advance new knowledge claims. The presence of genre agreements is as necessary for the understanding of narratives dealing with deep personal and direct experience as it is for those concerned with events or experiences distant in time or space from the writer. In both cases, we learn how to understand and respond to the particular kind of story that is being told. The stories we tell about ourselves, that is, are at least partly stories we have been acculturated to tell. But just as we learn generic stories, we are also able sometimes to change those stories and the genres that instantiate them. Personal experience, that is, is the product of powerful cultural scripts, such as those created by race, class, and gender. Though we can conform to or rebel against those scripts, we nevertheless construct our stories in some relation—conforming or transgressive—to other stories we have heard or read.

This brings me to my third point: Personal narratives in composition research are not inherently more authentic than other research modes. That is, an account is not necessarily genuine or adequate to the experience just because it is conveyed as a narrative. Individual instances of research based on experiential narrative may turn out to be more accurate or persuasive than instances of research based on other empirical methods. But the opposite is potentially true as well: Some narrative research is less compelling or persuasive than research in other modes. And while the value of personal stories is now widely accepted in composition, it is important to articulate what qualities of observation, analysis, or representation we require if we are to accept any particular narrative account as a persuasive instance of research.

Another View of Narrative

In order to suggest some of the qualities we might consider as we evaluate narrative in composition research, I turn now to issues of narrative epistemology and rhetoric as they have been theorized and practiced in other disciplines: particularly in historical sciences (such as paleontology, astronomy, or evolutionary biology) that are concerned with reconstructing the past. The goal of these disciplines is to create plausible narratives of unique events or clusters of events (such as why the dinosaurs became extinct), rather than general laws about invariant phenomena (such as how hydrogen and oxygen combine to create water). In constructing these narratives, researchers select (out of everything they know to have happened) those events they deem most significant and arrange them in terms of their temporal sequence and causal relations. The resulting narratives interpret the past from the perspectives of the researchers' present (their methodological, theoretical, and rhetorical commitments). Such narratives are not generalizable or verifiable in the way that research produced by experiments or statistical interpretation is. Rather, they describe and explain constellations of particular actions, persons, or material circumstances—things that only happened once. They are, to use another set of terms, "ideographic" rather than "nomothetic." The epistemological status of narrative knowledge consequently presents scientists with specific methodological and rhetorical challenges. If there is no critical experiment or statistical test to establish the veracity of a story, how does the writer convince readers to accept her representation?

Since there is no direct access to the past, scientific narratives, like other historical projects, are never completely established and always open to further interpretation. That is, no single piece of information or test definitively establishes the veracity of any particular narrative account. Instead, scientists rely on what is sometimes called "consilience," a process of assembling converging data that is akin to triangulation. However, despite the fact that the persuasive power of scientific narratives can be constantly renegotiated, scientists nevertheless want to write true stories about things that really happened in the world. As the biologist Richard Lewontin explains, "It is the purpose of [historical] sciences to provide a correct narrative of the sequence of past events and an account of the causal forces and antecedent conditions that led to that sequence" (481). How a scientist persuades readers that his is a "correct" narrative is a complex issue.

In his analysis of Charles Darwin's *On the Origin of Species*, for example, Robert Richards argues that Darwin persuades readers to accept his argument by establishing an "index of reality." This index consists of textual features that enforce the sense that the writer has accurately described and explained some aspect of the real world. Darwin's index was designed to be effective to his nineteenth-century audience; scientists writing at different times and to different audiences may establish the index differently. But typical constituents include references to extant research, standardized ways of describing data collection and analysis, shared metaphors, and visual conventions (e.g., Bazerman; Berkenkotter, and Huckin; Journet, "Writing"; Miller and Halloran; Myers). The index varies, that is, according to the range of genre commitments embraced by the particular disciplinary groups to whom the narrative is addressed. But when scientific narratives are persuasive (and they are always persuasive to some and not to others), it is because readers and writers share a set of assumptions that are textually manifested and that create "confidence regarding observations and theories" (Simpson 123).

Narrative Knowledge and Composition

The phenomena that historical scientists seek to explain exist independent of human interpretation (that is, they do not present themselves as already narrativized), and scientists must construct explanations that not only document what happened, when, and in what order but must also explain how or why those phenomena came to be as they are. Scientific narratives of the past are thus different in many ways from the narratives of direct experience produced so often in composition studies. Nevertheless,

I think that it is worthwhile to take note of disciplinary narrative practices from the perspective of historical sciences for at least two reasons. One is that although historical scientists understand that narratives are constructed, interpretive artifacts, they still go to great lengths to assure readers that their narratives correspond to the reality of the phenomena under discussion. And second, the validity of their narrative accounts is open to public debate: Other readers are able to bring conforming and nonconforming evidence to bear on what are publicly negotiated stories.

Turning to narrative research in composition, one might also ask if truth or veracity is an equally important component of the research narratives we tell. And if so, what kind of truth is it, and how is it conveyed to readers? Since, for many, one of the virtues of first-person narratives is that they dismantle or deconstruct the notion of accuracy or truth embedded in other more supposedly "objective" or "impersonal" accounts, the issue of veracity becomes complicated. But surely, even if our goal in personal narratives is to convey the multiplicity of truths or perspectives, we still want, in one way or another, to persuade readers that this story offers some version of the real world. These complex epistemological issues raise a number of methodological questions: Are personal narratives knowledge just because they're personal? Or are there differences in the kinds of personal narratives we value as disciplinary knowledge? And if there are differences, by what criteria do we evaluate personal narratives in order to determine how "truthful" or "correct" they are?

The scientists who write historical narratives have negotiated complex criteria by which the truth value of their work can be assessed. Such narratives are open to public scrutiny and debate because they are based in communal agreements about theory and method, as well as rhetoric. Unlike those of biologists, our ways of persuading often depend on tropes of authenticity. These tropes include certain kinds of identifying biographical and autobiographical details about the researchers and their participants, including often highly self-reflexive descriptions of the researchers' motives for conducting the research. Additionally, we see a range of canonical plots in composition narratives: a set of shared agreements about what kinds of events and agents are important to the story of composing. In particular, composition narratives are often marked by transformational arcs, in which students or teachers or researchers come to realize something significant about the nature of reading, writing, teaching, or learning. And increasingly, research narratives include (selected and edited) transcriptions or contributions from research participants in order to create what are sometimes called "heteroglossic" or "polyphonic" representations of multiple "voices." I am not arguing that these tropes are inappropriate or that they have not enriched our research practices. I believe they have contributed to research narratives that are increasingly complex, nuanced, and useful. But I also believe that it is important to recognize that we have invested a great deal of intellectual capital in rhetorical conventions that primarily use ethos (rather than method) to provide evidence that the researcher has produced an authentic account of her experiences or observations. That is, a great part of our "index of reality" rests on textual conventions to suggest that the researcher has "been there." But what aside from representational preferences convinces us of the emotional or experiential authenticity of the account? And a more difficult question: How do we decide if this account is worth building on, worth incorporating within what counts as disciplinary knowledge? These questions remain to be explored by composition researchers.

The Next Narrative Turn?

It is not an exaggeration to say that the work of rhetoric and composition is inescapably narrative. The ubiquity of our storytelling activities, though, makes it even more important to understand what is at stake in the various "narrative turns" in which we have engaged as a discipline. Stories may seem natural and relatively straightforward ways of understanding and recounting experience. But as scholarship—in narrative theory and in disciplines that depend heavily on narrative—reminds us, narratives are complex, mediated, and rhetorical.

As a discipline, we have considered narrative research primarily in terms of such questions as whose story we should tell or how various kinds of narrative reflect different ethical or ideological assumptions. However, we have not examined in detail the "index of reality," or the means by which researchers try to convince readers that they have offered a "true" account of things that really happened in the world. How, in other words, do researchers convince readers that this story is a good story, a story that is persuasive and adequate to the experiences the researcher is recounting?

The tropes and themes we employ in our narratives are at least partly conventional. Our most powerful disciplinary narratives are the ones that both conform to and expand generic possibilities of storytelling in rhetoric and composition. And if we are to evaluate these narratives—to adopt a critical stance—we need to identify what those generic possibilities are and how we want them to be used. At present, strong claims are being made about the power of personal narrative as an inherently progressive and libratory genre. I think this is only half true. Narrative genres do still carry revolutionary and progressive possibilities within them. But these possibilities are generated not because narratives are inherently libratory. Research genres, like research methods, are not inherently one thing or the other; they are used in one way or another (see chapters by Hesse and by Haswell, this volume, for a similar argument). Personal narratives are radical for many because they are still being written against older, more-established genres—just as for Mikhail Bakhtin the novel is a radical genre because of its parodic relation to other genres. Should we continue to write personal narratives, however, the day may come when writing experimental reports will be seen as a transgressive discursive move. Genres, even those that seem the most radical, are only operative within the shared agreements of groups.

If we are to base disciplinary knowledge on personal narrative, we need to understand what we are agreeing to. We also need to develop criteria to assess when those agreements are used well and when they are not. We need, therefore, to examine critically how narratives work in teaching and scholarship. What kinds of stories have we learned to tell? How are stories shaped by disciplinary preferences as well as cultural or theoretical commitments? How do the positions from which we write—particularly those of researcher or teacher—affect the kinds of stories we tell? What ethical obligations do we have to the people whose lives we narrate and the readers whom we are addressing? What qualities of observation, analysis, or representation should we expect if we are to accept any particular narrative as "research"? These are the sorts of questions narrative researchers are increasingly confronting and that will become even more complex in the next narrative turn as we start to focus on how narrative is shaped and transformed by globalization and digital media. In particular, as I argue elsewhere ("Literate Acts"), new digital genres introduce new forms of storytelling and, in turn, raise new questions about what constitutes a "text" and how we define concepts like "author" and "reader." These transformations increasingly challenge us not only to consider new forms of production and reception of narrative genres but also new kinds of stories about what it means to write and read.

Works Cited

Abbott, H. Porter. *The Cambridge Introduction to Narrative.* 2nd ed. New York: Cambridge UP, 2008. Print.

Bakhtin, M. M. (1981). "Discourse in the Novel." *The Dialogic Imagination: Four Essays.* Trans. C. Emerson and M. Holquist. Austin: U of Texas P, 1981. 259–422. Print.

Bazerman, Charles. *Shaping Written Knowledge*. Madison: U of Wisconsin P, 1988. Print.

Berkenkotter, Carol, and Thomas N. Huckin. *Genre Knowledge in Disciplinary Communication: Cognition/Culture/Power*. Hillsdale: Erlbaum, 1995. Print.

Bishop, Wendy. "I-Witnessing in Composition: Turning Ethnographic Data into Narratives." *Rhetoric Review* 11 (1992): 147–58. Print.

———. *Teaching Lives: Essays and Stories*. Logan: Utah State UP, 1997. Print.

Blyler, Nancy Roundly. "Narrative and Research in Professional Communication." *Journal of Business and Technical Communication* 10.3 (1996): 330–51. doi: 10.1177/1050651996010003003. Print.

Boehm, Beth A., and Debra Journet. "Teaching Narrative Theory in Rhetoric and Composition." *Teaching Narrative Theory*. Ed. James Phelan, David Herman, and Brian McHale. New York: MLA, 2010. 61–69. Print.

Booth, Wayne C. *The Rhetoric of Fiction*. 2nd ed. Chicago: U of Chicago Press, 1983. Print.

Brandt, Deborah, Ellen Cushman, Anne Ruggles Gere, Anne Herrington, Richard E. Miller, Victor Villanueva, Min-Zhan Lu, and Gesa Kirsch. "The Politics of Personal: Storying Our Lives against the Grain." *College English* 64.1 (2001): 41–62. Print.

Bridwell, Lillian S. "Revising Strategies in Twelfth Grade Students' Transactional Writing." *Research in the Teaching of English* 14 (1980): 197–222. Print.

Bruner, Jerome. *Acts of Meaning*. Cambridge: Harvard UP, 1990. Print.

Charney, Davida. "Empiricism Is Not a Four-Letter Word." *College Composition and Communication* 47.4 (1996): 567–93. Print.

———. "From Logocentrism to Ethnocentrism: Historicizing Critiques of Writing Research." *Technical Communication Quarterly* 7 (1998): 9–32. Print.

Clandinin, C. Jean, and F. Michael Connelly. *Narrative Inquiry: Experience and Story in Qualitative Research*. Hoboken: Jossey-Bass, 2004. Print.

Cortazzi, Martin. *Narrative Analysis*. London: Falmer, 1993. Print.

Couture, Barbara, and Thomas Kent, eds. *The Private, the Public, and the Published: Reconciling Private Lives and Public Rhetoric*. Logan: Utah State UP, 2003. Print.

Devitt, Amy. *Writing Genres*. Carbondale: Southern Illinois UP, 2004. Print.

Geertz, Clifford. *Works and Lives: The Anthropologist as Author*. Palo Alto: Stanford UP, 1988. Print.

Gilyard, Keith, ed. *Race, Rhetoric, and Composition*. Portsmouth: Boynton/Cook, 1999. Print.

Gould, Stephen Jay. *Wonderful Life: The Burgess Shale and the Nature of History*. New York: Norton, 1989. Print.

Haswell, Richard, and Min-Zhan Lu, eds. *Comp Tales: An Introduction to College Composition through Its Stories*. White Plains: Longman, 1999. Print.

Herman, David, ed. *Narrative Theory and the Cognitive Sciences*. Stanford: Center for the Study of Lang. and Information, 2003. Print.

Herndl, Carl. "Writing Ethnography: Representation, Rhetoric, and Institutional Practices." *College English* 53.3 (1991): 320–32. Print.

Hinchman, Lewis P., and Sandra K. Hinchman, eds. *Memory, Identity, Community: The Idea of Narrative in the Human Sciences*. Albany: State U of New York P, 2001. Print.

Hull, Glynda A., and Mira-Lise Katz. "Crafting an Agentive Self: Case Studies in Digital Storytelling." *Research in the Teaching of English* 41 (2006): 43–81. Print.

Journet, Debra. "Ecological Theories as Cultural Narratives. F. E. Clements's and H. A. Gleason's 'Stories' of Community Succession." *Written Communication* 8 (1991): 446–72. Print.

———. "The Limits of Narrative in the Construction of Scientific Knowledge: George Gaylord Simpson's *The Dechronization of Sam Magruder*." Perkins and Blyler, *Narrative and Professional Communication* 93–104.

———. "Literate Acts in Convergence Culture: Lost as Transmedia Narrative." *Rhetorics and Technologies*. Ed. Stuart Selber. Columbia: University of South Carolina Press, 2010. 198–218. Print.

———. "Synthesizing Disciplinary Narratives: George Gaylord Simpson's *Tempo and Mode in Evolution*." *Social Epistemology* 9 (1995): 113–50. Print.

———. "What Constitutes a Good Story? Narrative Knowledge i n Process, Post-Process, and Post-Post Process Composition Research." *Beyond Post-Process*. Ed. Sidney I. Dobrin, J. A. Rice, and Michael Vastola. Logan: Utah State UP, 2011. 41–60. Print.

———. "Writing within (and between) Disciplinary Genres: 'The Adaptive Landscape' as a Case Study in Interdisciplinary Rhetoric." *Post-Process Theory: Beyond the Writing Process Paradigm*. Ed. Thomas Kent. Carbondale: Southern Illinois UP, 1999. 96–115. Print.

Journet, Debra, Beth Boehm, and Cynthia Britt, eds. *Narrative Acts: Rhetoric, Race and Identity, Knowledge*. Cresskill: Hampton, 2011. Print.

Kirsch, Gesa, and Joy S. Ritchie. "Beyond the Personal: Theorizing a Politics of Location in Composition Research." *College Composition and Communication* 46.1 (1995): 7–29. Print.

Lewontin, Richard C. "Facts and the Factitious in Natural Sciences." *Questions of Evidence: Proof, Practice, and Persuasion across the Disciplines*. Ed. James Chandler, Arnold I. Davidson, and Harry Harootunian. Chicago: U of Chicago P, 1994. 478–91. Print.

Mayr, Ernst. *Toward a New Philosophy of Biology*. Cambridge: Harvard UP, 1988. Print.

McCarthy, Lucille, and Stephen Fishman. "Boundary Conversations: Conflicting Ways of Knowing in Philosophy and Interdisciplinary Research." *Research in the Teaching of English* 25 (1991): 419–68. Print.

Miller, Carolyn R. "Genre as Social Action." *Quarterly Journal of Speech* 70 (1984): 151–67. Print.

Miller, Carolyn R., and S. Michael Halloran. "Reading Darwin: Reading Nature." *Understanding Scientific Prose*. Ed. Jack Selzer. Madison: U of Wisconsin P, 1993. 106–26. Print.

Mitchell, W. J. T., ed. *On Narrative*. Chicago: U of Chicago P, 1981. Print.

Mortensen, Peter, and Gesa Kirsch, eds. *Ethics and Representation in Qualitative Studies of Literacy*. Urbana: NCTE, 1996. Print.

Myers, Greg. *Writing Biology*. Madison: U of Wisconsin P, 1989. Print.

Pagnucci, Gian. *Living the Narrative Life: Stories as a Tool for Meaning Making*. Portsmouth: Boynton/Cook, 2004. Print.

Perkins, Jane M., and Nancy Blyler, eds. *Narrative and Professional Communication*. Stamford: Ablex, 1999. Print.

Perl, Sondra. "The Composing Process of Unskilled College Writers." *Research in the Teaching of English* 13.4 (1979): 317–36. Print.

Polkinghorne, Donald E. *Narrative Knowing and the Human Sciences.* Albany: State U of New York P, 1988. Print.

Richards, Robert. "The Structure of Narrative Explanation in History and Science." *History and Evolution.* Ed. M. Nitecki and D. Nitecki. Albany: State U of New York P, 1992. 19–54. Print.

Robillard, Amy E. "It's Time for Class: Toward a More Complex Pedagogy of Narrative." *College English* 66.1 (2003): 74–92. Print.

Roen, Dwayne, Stuart C. Brown, and Theresa J. Enos, eds. *Living Rhetoric: Stories of the Discipline.* Hillsdale: Erlbaum, 1998. Print.

Rose, Mike. *Lives on the Boundary: A Moving Account of the Struggles and Achievements of America's Educationally Underprepared.* New York: Free Press, 1989. Print.

Rosner, Mary, Beth Boehm, and Debra Journet, eds. *History, Reflection, and Narrative: The Professionalization of Composition, 1963–1983.* Stamford: Ablex, 1999. Print.

Royster, Jacqueline Jones. *Traces of a Stream: Literacy and Social Change among African-American Women.* Pittsburgh: U of Pittsburgh P, 2000. Print.

Ruse, Michael. *The Philosophy of Biology.* Albany: State U of New York P, 1988. Print.

Simpson, George Gaylord. *This View of Life.* New York: Harcourt, 1964. Print.

Sommers, Nancy. "Revision Strategies of Student Writers and Experienced Adult Writers." *College Composition and Communication* 31.4 (1980): 378–88. Print.

Spigelman, Candace. "Argument and Evidence in the Case of the Personal." *College English* 64.1 (2001): 63–88. Print.

Swiencicki, Jill. "The Rhetoric of Awareness Narratives." *College English* 68.4 (2006): 337–56. Print.

Trimmer, Joseph, ed. *Narration as Knowledge: Tales of the Teaching Life.* Portsmouth: Boynton/Cook, 1997. Print.

Villanueva, Victor. *Bootstraps: From an American Academic of Color.* Urbana: NCTE, 1993. Print

2.

Reseeing and Redoing: Making Historical Research at the Turn of the Millennium

Liz Rohan

As a scholar who uses historical methods, I have a horrid daydream of a reporter from the *Daily News* calling me at my office and asking me to come up with some profound truism about what I know because my research in circulation indicates I'm an "expert" on some past event or trend relevant to current events. In this frightening, and hopefully perpetually fictional, moment, my mind is blank. Why? When I imagine a scholarly historian, I see a portly man with a gray beard, a pipe, and a wood study full of books about medieval England. Historians *know* the story. I, on the other hand, know how to *make* the story. Luckily, I arrived on the scene at a good time. As the century turned so has the "archival turn" inspired scholars to show readers how their scholarly questions and personal identities shape their production of knowledge (Schultz vii). Historical work is, after all, rhetorical work, that is, the *making* of research.

The late Robert Connors was therefore arguably ahead of *his* time when he introduced us to the concept of history making as a subject *and* a process in his landmark 1992 essay, "Dreams and Play: Historical Method and Methodology." Through his oft-cited description of work in the archives as "a kind of directed ramble, something like an August mushroom hunt" (23), he inspired burgeoning composition historians like me to reflect upon their scholarly questions and their discoveries while in the archives. When I began doing historical work, I, for example, wrote about history making, using the metaphor of sewing as I "stitched together" a narrative about my research subject, Janette Miller (1879–1969). Later in my research, I coined the term "imagined communions" to theorize my felt connection to Janette, a concept I will discuss. My favorite and newer metaphor for archival research is composition

imagined communions

25

historian David Gold's. It's like a "jigsaw puzzle," he claims, "except that you don't have a picture on the book for reference, there's more than one puzzle in the box, the picture keeps changing depending on how you put the pieces together, and the pieces themselves change shape when your back is turned" (15). Connors reminded us how historians are coaxed into intoxicating contact zones as agents who introduce and sometimes even marry the present to the past, a phenomenon for which we could use a metaphor and, more formally and sometimes related, a *method* for interpreting texts and posing questions.

Connors's approach to history making thus remains inspiring years later as we use his metaphors and develop our own, reflect upon and generate scholarly questions, and identify our biases. However, the bias that shapes Connors's data analysis in this same essay is now *itself* an archive; it tells us about questions compositionists asked when the field was newer. For example, when outlining what "constitutes data in historical studies," Connors defines sources broadly as "library" and "archival," but his description of these sources—historical textbooks like the 1907 *Heath Handbook,* historical editions of journals like *College English,* general-interest periodicals such as the *Atlantic Monthly,* students papers, and faculty syllabi—reflects a limited scope of inquiry from our more contemporary perspective. This history tells us that during a particular time and place leaders in the field of composition like Connors were most curious about historical college classrooms and writing undertaken for teachers as told by dominant institutions.

Although Barbara L'Eplattenier rightly argues recently that composition scholars who do historical methods need to be better trained (68), many composition scholars who have done historical work in the past two decades have crafted significant conversations about the value and purpose of historical work. For example, with the backdrop of a more postmodern landscape, composition historians have more recently been writing histories of composition by expanding *whom* they study. Scholars today are more likely to study data that chronicles stories of writing outside of classrooms. They also gather data outside of paper archives, outside of institutional archives, and even outside of the library—quite literally—when they engage with geographical places as living archives. Scholars have also become even more interested in *how* they study subjects. Feminist scholars in particular have been in the forefront of inventing these new methods and have theorized, for example, about the role of emotion in research design (Bizzell). New ways of thinking among these feminist scholars have led to new ways of seeing and interpreting the past. These scholars who study dead people are theorizing about the live people they bring to the archives, themselves, and what it means to perpetuate a legacy when representing subjects who can no longer speak for themselves, let alone chronicle their lives. They have also generated questions about scholars' responsibilities towards their subjects beyond the standard academic practice of introducing and contextualizing new subjects and new ideas.

Integral to these new methods for these scholars is a concern for ethical representations of research subjects, which I boil down to caring for others, no matter which side of grave, and acknowledging the benefits garnered from research and writing, even the pain that can come with self-awareness. This new awareness has also shaped how feminist scholars represent their subjects in their research reports, reports that do not necessarily conform to traditional academic conventions dictating detached objectivity and its voice. In fact, some of these scholars insist on showing readers that they are neither detached nor objective about their research subject. Skeptics might comment that these feminist scholars have abandoned classic criteria of responsible scholarship. On the contrary, these historical-research methods and their products indeed *foreground* responsible research and model how to gracefully manage the gift of hindsight as a tool and not a weapon. These methods can also potentially change the way any or all scholars of historical research think about, conduct, and publish their data.

Reseeing among Feminist Historians

Connors outlined methods for writing the history of composition just as proliferating personal computers made text production easier and online databases began changing how scholars find information and just before the World Wide Web introduced opportunities for reading and producing vernacular and essentially *public* texts. As opportunities for self-sponsored literacy proliferated on the web, scholars studying the history of composition became interested in what Anne Ruggles Gere calls the "extra curriculum of Composition," the history of literacy, writing, and writing instruction outside of formal school settings. In her 1994 article about the "extra curriculum," Gere encourages scholars to "uncouple composition and schooling, to consider the situatedness of composition practices, to focus on the experience of writers not always visible to us inside the walls of the academy" (80). Gere's scholarship about women making culture through the turn-of-the-twentieth-century club movement in her monograph *Intimate Practices: Literacy and Cultural Work in U.S. Women's Clubs, 1880–1979* models how studying text produced outside of

Gere—Comp's extracurricula

school settings broadens categories of authorship (251). She encourages readers to recognize the historical efficacy of these "amateur" writers' texts; the women wrote plays, poems, and policies and also budgets and board-meeting minutes that had consequences in the world by moving audiences and shaping culture. Reconstituting who "counts" as authors helps us identify text production we may not have valued or even noticed when concentrating our studies on what happens *in* the classroom. As Maureen Daly Goggin argues in her study of historical needlework sample making, a new lens can help scholars resee what "counts as texts," what counts as rhetorical practice, and "who counts in its production" (310).

While scholars working with historical documents excavated and interpreted the work of so-called amateurs, scholars like Elizabeth (Betsy) Birmingham were reseeing the work of women who were inarguable experts, such as Marion Mahony Griffin, one of the first women architects whose known influence on architecture had more or less died with her. Unlike Gere's modest subjects who likely never dreamed their interpretation of *Macbeth* performed at the high school auditorium to raise money for books at the local library would become scholarly fodder, Mahony Griffin was a conscious archivist whose sprawling, then-unpublished multimodal autobiography, "The Magic of America," documented both her career and a love story between herself and her husband and collaborator, fellow architect Walter Burley Griffin. Despite Mahony Griffin's remarkable life and the rich archives that document this life, when Birmingham discovered this life and its texts, housed at the Art Institute of Chicago, as an undergraduate in the late 1980s, her senior advisers in her then field of historical architecture discouraged her interest in the woman's work. The dismissive attitude about Mahony Griffin's work by Birmingham's mentors paralleled the sexist and even scathing description of Mahoney Griffin's career and personality in the secondary scholarship about her. Aside from Birmingham's own instinct and observation, there was simply no scholarly infrastructure available for her as a young scholar to "see" Mahony Griffin for what she was: a successful professional woman working in a male-dominated field. Eventually, when she became a scholar of composition, Birmingham eventually wrote about Mahoney Griffin. As of 2011, Mahony Griffin's "Magic of America" was published online, and numerous other scholarly articles, including those authored by Birmingham, were published about Mahony Griffin—including a book-length monograph *Marion Mahoney Reconsidered.* The apparatus influencing Birmingham as a young scholar taught her how contemporary blinders, and in this case a male-dominated discipline, can hide even the shiniest of stars: "As a scholar, I had to make up an implausible story so that I could be wrong in good company" (143). Birmingham could not follow her own instincts as a young scholar because her academic power brokers literally forbade her to.

Birmingham's experience as a novice scholar reinforces Christine Sutherland's observations about the power, and also limits, of personal reactions to archival material. Sutherland's mentors encouraged her to study primary sources first and secondary sources later so that she might rely on her own instincts about a text, however naïve (112). My experience studying the lives and texts of Janette Miller parallels Birmingham's experience and reinforces Sutherland's advice. I "met" Janette through the diaries she produced as a girl and later as a young woman working at the Detroit Public Library. As a fellow diarist and a fellow Metro Detroiter, I was sucked into the details she shared in a genre I felt comfortable with and about subjects with which I could vaguely relate—after all, I was reading her diaries in a library, and Janette worked in a library. When Janette moved to Africa to become a missionary when she was thirty, she quit writing in her diary and instead wrote articles in female-authored and female-edited missionary magazines. These magazines, in vogue at the time, featured articles and photographs about "converting natives," and I struggled to engage with these texts that chronicle now obviously politically incorrect observations about third-world "Others." Yet, my initial relationship with Janette via "our" diaries inspired me to withhold judgment about her work ever after and even if it felt unnatural. I came to share Sutherland's claim that "[w]hat we modern women see as ethically correct is not necessarily consistent with the values of women belonging to other cultures and other times" (115). Although I would have felt more comfortable if Janette had continued her life as a librarian, because this life was easier to write about, her lifetime career as a missionary allowed her opportunities as a writer, teacher, and preacher that were more dynamic than her duties as a librarian. While complicating her role as a colonizer who in fact "went native," I ultimately concluded that she was brave to seek such a life.

"Befriending" Our Subjects: Passionate Attachments

Birmingham describes Mahony Griffin as a friend, a subject with whom she collaborated, and arguably grew up with, whom she literally "met" on paper. She admits being emotionally moved by gaining the long view of Mahony Griffin's love affair with her husband, after reading about Griffin falling in love at forty and later mourning her husband's untimely death,

research subject as "friend"
& historical

all told to Birmingham from the archives and from the grave. While traditional methods encourage critical distance from a subject, scholars like Birmingham demonstrate that empathy and identification with a research subject can be integral to the research process; emotions can drive and inspire scholarly questions. Sutherland emphasizes historical research as a collaboration with a deceased other. This deceased subject may not share the lived context of the scholar who studies her but obviously shares the experience of being human or in most of the cases cited here as women. Thus, Sutherland argues, "One should begin with one's experience" when studying historical subjects (112–13).

Birmingham testifies about the power of the archives to persuade the living to study the dead, what she calls the "researcher's sixth sense," as well as the bodily involvement of the researcher herself in the process: "The researcher's sixth sense isn't the ability to see the dead but our potential to help the dead, who do not know they are dead, finish their stories, and we do this in the moment in which we realize that their stories are ours" (144). Jacqueline Jones Royster, too, argues for making explicit and scholarly what she calls "passionate attachments" (283). Outlining the impact of discovering her great-great-great aunt Annie's very ordinary diary, scholar Jennifer Sinor in fact makes such "passionate attachments" explicit in her book *The Extraordinary Work of Ordinary Writing* through essays that link her experiences as a writer, daughter, and wife to similar roles described by her long-deceased aunt in her diary. Royster recognizes that personal writing such as Sinor's essays can be integral to ethically sound and also theoretically appropriate methods for studying the past, a process for making the "familiar strange and the strange familiar" (283). Recent scholarly projects therefore demonstrate that a scholar's bias, empathy, or felt connection with a deceased other need not be edited from a research agenda or even a research report. As Royster points out, subjects of the past can act as "mentors" or "guides" for researchers who share similar experiences, and communities, with their subjects and whose shared identities therefore unearth persisting experiences over time that can educate ourselves and audiences about prevailing power structures (278). Birmingham's more contemporary power struggles and disciplinary conflicts, for example, no doubt shed light on similar struggles experienced by women working in historically male-dominated fields, such as Mahoney Griffin in the field of architecture. Connections between lived lives and the lives of deceased subjects can therefore produce useful knowledge about the past, the present, and culture generally, even if not written in the conventional voice of academic discourse.

Scholars of history in composition have also theorized methods that bridge the present with the past by acknowledging gaps, what can't be known about a scholarly subject. Personal writing, the account of excavating a research subject, as modeled by Sinor, can do the work of acknowledging these unknowns, making them explicit. Sinor shows that creative writing is one method for showing how deceased subjects can affect the lived lives of the scholars who study them. Sinor describes this method as "[b]eing accountable for your own presence in the recovery of the text" (17). Royster also promotes the imagination as a source for representation and as important when recovering the lives of historical African American women who lacked the privileges of Mahoney Griffin and even the modest resources of a farmwife like Annie and therefore left no material evidence of their lives behind at all.

Sutherland professes the study of place as a concrete method for imaginatively bridging the past and the present, a way to better imagine the context experienced by a deceased subject. When studying the work of British Quaker Margaret Fell, Sutherland was able to connect with her subject via Fell's old stomping grounds: the buildings at the University of Durham. Sutherland claims, "Simply being there put me in touch with the object of my research in a new way. I began to share her context. My contact with her, then, was not purely intellectual, but spiritual and emotional as well" (113). Gesa E. Kirsch describes a similar experience of using a place as an archive when studying the work and life of Mary Bennett Ritter, a physician and woman's rights advocate, who worked and lived in historical Berkeley, California. Kirsch describes the impact of place on her research: "The simple fact of being there, in Berkeley, walking across campus many times, jogging on the local trails, joining in a campus tour, reading street and building names—all these activities made it much easier for me to read handwritten correspondence and diary entries that prominently featured places and events" (22). Contemporary landscapes that embody memories of the dead helped these scholars to better imagine the lives of their subjects and better interpret these lives by noting the differences between the past and present: when a religious career was the highest achievement for a studious and ambitious intellectual woman and when a smart woman doctor was a radical presence in a medical school and in the operating room.

Scholar Malea Powell also draws attention to how layers of place can inform and interface with recovery projects in the particular case of studying texts by Native Americans within the otherwise pleasant Newberry Library in Chicago. While studying the texts of Native American Charles Eastman, she was chilled not only by the air conditioning but the

how place can influence research

realization that the library sits on the land where Miami Indians "hunted, gathered and celebrated long before any city was built there" (121). Powell's interface with texts, place, and the task at hand was ironic for her, an "Indian, and mixed blood," and made her "think about empire" as she felt "puny and insignificant in the face of imperialism" (120). Place, in this case a library built in a city that has so naturalized colonization that its previous destiny as a hunting grounds is literally invisible, encouraged Powell's self-reflexivity about giving her ancestors a voice for contemporary audiences. Considering her inevitable comfort in a colonized space, how could she avoid colonizing moves herself as an author during her recovery project? For Powell, insights about her location, both literally and ideologically, birthed questions about innovative methods, and she in fact used poetry to express her felt responsibility for and connection to her ancestors. Thus, scholars like Sutherland, Kirsch, and Powell advocate that studying geographic places not only helps them to imagine the past but also encourages the self-reflexivity that inevitably shapes how they frame and render historical lives.

Considering scholars' public admittance about their felt connection to their research subjects, through their emotions, imagination, and a combination of intellectual processes, they at the same time obviously experience a sense of accountability toward their deceased subjects. Birmingham claims outright that she feels responsible for telling the story of Mahoney Griffin's life, a felt obligation that might connote a love affair but more practically helped Birmingham generate scholarly questions. Birmingham describes the difference: "My responsibility as a researcher has led to my interest not in teasing apart some truth of her life, not in seeing it as a life that needs me to ride in like the cavalry to discover its importance, but to ask why it is a life that should need recovering at all" (144). As Birmingham and Powell attest, a felt responsibility towards a research subject is not the end of a research process, it generates questions about culture. Powell writes about an "alliance" with her ancestors "that requires care, respect, and gift-giving for the things I take away" (121). Royster observes the interconnectivity between recovering and gaining insight about a subject, this felt responsibility towards this subject coupled with a method of representation: "As researchers and scholars, we are responsible for its uses and, therefore, should think consciously about the momentum we created when we produce knowledge or engage in knowledge-processes" (281). A scholar's sense of responsibility towards her subjects in the best case and when employing the best practices results in better questions and therefore more-innovative research products.

Sinor's project is a good example of how a felt connection and an obligation to a research subject, imagination, and the so-called spirit of a subject's life can birth a method of representation. Annie's writing is by definition ordinary—that is, it does not tell a story. If read with the framework of literary analysis, Annie's diary would only invite critique. It is a repetitive and boring story of a lonely farmwife whose most interesting entry recounts a dream she had about her husband's infidelity, a drama she only hints at in her other diary entries. Thus, Sinor developed a method of reading Annie's texts that honors ordinary writing. In advocating for Annie, Sinor advocates for all ordinary writing, writing that "becomes a highly productive site for investigating how both writing and culture get made *every day*" (10). Gere theorizes, on the other hand, for the importance of silence when representing some subjects, partly as a result of her experience reading the private texts of anonymous deceased women who authored the myriad documents she read when researching *Intimate Practices*. As she describes her sense of responsibility, "I became nervous because I realized that these now dead and defenseless women depended on my ethical choices in textualizing their interior lives" (214). By drawing attention to the role of silence when rendering others' texts, Gere also suggests the limits of the imagination when representing ordinary lives; some ordinary texts are not fit for scholarly analysis or publication because they have been composed in haste, without a public audience in mind and/or strictly for the self. Gere promotes a healthy respect for the unknown and for vulnerable subjects; omission about a researcher's self or her research subject can therefore also shape a scholar's representation of her subject.

These feminist composition scholars who do historical work have shown how their affection for their research subjects has not automatically resulted in glowing hagiography. They have theorized what it means to resee the past and why reseeing must often result in redoing when scholars employ nontraditional genres to represent their subjects and their own subjectivities. Yet, composition scholars have not invented these ideas. As early as 1975, feminist scholar Teresa de Lauretis for example, discovered a researcher of archival data in Italy, Adele Cambria, who developed methods that acknowledged this writer's passionate attachments to her subject: Antonio Gramsci's mentally ill wife, Giulia. In Cambria's narrative, she "shares her emotion at discovering the letters, looking at the faded colors of the paper, the elegant old-fashioned handwriting" and her "feelings as she approached the Moscow house where Giulia lived" (de Lauretis 90). Cambria also used creative writing to emphasize and make concrete her passionate attachment to Giulia similar to methods of representation employed by Sinor and Powell. Cambria wrote a play about Giulia and also created a contemporary character who responds to Giulia's historical dilemmas, much as scholars cited in this chapter employed methods to engage with their deceased subjects through their imaginations or by using physical places to build mental pictures of the past lives of their subjects.

At the same time, innovative presentations are not as yet "required" for those using feminist methods, and experimental academic discourse should not become automatically conflated with these methods. In fact, as early as 1987, de Lauretis warned against codifying particular feminine products or modes of analysis, insisting that "we must not accept a priori categories" when studying or representing others, in this case women (93). Although scholars might emulate the work of other scholars, each subject requires a fresh lens. Recent scholarship among feminist scholars in composition, however, indeed demonstrates that self-reflective practices often inspire scholars to question or abandon the rhetorical voice of detached objectivity when recovering and representing their research. If it has unfortunately taken more than three decades to norm the arguably useful intellectual work of admitting and using both emotions and the imagination for scholarly projects, I predict this scholarly work will likely transform not only who counts as subjects but also "what" counts as academic practice in the years to come.

Works Cited

Birmingham, Elizabeth (Betsy). "'I See Dead People': Archive, Crypt, and an Argument for the Researcher's Sixth Sense." Kirsch and Rohan, *Beyond the Archives* 139–46.

Bizzell, Patricia. "Feminist Methods of Research in the History of Rhetoric: What Difference Do They Make?" *Rhetoric Society Quarterly* 30.4 (2000): 5–18.

Connors, Robert J. "Dreams and Play: Historical Methods and Methodology." *Methods and Methodology in Composition Research*. Ed. Gesa Kirsch and Patricia A. Sullivan. Carbondale: Southern Illinois UP, 1992.

de Lauretis, Teresa. *Technologies of Gender: Essays on Theory, Film and Fiction*. Bloomington: University of Indiana, 1987.

Gere, Anne Ruggles. *Intimate Practices: Literacy and Cultural Work in U.S. Women's Clubs, 1880–1920*. Urbana: U of Illinois P, 1998.

———. "Kitchen Tables and Rented Rooms: The Extracurriculum of Composition." *College Composition and Communication* 45.1 (1994): 75–92.

———. "Revealing Silence: Rethinking Personal Writing." *College Composition and Communication* 53.2 (2001): 203–23.

Goggin, Maureen Daly. "An Essamplaire Essai on the Rhetoricity of Needlework Sampler-Making: A Contribution to Theorizing and Historicizing Rhetorical Praxis." *Rhetoric Review* 21.4 (2002): 309–38.

Gold, David. "The Accidental Archivist: Embracing Chance and Confusion in His-torical Research." Kirsch and Rohan, *Beyond the Archives* 13–19.

Kirsch, Gesa E. "Being on Location: Serendipity, Place, and Archival Research." Kirsch and Rohan, *Beyond the Archives* 20–27.

Kirsch, Gesa E., and Liz Rohan, eds. *Beyond the Archives: Research as a Lived Process.* Carbondale: Southern Illinois UP, 2008.

L'Eplattenier, Barbara. "Opinion: An Argument for Archival Research Methods: Thinking beyond Methodology." *College English* 72.1 (2009): 67–79.

Powell, Malea. "Dreaming Charles Eastman: Cultural Memory, Autobiography, and Geography in Indigenous Rhetorical Histories." Kirsch and Rohan, *Beyond the Archives* 115–27.

Royster, Jacqueline Jones. *Traces of a Stream: Literacy and Social Change among African American Women.* Pittsburgh: U of Pittsburg P, 2000.

Sinor, Jennifer. *The Extraordinary Work of Ordinary Writing: Annie Ray's Diary.* Iowa City: U of Iowa P, 2002.

Sutherland, Christine Mason. "Feminist Historiography: Research Methods in Rheto-ric." *Rhetoric Society Quarterly* 32.1 (2002): 109–22.

3.

Exceeding the Bounds of the Interview: Feminism, Mediation, Narrative, and Conversations about Digital Literacy

Cynthia L. Selfe and Gail E. Hawisher

Most researchers recognize that large-scale statistics provide one picture of salient educational trends, but such a picture, as Donna Haraway notes, can prove problematic if it seduces us into the "God Trick" (584), the arrogant and mistaken belief that we can know objectively, completely, transcendently. If we, as researchers, depend solely on such information, we tend to miss the human and very personal face of social, cultural, economic phenomena that so fundamentally shapes the project of education and the nature of institutions, departments, and classrooms. We miss the powerful, vernacular sense of what social change looks like from the perspective of individuals in their own experiences and lives, in their relations with other humans. This kind of intimate and richly situated information, many feminist researchers argue (e.g., Belenky, Clinchy, Goldberger, and Tarule; Nielson; Oakley; Reinharz), emerges most productively from interviews, especially when such exchanges are structured or semi-structured (e.g., Gubrium and Holstein; Ritchie and Lewis) as conversations (e.g., Palmer; Burgess; Lofland and Lofland; Shepherd) in which all participants—researchers *and* informants—understand that they are engaged in mutually shaping meaning and that such meaning necessarily is local, fragmentary, and contingent.

This chapter describes interviewing as a research strategy and details the ways in which our use of the interview has evolved and changed in the more than ten years in which we have taken up this research practice. We draw, in particular, on feminist understandings of interviewing as a process not of extracting information but of sharing knowledge (Olesen; Reinharz; Visweswaran; Nielson; Oakley). Within such exchanges, we believe researchers and participants engage in a reciprocal, and often intimate, shaping of information, one fundamentally influenced by the material realities and situated perspectives of multiple partners (Ritchie and Lewis). The relationships forged within these conversations, we believe, construct a participatory model of research that challenges more conventional understandings of investigations and the power relations between the researcher and researched subjects (Kirsch; Landman; Oakley). As we know from personal experience, interviews informed by such feminist principles quickly escape the boundaries of a single session, a single model or location, or a single medium. They proceed best when participants forge relationships over time, across conventional spatial and geopolitical boundaries, and around conditions of mutual interest (Kivits; Shepherd).

Coming to a Feminist Understanding of Interviews

In 1998, inspired by an outstanding talk that Deborah Brandt gave at the University of Louisville's Thomas R. Watson Conference on her oral-history literacy project, we began first interviewing individuals in the United States and then abroad about their digital literacy practices and values. Our interest was in characterizing how and why different people in different situations and cultural contexts acquired and developed (or, for various reasons, failed to acquire and develop) digital literacies at a time in history when the United States and many other parts of the globe were becoming increasingly dependent on networked systems of digital communication.[1]

The project that we finally settled on, like Deborah Brandt's scholarship, was grounded in oral-history and life-history research (e.g., Bertaux; Bertaux and Thompson; Thompson; Lummis). The research coming out of this ongoing project began first with our attempts to investigate the digital literacy experiences of U.S. citizens by interviewing them in face-to-face settings using a standard list of interview questions—a conventional interview protocol—that asked for demographic data and for information about family history, stories about literacy practices and values, memories of schooling environments and workplace experiences, and descriptions of technology use and avoidance. Our goal in this project was to conduct interviews with individuals and to collect what we called initially "technological literacy autobiographies" from a wide range of people of differing ages, genders, ethnic and racial groups, and geographical backgrounds in order to explore the "literacies of technology" (Selfe and Hawisher; Hawisher, Selfe, Moraski, and Pearson). Our understanding of interviewing as a research methodology at this point in time was fairly conventional (e.g., Mishler); we understood interviews as carefully planned and controlled sessions that unfolded along an easily recognized and generally accepted *storyline*,[2] in which a *researcher* asked a *subject* a standard set of questions and then analyzed and interpreted these focused responses in a coherent way, thereby making sense of what the *subject* said. In our early interviews, we asked questions, audiotaped individuals' responses, and later had the sessions transcribed so that we could study and report on them. We continued this approach for a few years, working primarily with colleagues, graduate students, and undergraduates whom we encountered at our respective institutions and at other institutions that participated in events connected with the field of rhetoric and composition.[3]

These early interviews we have agreed were useful—even as relatively structured question-and-answer sessions (Burgess; Ritchie and Lewis). However, as we became more comfortable with the process of interviewing and clearer about the limits of our roles within such settings, we came to appreciate the importance of making these exchanges less formal and less predictable and more like conversations that involved participants in a joint project of inquiry. In particular, we discovered in these early sessions, the importance of paying close attention not only to participants' direct responses to our targeted protocol questions but also to the small stories (Georgakopoulou) they told us about their digital literacy practices and values. Through such narratives, which are suppressed or go underinterrogated in more conventional forms of interview research (Mishler), we came to realize that these individuals were engaging with us in making sense of their own digital media practices, even as we, too, were trying to do so.

The value of eliciting autobiographical stories in interview-type settings has been well documented by scholars from cognitive theory, social theory, and narrative theory, among many other disciplines. As Jerome Bruner maintains, in autobiographical narratives, individuals have the opportunity to "set forth a view of [the] . . . Self and its doings" (66) and in telling stories to create the texts of their lives. So, against the ground of their narratives about digital literacy values and practices—at home, in school, and in community settings—we understood participants not only to be helping us understand how they used digital technologies but also to be engaging in a kind of "self-fashioning" (Brockmeier and Carbaugh 10) and self-performance (Goffman), composing themselves into the fabric of an increasingly technological world through their utterances and actions. In this important sense, we came to understand participants to be using the interview settings and the narratives they told within these settings as their own personal form of social action, a narrative strategy available to all humans as Brockmeier and Carbaugh point out. Revealed in these stories were not only glimpses of the challenges with which participants struggled when they sought access to technology or assistance in learning to use technology but also tacit and often unconscious acts of world making, of discursive and rhetorical codings that helped them both to articulate the cultural conventions of the technological world in which they lived and to shape that world to their needs.

By the time we had worked for a year or more with various participants to explore their digital literacy practices, however, both of us also had come to recognize the limitations of conventionally structured interviews within the context of our larger project. For one thing, we had grown increasingly dissatisfied with containing our questions to a standard set of prompts that elicited information but did not easily encourage follow-up questions and did not always encourage the kinds of narrative responses we found so richly laden with information (Mishler). With these goals in mind, we continued to modify our exchanges to more closely follow the format of semi-structured (Ritchie and Lewis) or unstructured interviews (Burgess), asking participants to tell us stories, trusting what seemed, at times, like lengthy narrative digressions and paying much-closer attention to the performative aspects of their interview responses (Goffman).

We also began to attend more closely to the social nature (Mishler) of the semi-structured and unstructured interviews and to understand that participants' responses and the meanings we attached to these responses emerged in an ongoing dialogic space constituted by our continued interactions and within our conversations with participants. In the context of this understanding, it became increasingly clear that the findings growing out of our interviews did not consist simply of our own interpretations of participants' responses but rather that participants themselves—in the less-formal exchanges and conversations we had begun to have with them—were dialogically and discursively engaged *with* us in making meaning and formulating interpretations of their experiences. It became increasingly clear, moreover, that our interactions with participants were resistant both to the boundaries of single-session conversations and to single geopolitical locations like the United States.[4] For example, we first interviewed our colleagues Safia el Wakil and Kate Coffield, who taught at the American University of Cairo, by meeting face-to-face in Egypt, and we continued to exchange life narratives with them through online conversations via e-mail, strengthening our relationships during an annual meeting of the Computers and Writing Conference in South Dakota, and learning still more about the lives of these remarkable women in Houghton, Michigan, at yearly workshops (see Hawisher, Selfe, Coffield, Wakil).

It was our regard for women like Kate and Safia, and the many others we met as we continued our multifaceted project that convinced us to begin the practice of coauthoring with the participants we interviewed, most of whom contributed at least as insightfully and fully to our research projects as we ourselves did and many of whom continued to share cogent interview information with us long after our initial exchanges. Given our growing understanding of this fact, we sought ways to demonstrate the active and continuing involvement of participants with whom we worked as a way that more materially and visibly acknowledged the full range of their contributions as participants in our interview-based research project.

Thus, by the time we began our book *Literate Lives in the Information Age: Narratives of Literacy from the United States*, we had added coauthorship as a major component to our research approach. We were influenced in this decision not only by our increasing awareness of the dialogic structure of unstructured and semi-structured interviews but also by Caroline Brettell's collection *When They Read What We Write*, which presents a series of perspectives on studies like ours—interview-based ethnographies and life histories—and talks about the ways in which modernist approaches to reporting on such research have often suffered from the limited perspectives of academics and professional scholars who, as Donald Schoen notes, still cling to an understanding of "the superior academic value of 'pure knowledge' inherited from the 'model of technical rationality' that has been influential in all American social sciences" (27). As Alexandra Jaffe argues in this same collection, such an approach to research claims a "distance between observer and observed" that is, to a great extent, an "ethnographic fiction," one that scholars have employed to "maintain control over . . . 'subjects'" (51). As a corrective to this modernist approach, Brettell and others in her collection suggest the alternative method of having subjects "talk back," that is, comment on, modify, change, and/or correct scholars' interpretations of what the subjects said (9). Talking back, Jaffe goes on to say, helps to "undermine" professional ethnographers' "ability to construct an unproblematic other, and hence, an unproblematic self" from interviews and observation encounters (52). In our experience, the reflexivity established by this dialogue is not only a positive and productive characteristic of postmodern anthropology but, as Jaffe points out, a realistic and "essential condition of interaction with the people we study" (51).

let subjects talk back

Other feminist researchers who questioned their own abilities to represent accurately the narratives of interview participants also shaped our thinking. From Deborah Britzman, for instance, we learned that although, like her, we desired to tell "good stories filled with the stuff of rising and falling action . . . that there is a contradictory point of no return, of having to abandon the impossible desire to portray the study's subjects as they would portray themselves" (32). We recognized this dilemma and decided that coauthorship, as a refinement in method, would give the participants more say in the politics of interpretation. We looked, too, to experimental sociologist Laurel Richardson, whose work encouraged us to ask how the "theoretical concepts of feminist poststructuralism—reflexivity, authority, authorship, subjectivity, power, language, ethics, representation" (153)— played out in our study. And we turned to Patti Lather and her decision to situate her research on women living with HIV/AIDs in a "feminist poststructural problematic of accountability to stories that belong to others," all the while attending to "the crisis of representation" (285). How, in other words, we asked, could we change our actual ways of writing and interpreting the results of our interview-based project to learn more *from* and *with* the participants we studied rather than just *about* them (Reinharz)? To our minds, coauthorship seemed a viable, practical, and ethical resolution. In thinking through our decision, we also slowly came to the realization that the project we had undertaken was no longer our own. It belonged, as well, to the people we interviewed and surveyed—their words and their stories were continual reminders that they had claimed the intellectual ground of the project as their own. When we turned to the participants featured in the *Literate Lives* project, finally, and asked if they would be willing to coauthor their chapters, almost all accepted, only a few preferring to maintain their anonymity and privacy.

Such feminist understandings of the interview-based work in which we were engaged encouraged us to leave behind many of our more structured, interviewer-directed research goals and to commit—philosophically and pragmatically—to more-interactive exchanges, in which we encouraged participants not only to tell us stories but to help us make sense of them. What had been our relatively structured approach to interviews, thus, gradually became less structured. In many instances, we began a session with an unfocused prompt, such as, "Can you tell us some stories about how you learned to read and compose?" and followed from there, sometimes over the course of multiple sessions, the multiple, loosely connected—and sometimes, seemingly unconnected, small—stories that participants began to relate. Our approach, increasingly, has become closer to that of interested others engaged in one or more conversations with individuals on a topic of interest. Our job involves asking participants for elaboration, encouraging them to reflect on stories they tell, and, occasionally, telling stories of our own when we find points in common. We also ask participants if the ways in which we understand their stories make sense to them. Occasionally, like Katherine Borland's interviewees, they dispute our understanding and assert their own in conversations about their stories, thus involving us in a more "negotiated interpretive process" (311). These untidy, discursive, and dialogic exchanges highlight individual conversations and make us increasingly aware of the collaborative role that we play with participants in making meaning of their narratives. In these relatively unstructured interviews, although we can never completely abandon the role of researcher or the power attendant to that position, we have become much more comfortable working with participants to understand their stories dialogically as they emerge in the conversational moment. And, we believe, the resulting interviews have yielded richer and more-insightful understandings than those growing out of sessions that are more structured, focused, and constrained and focus only on questions and direct responses. As Haraway might characterize our efforts, we have become less interested in the God stories that yield coherent narratives of complex phenomena and more interested in the coyote knowledge of individuals, which provides small but potent glimpses of the meaning people attach to the everyday practices of their literate lives.

Coming to a Mediated Understanding of Interviews

In the second year of our study, the interviews, increasingly, began escaping the boundaries of face-to-face exchanges. In one project, for instance, we interviewed a group of fifty-five technical communicators on the Techwr-1 listserv, asking them to tell us how they acquired electronic literacy from 1978 to 2000, a period during which personal computers became increasingly ubiquitous in the United States in educational settings, homes, communities, and workplaces. To supplement these findings, we also conducted face-to-face interviews with four case-study participants: a faculty member, a professional communicator, and two students of different backgrounds majoring in technical communication.[5]

These face-to-face interviews, although they did supplement our understanding of participants literacy practices and histories, further corroborated our sense that no one method of collecting interview information, no single session, regardless of how long it lasted, and no one interpretation of participants' stories was sufficient to the task of exploring

no one interview session
is sufficient

participants' literacy practices, values, and histories. Thus, between 2004 and 2009, our collection expanded beyond the bounds of print as a venue for both gathering information and reporting on what we—and participants—have discovered in interviews.

In 2004 during an invited lecture at the University of Oslo, Norway, we became acutely aware that our interview research was limited both in method and by location. The audience in Oslo received our talks with great interest but also asked questions and brought up issues that subsequently had a direct impact on our research.[6] Their suggestions ultimately led us to rethink the ways in which we worked with informants and the ways in which we presented the research itself. The audience asked why we didn't present our interview research on the web, why we didn't make more use of images and especially moving images or video clips in conducting and showing our research. As we pondered these questions, we realized that although we had worked hard to ground our interview approaches in feminist contentions, we were perhaps neglecting in practice the very technology—digital media—that formed the core of our research interests. In the year that followed, one of the participants at our Norwegian symposium began completing an online autobiographical account of her life history with technology and multimodal composition while also videotaping her interactions with technology over the course of a typical day. For her and us, the use of the video clip represented an additional strategy that could be used to capture the digital writing life of research participants and coauthors. Eventually, this combination of an online life-history interview juxtaposed with video clips was first featured in a 2006 College Composition and Communication conference presentation (Hawisher, Selfe, Skjulstad, and Berry) and its methods became a prominent component of our research practice here and abroad.[7]

In 2007, then, working both with contributors in the United States and Sydney, Australia, we took up with some regularity the practice of videotaping our interview conversations—a practice that is being increasingly employed across the disciplines.[8] Over the last decade, for example, scholars in a number of disciplines—among them, social sciences, linguistics, and disabilities studies; folklore (Schüller); musicology (Stock); history (Frisch); education (Hitchcock, Prater, and Dowrick; Erickson); psychology (Goodwin and Goodwin); international policy and development (Braden); anthropology (Pink, Kürti, and Afonso)—have begun using both digital video and audio to record interviews and other kinds of research observation. These researchers note that videotaping provides the potential for recording a fuller range of information about

Videotaping

human interaction, language, and behavior than they could gather using conventional observation and note-taking approaches alone. With the use of digital video, for example, researchers can record more of what is said and to whom and how social exchanges of information happen among researchers and participants through speech, facial expressions, gestures, and glances, among other paralinguistic data (Erickson). Perhaps of the greatest interest to us, however, were those researchers who were using audio and video not only to *conduct* their interview-based research but also to *report* on this work, producing texts that tend to be more robust, informative, and richly descriptive than those which rely on the researchers' and participants' transcribed words alone. Although video and audio have been used for a number of years to collect and report on data in disciplines such as anthropology, biology, and political science, such methods have not seen widespread use in other humanities disciplines like rhetoric and composition studies, in part due to the limitations of publication venues like printed journals and books. With the advent of digital-media publications, however, it is now possible for researchers to expand their reports beyond the range of the alphabetic.

In our recent interviews with those who inhabit transnational contexts, for example, we have used digital video and audio to both record and report on interviews in which individuals shared narratives about their use of various digital technologies to maintain their relationships with family, friends, and coworkers. Rendered in a more conventional form—that is, through printed transcripts and quotations—such narratives would not only be monodimensional but much less complete, accurate, and informative. Transcribed accounts of these interviews, for instance, would contain the students' words, but the transcripts would fail to convey other important information that video-recorded interviews can help convey: the multilingual abilities of speakers from various regions and parts of the world; the rhythm and pace of their voices as they talk about particular incidents involving their parents, their friends, or their siblings; the vocal emphasis they place on some words and phrases as they tell their stories about emigration, the violence of war, and the challenges of adapting to a new culture; the revealing gestures and facial expressions they use to accompany a specific narrative about a mother, a father, a sister; and the bodily presence they invest in conversations about school, travel, and technology as they immerse themselves in multiple cultures and locations.

Like Judith Mousley, we argue that video and audio clips of interviews not only add additional semiotic information to alphabetic representations of our interview-based research but also can have the added benefit of supporting readers in performing their own validity checks on the information and interpretations we provide, thus offering some triangulated perspective on our own explanations of human communication and behavior (Walker 119). Indeed, Roy Pea and Jay Lemke suggest that such representations of research data—for example, the use of digital video clips to represent instances of communicative exchanges—should be used in tandem with written descriptions of specific phenomena to support closer and more detailed readings.

An Emerging Approach

Our understanding of and conduct in collecting interviews has changed over time from a more structured question-response exchange with a participant to a more loosely structured dialogic exchange in which both we and participants engage in making and interpreting meaning; from a session structured and controlled by the researcher to a less-structured conversation in which meaning is made, negotiated, and interpreted collaboratively; from a single session in one location conducted solely through a face-to-face exchange to multiple and continuing conversations conducted over time and across national boundaries that occurs both in person and in digital communication environments. Interviewing has remained, for us, however, the primary means by which we engage in our investigations of literacy. We cannot imagine any other method that allows us to assemble more-direct information of personal literacy values, more-intimate glimpses into what literacy means in the lives of individuals, and more-meaningful ways of testing our theories about language use against the realities of peoples' literate practices and their understandings about these practices. We think other literacy researchers, too, would identify similar benefits of using semi-structured and unstructured interviews as a research method.

Although we clearly do not imagine the reports of the interviews we have conducted as *data* in the more traditional and objective sense of that word, we are attracted to the concept of entering into a collaborative engagement around shared digital representations of research evidence—not only with interview participants themselves but also with colleagues who are willing to help us make sense of interview-based narratives and our interpretations of these stories. Potentially, we believe this kind of digital media representation of interview conversations—which might find their way into hybrid mixes of alphabetic text, audio clips, and video texts for publication—could challenge the ways in which

English departments and rhetoric and composition scholars typically understand research and the knowledge that accrues from it, prompting questions informed by feminist ways of thinking about who owns the information resulting from interviews and at what stage of the research process, how knowledge is produced and by whom, and how scholars engage with the findings of their colleagues. Such approaches, as Rob Walker points out, could also help de-emphasize a tendency to rely on received knowledge from authors who have arrived at one interpretation of research-based information and could encourage a more active and open engagement through the creation of multiple alternative interpretations of interview conversations.

Notes

1. For additional perspectives on technology use, see in the current volume Haas, Takayoshi, and Carr; Blair; McKee and Porter.

2. Here we employ Holland and her colleagues' concept of storylines, central narratives that organize the world into a "taken-for-granted unfolding of particular activities" (297). Storylines are not entirely prescriptive, but they do provide an important "backdrop for interpretation." As these authors point out, "The meanings of characters, acts, and events in everyday life are figured against storylines" (54).

3. For other examples of research approaches that feature collaboration, see in the current volume Haas, Takayoshi, and Carr and Blair.

4. For an additional example of international research, see Lunsford in the current volume; Hawisher, Selfe, Guo, and Liu, "Globalization and Agency: Designing and Redesigning the Literacies of Cyberspace," and Selfe, Hawisher, Lashore, and Song, "Literacies and the Complexity of the Global Digital Divide."

5. See Selfe and Hawisher, "Historical Look."

6. We are especially indebted to Synne Skjulstad, University of Oslo, for insisting that our research would greatly benefit by our moving the interview segments from print to digital media, specifically making use of videos to be shown on the web.

7. Computers and Composition Digital Press (CCDP) was established in part to address the need for publishing book-length, digital multimodal texts that could make use of the videotaped interview. See http://ccdigitalpress.org/, an imprint of Utah State University Press. See Berry, Hawisher, and Selfe; Computers and Composition Digital Press," http://ccdigitalpress.org/transnational/.

8. See also Hawisher, Selfe, Kisa, and Ahmed.

Works Cited

Belenky, Mary F., Blythe M. Clinchy, Nancy R. Goldberger, and Jill M. Tarule. *Women's Ways of Knowing*. New York: Basic Books, 1997. Print.

Berry, Patrick W., Gail E. Hawisher, and Cynthia L. Selfe. *Transnational Literate Lives in Digital Times*. Logan: Utah State UP, 2012.

Bertaux, Daniel. *Biography and Society: The Life History Approach*. Beverly Hills: Sage, 1981. Print.

Bertaux, Daniel, and Paul Thompson. *Between Generations: The Life History Approach.* Beverly Hills: Sage, 1993. Print.

Borland, Katherine. "'That's Not What I Said': Interpretive Conflicting Oral Narrative Research." Perks and Thomson, *Oral History Reader* 311–21.

Braden, Su. "Using Video for Research and Representation: Basic Human Needs and Critical Pedagogy." *Learning, Media, & Technology* 24.2 (1999): 117–30. Print.

Brettell, Caroline B., ed. *When They Read What We Write: The Politics of Ethnography.* Westport: Bergin, 1996. Print.

Britzman, Deborah. "'The Question of Belief': Writing Poststructural Ethnography." St. Pierre and Pillow, *Working the Ruins* 27–40.

Brockmeier, Jens, and Donal A. Carbaugh, eds. *Narrative and Identity: Studies in Autobiography, Self, and Culture.* Amsterdam: Benjamin, 2001. Print.

Brockmeier, Jens, and Rom Harre. "Narrative: Problems and Promises of an Alternative Paradigm." Brockmeier and Carbaugh, *Narrative and Identity* 39–58.

Bruner, Jerome. "Self-Making and World Making." *Journal of Aesthetic Education* 25.1 (1991): 66–78. Print.

Budwig, Nancy, Ina Užgiris, and James Wertsch, eds. *Communication: An Arena of Development.* Westport: Greenwood, 1999. Print.

Burgess, Robert G., ed. *Field Research: A Sourcebook and Field Manual.* London: Allen, 1982. Print.

Cantoni, Lorenzo, and Catherine McLoughlin, eds. *Proceedings of Ed-Media 2004 World Conference on Educational Media, Hypermedia, and Telecommunications.* Norfolk: Assoc. for the Advancement of Computing in Education, 2004. Print.

Daniels, Beth, and Peter Mortensen, eds. *Women and Literacy: Local and Global Inquiries for a New Century.* New York: Erlbaum, 2007. Print.

Denzin, Norman, and Yvonna Lincoln, eds. *Handbook of Qualitative Research.* 2nd ed. Thousand Oaks: Sage, 2000. Print.

Derry, Sharon L., ed. *Guidelines for Video Research in Education: Recommendations from an Expert Panel.* Data Research and Development Center, Arlington, Virginia. July 2007. Web. <http://drdc.uchicago.edu/what/video-research-guidelines.pdf>.

Erickson, Frederick. "Definition and Analysis of Data from Videotape: Some Research Procedures and Their Rationales." Green, Camilli, Elmore, and Skukauskaite, *Handbook of Complementary Methods* 177–93.

Frisch, Michael. "Oral History and the Digital Revolution." Perks and Thomson, *Oral History Reader* 102–14.

Georgakopoulou, Alexandra. "Thinking Big with Small Stories in Narrative and Identity Analysis." *Narrative Inquiry* 16 (2006): 129–37. Print.

Goffman, Erving. *The Presentation of Self in Everyday Life.* New York: Penguin, 1969. Print.

Goodwin, Marjorie Harness, and Goodwin, Charles. "Emotion within Situated Activity." Budwig, Užgiris, and Wertsch, *Communication* 33–53.

Green, Judith, Gregory Camilli, Patricia Elmore, and Audra Skukauskaite, eds. *Handbook of Complementary Methods in Educational Research.* London: Routledge, 2006. Print.

Gubrium, Jaber F., and James A. Holstein. *The New Language of Qualitative Method.* Oxford: Oxford UP, 1997. Print.

Haraway, Donna. "Situated Knowledges: The Science Question in Feminism and the Privilege of Partial Perspective." *Feminist Studies* 14.3 (1988): 575–99. Print.

Hawisher, Gail, E., and Cynthia L. Selfe, with Brittney Moraski and Melissa Pearson. "Becoming Literate in the Information Age: Cultural Ecologies and the Literacies of Technology." *College Composition and Communication* 55.4 (2004): 642–92. Print.

Hawisher, Gail E., and Cynthia L. Selfe, with Gorjana Kisa and Shafinaz Ahmed. "Globalism and Multimodality in a Digitized World." *Pedagogy: Critical Approaches to Teaching Literature, Language, Composition, and Culture* 10.1 (2010): 55–68. Print. doi:10.1215/15314200-2009-020.

Hawisher, Gail, E., and Cynthia L. Selfe, with Katherine Coffield and Safia El-Wakil. "Women and the Global Ecologies of Digital Literacies" Daniell and Mortensen, *Women and Literacy* 207–28.

Hawisher, Gail E., and Cynthia L. Selfe, with Yi-Huey Guo and Lu Liu. "Globalization and Agency: Designing and Redesigning the Literacies of Cyberspace." *College English* 68 (2006): 619–36. Print.

Hawisher, Gail E., Cynthia L. Selfe, Synne Skjulstad, and Patrick W. Berry. "Global Feminist Encounters on the Internet and Beyond." Conference on College Composition and Communication. Chicago, Illinois. 22–25 March 2006. Reading.

Hine, Christine, ed. *Virtual Methods: Issues in Social Research on the Internet.* Oxford: Berg, 2005. Print.

Hitchcock, Caryl H., Mary Anne Prater, and Peter W. Dowrick. "Comprehension and Fluency: Examining the Effects of Tutoring and Video Self-Modeling on First-Grade Students with Reading Difficulties." *Learning Disability Quarterly* 27.2 (2004): 89–104. Print.

Holland, Dorothy, William Lachicotte, Debra Skinner, and Carole Cain. *Identity and Agency in Cultural Worlds.* Cambridge: Harvard UP, 1998. Print.

Jaffe, Alexandra. "Involvement, Detachment, and Representation on Corsica." Brettell, *When They Read* 51–66.

Kanes, Clive, Merrilyn Goos, and Elizabeth Warren, eds. *Teaching Mathematics in New Times.* Brisbane: Mathematics Educ. Research Group of Australasia, 1998. Print.

Kirsch, Gesa E. *Ethical Dilemmas in Feminist Research: The Politics of Location, Interpretation, and Publication.* Albany: State U of New York P, 1999. Print.

Kivits, Joelle. "Online Interviewing and the Research Relationship." Hine, *Virtual Methods* 35–64.

Landman, Maeve. "Getting Quality in Qualitative Research: A Short Introduction to Feminist Methodology and Methods." *Proceedings of the Nutrition Society* 65 (2006): 429–33. Print.

Lather, Patti. "Drawing the Line at Angels: Working the Ruins of Feminist Ethnography." St. Pierre and Pillow, *Working the Ruins* 284–311.

Lofland, John, and Lyn Lofland. *Analyzing Social Settings: A Guide to Qualitative Observations and Research.* Belmont: Wadsworth, 1984. Print.

Lummis, Trevor. *Listening to History: The Authenticity of Oral Evidence.* London: Hutchinson, 1987. Print.

Mishler, Elliot G. *Research Interviewing: Context and Narrative.* Cambridge: Harvard UP, 1986. Print.

Mousley, Judith. "Ethnographic Research in Mathematics Education: Using Different Types of Visual Data Refined from Videotapes." Kanes, Goos, and Warren, *Teaching Mathematics* 397–403.

Nielson, Joyce McCarl. *Feminist Research Methods: Exemplary Readings in the Social Sciences*. Boulder: Westview, 1990. Print.

Oakley, Ann. "Interviewing Women: A Contradiction in Terms." Roberts, *Doing Feminist Research* 30–61.

Olesen, Virginia L. "Feminisms and Qualitative Research at and into the Millennium." Denzin and Lincoln, *Handbook of Qualitative Research* 215–55.

Palmer, Vivien M. *Field Studies in Sociology: A Student's Manual*. Chicago: U of Chicago P, 1928. Print.

Pea, Roy, and Jay Lemke. "Sharing and Reporting Video Work." Derry, *Guidelines for Video Research* 39-46.

Perks, Robert, and Alistair Thomson, eds. *The Oral History Reader*. London: Routledge, 1998. Print.

Pink, Sarah, László Kürti, and Ana Isabel Afonso. *Working Images: Visual Research and Representation in Ethnography*. London: Routledge, 2004. Print.

Reinharz, Shulamit. *Feminist Methods in Social Research*. New York: Oxford UP, 1992. Print.

Richardson, Laurel. "Skirting a Pleated Text: De-Disciplining an Academic Life." St. Pierre and Pillow, *Working the Ruins* 153–63.

Ritchie, Jane, and Jane Lewis. *Qualitative Research Practices: A Guide for Social Science Students and Researchers*. London: Sage, 2003. Print.

Roberts, Helen, ed. *Doing Feminist Research*. London: Routledge, 1981. Print.

Schoen, Donald. *The Reflexive Practitioner*. New York: Basic Books, 1983. Print.

Schüller, Dietrich. "Audiovisual Research Collections and Preservation." *Phonogrammarchiv, Austrian Academy of Sciences*. 4 Feb. 2008. Web. <http://www.knaw.nl/ecpa/TAPE/docs/audiovisual_research_collections.pdf>.

Selfe, Cynthia L., and Gail E. Hawisher. "A Historical Look at Electronic Literacy." *Journal of Business and Technical Communication* 16.3 (2002): 231–76. Print.

———. *Literate Lives in the Information Age: Narratives of Literacy from the United States*. Mahwah: Erlbaum, 2004. Print.

Selfe, Cynthia L., and Gail E. Hawisher, with Oladipupo Lashore and Pengfei Song. "Literacies and the Complexity of the Global Digital Divide." Van Waes, Leyten, and Neuwirth, *Writing and Digital Media* 253–85.

Shepherd, Nicole. "Interviewing Online: Qualitative Research in the Network(ed) Society." AQR Qualitative Research Conference. Sydney, Australia. 16–19 July 2003. Reading.

Shunk, Sandy, and Matthew Kearney. "Digital Video as a Tool in Research Projects: Zooming In on Current Issues." Cantoni and McLoughlin, *Proceedings of Ed-Media* 2085–92.

Stock, Jonathan P. J. "Documenting the Musical Event: Observation, Participation, Representation." *Empirical Musicology*. Ed. Eric Clarke and Nicholas Cook. Oxford: Oxford Scholarship Online Monographs, 2004. 15–35. Web. <http://www.oxfordscholarship.com/view/10.1093/acprof:oso/9780195167498.001.0001/acprof-9780195167498-chapter-2>.

St. Pierre, Elizabeth, and Wanda Pillow, eds. *Working the Ruins: Feminist Poststructural Theory and Methods in Education*. New York: Routledge, 2000. Print.

Thompson, Paul. R. *The Voice of the Past: Oral History*. Oxford: Oxford UP, 1988. Print.

Van Waes, Luuk, Marielle Leyten, and Chris Neuwirth, eds. *Writing and Digital Media*. Amsterdam: Elsevier, 2007. Print.

Visweswaran, Kamala. *Fictions of Feminist Ethnography.* Minneapolis: U of Minnesota P, 1994. Print.

Walker, Rob. "Case Study, Case Records and Multimedia." *Cambridge Journal of Education* 32.1 (2002): 109–27. Print.

4.

Analytic Strategies, Competent Inquiries, and Methodological Tensions in the Study of Writing

Christina Haas, Pamela Takayoshi, and Brandon Carr

> Knowledge is . . . the product of competent inquiry.
> —John Dewey (1938)

While knowledge making is imperative for any disciplinary field (as Haswell, "NCTE/CCCC's Recent War on Scholarship," rightly notes), it is particularly important for the field of writing studies, where the object of study—contemporary writing practice—is not fixed but fluid and changing. This knowledge making depends on what John C. Dewey calls "competent inquiries," which we understand to be inquiries that are systematic, self-conscious, clearly articulated, and warranted. Hence, the nature of inquiry and the methodological issues associated with it are becoming increasingly salient—as this volume's editors so clearly argue.

This chapter describes and discusses five analytic strategies for inquiry and knowledge making in the study of writing. These strategies grew out of and became a key component of our long-term and ongoing research on new-media writing in contemporary youth culture. Specifically, our project focuses on the language (linguistic forms) and discourse (social practices) of instant messaging (IM).[1] Working out research practices has been a central feature of this project as it has unfolded over the last several years. Inspired by Dewey's call for building knowledge through competent inquiry, the strategies outlined below have, we believe, moved us some distance toward making our research on digital writing in IM systematic, self-conscious, clearly articulated, and warranted. The chapter concludes by reflecting on the productive tensions that lie at the heart of inquiry and on the need for "homegrown" methods in writing studies.

Although we developed these strategies in the conduct of our research, they have their genesis in two traditions within writing studies: linguistic-based discourse analysis[2] (e.g., Fahnestock and Secor; MacDonald; Swales) and field-based studies of literacy (e.g., Cushman; Heath). The linguistic-based discourse analysis approach is exemplified in writing research in 1990 by John M. Swales's research on the construction of the scholarly article, Jeanne Fahnestock and Marie Secor's 1988 analysis of the rhetorical moves in literary arguments, and Susan P. MacDonald's 2005 study of the linguistic features of journalistic accounts of medicine. Field-based studies of literacy include Ellen Cushman's 1996 action research with community members and Shirley Brice Heath's 1984 study of family literacies in Appalachia. Given their genesis in research traditions familiar to writing scholars, we do not expect that the strategies will be entirely new to other researchers. However, presenting these strategies in detail and in tandem will, we hope, make them useful and applicable to future projects. The five strategies are:

1. Use an inductive approach.
2. Quantify.
3. Employ the technology under study.
4. Work with insiders.
5. Integrate talk and text in the conduct of collaborative writing.

The first two strategies grow out of the tradition of linguistic-based discourse analysis, while the third and fourth are similar to some of the procedures of field-based studies of literacy. The fifth strategy is one that helps to manage the tensions between the two traditions in the conduct of research activity.

These strategies as we have developed and practiced them are particularly well suited to descriptive studies using what are generally understood to be qualitative methods, that is, studies designed to generate accounts of writers' experiences, writing practices and contexts, and written texts. The strategies are meant to be used in the analytic phases of research, that is, when researchers attempt to make sense of data. Although we used these strategies with transcripts of instant-messaging sessions (and, with strategy 5, transcribed conversations within a work group), we believe they can be applied to many kinds of data: student texts, transcribed oral discourse, interview data, systematic observational field notes, open-ended survey responses, and even video transcripts.

Background: The Instant-Messaging Project

This project grew out of our belief that detailed accounts of the forms and features of the ubiquitous discourse of IM could contribute to robust understandings of literacy as it is practiced in people's everyday, nonacademic lives.[3] Understanding everyday literacy practices can, in turn, suggest ways that academic practices and writing instruction could be modified in order to better teach students the composition and communicative skills needed in an increasingly digital world.

We collected almost sixty naturally occurring IM sessions of college students (i.e., IM sessions that had not been generated for the purposes of our study) for a total corpus of over thirty-two thousand words. From these data, we inductively developed a taxonomy of IM features, features that might in some contexts be seen as nonstandard but that we came to understand as standard conventions of IM discourse. These features included, for example, repeated punctuation (!!!!, ...); substitutions of numbers or letters for words (I'll wait 4 you; B right back); slang (profanities and swear words, as well as words like "geez" and "cutie"); repeated or deleted letters (realllly, ppl [for people]); emoticons (:-), ;o); and sound words (eeeekkk, argg). We also determined frequencies of occurrence of the IM features in the taxonomy. The results of our project are available in Haas and Takayoshi (with Carr, Hudson, and Polluck) and in Haas, Carr, and Takayoshi.

Many of our analytical choices were made via in situ methodological decision making. Our research team comprised at different points in our project two associate professors, Christina Haas and Pamela Takayoshi; three writing-studies PhD students, Diana Awad, Emily Dillon, and Elizabeth Feltner; and/or four undergraduate students, Brandon Carr, Jessica Heffner, Kimberley Hudson, and Ross Pollock. Methodological decisions involving the taxonomizing, coding, and analyzing of features were often negotiated in lengthy conversations among the research-team participants. Our in situ methodological decisions—which are, of course, a part of any research program—were made in the situational and temporal contexts of our own research practice.

Research is, in a very important way, learning what you don't already know. It requires putting oneself in an always uncomfortable position, a position of uncertainty. For us, this meant a kind of shift in how we understood ourselves vis-à-vis writing. We are writing teachers and researchers, we are writers ourselves, and we hold positions of authority in institutions that see us as writing experts. And indeed, we know something about what writing is and how it is done. But trying to understand new media and the young people who use it so facilely meant that we were often in a knowledge-down (if not power-down) position vis-à-vis others. At this historical moment, characterized by rapid technological change and the rise of new writing media, writing researchers are not experts in the discourse forms that young people have integrated so seamlessly into their everyday lives. This specific research context, one in which we were studying practices and forms with which we were not expert, caused us to rethink some of our research practices, views about knowledge making, and understandings of "competent inquiry." The five strategies grew out of this process of rethinking.

The Analytic Strategies

1. Use an inductive approach.

After gathering the transcripts, removing identifying marks, and standardizing the format, we began with a very fine-grained look at the "thing itself"—the words and symbols that constituted the instant-messaging sessions. Working independently at first, then discussing and comparing, we incrementally built a coding scheme that accounted for each and every instance of "nonstandard" usage in the transcripts. (The quotes around *nonstandard* are meant to suggest that although such usages are not part of standard written English [SWE], we came to understand them as conventions within IM discourse.) The categories were emergent (Glaser and Strauss), meaning that we did not bring to the analysis any specific, previously developed schemes for analyzing discourse, although we each had implicit theories of language and we were all well-schooled in the features of SWE. We attempted to bracket previous assumptions, and working collaboratively helped in this regard. This inductive, from-the-ground-up strategy was particularly apt for our project, which focused on textual forms that had not been previously studied in much detail.

The watchwords for this inductive phase of the project were *be thorough* and *be generous*. In other words, we tried to avoid taking any feature or data point off the table—we wanted our coding scheme to account for virtually all the discourse features we encountered. So if we found a feature that we were tempted to categorize as "other," we set that instance aside as we continued to analyze the transcript, returning to the item later. Often, being able to contextualize the feature in the larger discourse allowed us to understand how to code it. Or, we conferred with one another to determine if other similar instances had been found and could justify the creation of a new category.

Generosity came into play in that we treated every feature as essentially meaningful. Certainly, IM gets a bad rap in the popular literature, where it is seen as either a contributing factor to and/or evidence of young people's poor control over the English language. But we resisted coding particular features as error. Indeed, in one of the early codings of the data, we systematically and collaboratively attempted to read every error (as understood in the context of SWE) as a meaningful utterance or at least understand it as part of the emerging conventions of IM. So, for example, we treated missing capitals and missing end punctuation—because they were so common—as standard for instant-messaging discourse. In most cases, we tried to grant the benefit of the doubt: If a particular instance could be coded as meaningful and intentional (i.e., part of the coding scheme), then we did. Take the case of repeated letters: We coded items like "lllovvve" and "ccoool" as instances of this category, but we also included "rreally" and "cllass," since we wanted to assume meaningfulness.

2. Quantify.

As the project proceeded, we came to understand—or to rediscover—the importance of quantitative methods of analysis. In this project, quantitative analysis simply consisted of determining frequencies and means. But even deciding to calculate frequencies and means was a move beyond description and a conscious choice to be systematic.

This move to the quantitative was important in our project for two reasons: It allowed us to understand our object of study in a way that mere description did not, and it helped us see what kinds of arguments were really supported by the data—or were not. For instance, a common conception about IM discourse is that it consists almost exclusively of slang and abbreviations. And indeed, the largest category of IM features was slang; the third largest was abbreviations. But determining means and frequencies allowed us to say more than that these two kinds of features were common. That is, even though slang was common, it was only relatively common. Slang expressions constituted about 20 percent of the IM features (and we can imagine different readers, with different expectations, saying, "Wow, that much?" or "Wow, that little?"), but this was only about 1.8 percent of the total words in the corpus. [4]

Our watchwords for working with this strategy were *differentiate* and *consolidate*. Again, in the case of slang, we differentiated the actual slang words used, and our analysis revealed that same set of core slang words came up over and over again in the analysis. In other words, there was a whole lot of "standard slang" (if that's not a contradiction in terms) and very little "creative" slang. In another analytic move, we consolidated three categories that had to do with temporality relations: transcribed speech (in which letters were added or dropped to represent the cadence of speech through the options allowed by a conventional keyboard), punctuation (such as long dashes or ellipses, to indicate the passage of time), and metamarkings (a relatively rare category in which people used keyboard letters and symbols to indicate a temporal or spatial distance from their own discourse). This move allowed us to see that almost 30 percent of the features were concerned with representing time. These findings could, in turn, lead to claims about the role of time in IM practice or about the ways in which students tried to mimic speech (a temporal rather than spatial mode) in their IM discourse. In short, quantifying the data in just these simple ways helped us understand the phenomenon under study more clearly by indicating various features' relative occurrence and, at the same time, suggested lines of argument that might, or might not, be supportable.

Strategies 1 and 2—induction and quantification—are staples of linguistic-based discourse analysis. Strategies 3 and 4, however, are drawn from field-based studies of literacy and emphasize insider knowledge and the experiential learning of the researcher.[5]

3. *Employ the technology under study.*

This strategy emphasizes the experiential knowledge of researchers, a characteristic of field-based research (Lincoln). Of course, writing researchers—by virtue of their objects of study—use the tools they study. But here we mean "use" in a very particular way: building our experiential knowledge of IM by employing it in the conduct of purposeful activity and being self-conscious about the use of that technology.

We had all heretofore seen ourselves as IM users—we had enjoyed picking screen names and playing with color and font to express the "personality" of those screen names, and we had come to regularly (if not habitually) use the program to say "hello" to family members and friends, to plan meetings with colleagues, or to check schedules with kids. But we also used IM to discuss coding decisions and adjudicate disagreements. In this new context of use within conceptual activity, we came to understand—from a user's point of view—how and why certain IM features might be used: how the repeated punctuation to indicate time was used to suggest thought time or uncertainty; how the speed of IM conversations virtually required the use of abbreviations, dropped letters, and replacing letters or numbers for entire words; how employing the medium seemed to invite the use of emoticons, sound words, or emphasis marking to indicate paralinguistic cues, that is, how a message should be "taken."

In addition to learning the lexicon of IM, the experience of using it in the conduct of our work reinforced our notions about the purposefulness and intentionality of this innovative form. That is, while we held certain theoretical assumptions about the purposefulness and intentionality of language use, the experience of using it ourselves gave us first-hand experience to ground these assumptions. Equally important, however, was how this experience showed us that while the form was innovative, it was not the case that anything goes in IM. The students we worked with teased us about some of our more "innovative" (that is, incomprehensible) abbreviations and emoticons and, in so doing, helped us to understand certain social and cultural norms for IM.

4. Work with insiders.

Very much related to the previous strategy, the strategy to work with insiders was based in the strong collaborative nature of our project. Envisioning a large, multiyear, corpus-based study from the outset, we had assembled a research team to work on the project, including some undergraduate English majors, initially drawn from Haas's seminar. These students were integral to the project, and they worked much more than typical research assistants. This was partly out of design (we had worked on several collaborative projects before and had become committed to the team approach to research) and partly out of necessity (the students were receiving upper-division credit, so we had to give them something to do besides photocopy and run to the library).

The students were involved in virtually every aspect of the project: They helped draft consent forms and institutional-review-board documents; they visited classes to recruit participants; they helped to standardize the transcripts in preparation for analysis; they served as coders, both for the data set as a whole and for determining interrater reliability; they created spreadsheets and tables of findings; they were coauthors on conference papers; they were intimately involved in the writing of articles.

The intimate involvement of the students in the research meant that they were in a position to provide important insights on an almost daily basis. They explained aspects of youth culture at our university, such as local hangouts, shorthand references to campus locations, or allusions to current movies, television shows, and music. They also provided "native" or insider knowledge about IM, in that they helped us read various abbreviations and emoticons and explained the nature of "poke wars."

Most important, they provided specific, deep understandings of the transcripts. That is, they added contextual information to explain aspects of the data that we found otherwise inexplicable, such as one session into which a participant had embedded the content of another IM session to share aspects of the prior conversation with her friend. Or, in another case, explaining that what seemed to us to be random insertions of "away messages" into ongoing conversations actually revealed when a participant went off task to check e-mail or to participate in a parallel IM session. Early in the project, one of the students (who was an active online gamer) casually asked us if we would like to see what messaging looked like in game environments. In so doing, he helped us to begin to see the ways that messaging technology is embedded in other contexts we had not thought of.

The point here is that the students we worked with were "insiders" in university life and IM culture in a way that we could not and cannot be. That is, this project needed to be cross-generational, not just because young people tend to be more tech-savvy than their professors but because they are hooked into a youth culture in a way we could not be. And it is only through including them in all aspects of the research—from scholarly reading to coding to writing—that we were able to tap into and take advantage of their insider knowledge. Had they been only photocopying and running to the library, we would never have known what they knew—and what we did not know.

5. Integrate talk and text in the conduct of collaborative writing.

This strategy concerns the process of collaboratively producing documents, not analysis per se. It was born of necessity and out of logistical concerns. We had been making notes from time to time about the piece we envisioned on methodology for new-media writing studies, and we each brought these notes to our initial brainstorming meeting about the argument we hoped to make in such a piece. As this scheduled one-hour meeting stretched to two and as we realized the variety of potential ideas we had about the planned text, the scope of the task became somewhat daunting. Since, for us, writing was at least as much about talking through ideas as it was about the generation of text, all three of us had lots to say and were often saying it over one another. The resulting wide-ranging discussion proved to be difficult to capture in notes, and the note-taking, even on a laptop, became increasingly cumbersome. Ultimately, the note-taker couldn't keep up with the conversation, and the note-taking was abandoned.

While we had focused on form in our analysis of data, now we needed to keep track of content. So we turned to a better technology for this purpose, and we began audiotaping our writing sessions and taking turns transcribing the tapes between meetings. This eliminated the need for a note-taker (although it added the additional labor of transcribing; we have since attempted to use speech recognition software for this task, with mixed results), but it also had an additional benefit: The transcript provided a material record that we could return to again and again. The process became aggregative in that we could use the data (in this case, the transcribed writing sessions) to determine what ideas might be worth building upon and extending. In essence, our verbalized ideas became materialized and objectified so that they could, in turn, become the basis of reflection, text production, and further discussion.

This writing strategy in fact allowed us to analyze these meeting transcripts the way we had the IM transcripts—taking multiple passes through the text, following topic threads, looking for patterns, judging the relative depth of different ideas. This strategy was also a reminder of the fluid boundaries between modes in the conduct of human activities—just as the students whose instant messaging we studied developed conventions to create some of the dynamics of talk in the textual form, so we systematically turned talk into text, which then became the basis of more talk and, ultimately, this published text.

Some Concluding Thoughts

In closing, this project has reminded us again of the inherent and productive tensions that lie at the heart of research, tensions between a focus on the object of study and a focus on the process of inquiry, tensions between a fine-grained focus on the object itself (as employed within linguistic-based discourse analysis) and a more wide-angle view of the object-in-context (as understood within field-based studies of literacy). While the first two strategies each concern "the thing itself," the third and fourth strategies are part of the process of contextualizing. Further, the strategy for working inductively and the strategy for quantifying both invite synchronic analysis; they provide a slice of time and focus on formal qualities—and they lead to the development of categories and taxonomies (as in our IM study). The strategies for employing the technology of study and working with insiders are both diachronic; they focus on experiential knowledge in real-time contexts and thereby provide a view of process; rather than a taxonomy, these strategies yield a narrative.

An analytic movement from the object itself to the object's "habitat" and our experience of that habitat allows critical distance. But, at least as important, so does the move back to the object itself. This ongoing pulling apart and bringing together constitutes, in our view, the nature of analysis—and the basis for competent inquiries, as Dewey terms them—in the study of writing.

Finally, we have come to be convinced that the field of writing studies needs to develop methods for the study of writers and writing that are specific to our own enterprise—"homegrown" methods, as it were. One way to develop such homegrown methods is in the combining of research traditions as we have tried to do here.[6] Another way is in the action-reflection, talk-text movement that is at the heart of the strategies we present above and that is encapsulated in the fifth strategy about writing—an integration of doing, writing, reflecting. But the reflection has to be intentional, it has to be systematic, it has to be overt, it has to be built into the process. Our hope is that what we have presented here—not just the strategies but the reflections on method—might become an opening move in discussions about homegrown methods for the study of writing.

Notes

1. While a review of recent research on IM is beyond the scope of this chapter, exemplary recent studies include: Baron, "See You Online"; Bryant, Sanders-Jackson, and Smallwood, "IMing, Text Messaging, and Adolescent Social Networks"; Jacobs, "Fast Times and Digital Literacy" and "Complimenting Contexts"; Lee, "Affordances and Text-Making Practices in Online Instant Messaging"; Lewis and Fabos, "Instant Messaging, Literacies, and Social Identities"; Nardi, Whittaker, and Bradner, "Interaction and Outeraction"; and Nastri, Pena, and Hancock, "Construction of Away Messages." An important early study is Ferrara, Brunner, and Whittemore, "Interactive Written Discourse as an Emergent Register."

2. We use the term *discourse analysis* to mean textually based analysis of extended, intact written language; this is how the term is used in Bazerman and Prior, *What Writing Does and How It Does It.* This is distinguished from *critical discourse analysis* (e.g., Fairclough, *Critical Discourse Analysis*), which is also sometimes called discourse analysis.

3. Our research was funded by the National Council of Teachers of English, Kent State University's Office of Research and Graduate Studies, and the Faculty Professional Development Center at Kent State.

4. This example also illustrates nicely that "data don't speak for themselves." Although we have hard numbers about the frequency of slang (in this case), how those numbers are interpreted can vary, and there are many different arguments for which such numbers might be used in support.

5. For more about insider knowledge, see Heath's ethnographic work with schools and families in Appalachia. For more about the experiential learning, see Cushman's action research.

6. See Greene and Caracelli, "Making Paradigmatic Sense of Mixed Methods Practice."

Works Cited

Baron, N. "See You Online: Gender Issues in College Student Use of Instant Messaging." *Journal of Language and Social Psychology* 23.4 (2004): 397–423. Print.

Bazerman, Charles, and Paul Prior. *What Writing Does and How It Does It.* Mahwah: Erlbaum, 2004. Print.

Bryant, J. Alison, Ashley Sanders-Jackson, and Amber M. K. Smallwood. "IMing, Text Messaging, and Adolescent Social Networks." *Journal of Computer-Mediated Communication* 11.2 (2006). Web. 18 Aug. 2010. <http://jcmc.indiana.edu/vol11/issue2/bryant.html>.

Cushman, Ellen. *The Struggle and the Tools: Oral and Literate Strategies in an Inner City Community.* Albany: State U of New York P, 1996. Print.

Dewey, John. *Logic: The Theory of Inquiry.* New York: Holt, 1938. Print.

Fahnestock, Jeanne, and Marie Secor. "The Stases of Scientific and Literary Argument." *Written Communication* 5.4 (1988): 427–43. Print.

Fairclough, Norman. *Critical Discourse Analysis: The Critical Study of Language.* Harlow: Longman, 1995. Print.

Ferrara, Kathleen, Hans Brunner, and Greg Whittemore. "Interactive Written Discourse as an Emergent Register." *Written Communication* 8.1 (1991): 8–34. Print.

Glaser, B. G., and A. L. Strauss. *The Discovery of Grounded Theory: Strategies for Qualitative Research.* Piscataway: Transaction, 1967. Print.

Greene, Jennifer, and Valerie J. Caracelli. "Making Paradigmatic Sense of Mixed Methods Practice." *Handbook of Mixed Methods in Social and Behavioral Research.* Ed. A. Tashakkori and C. Teddlie. Thousand Oaks: Sage, 2003. 91–110. Print.

Haas, Christina, and Pamela Takayoshi, with Brandon Carr, Kimberley Hudson, and Ross Pollock. "Young People's Everyday Literacies: The Language of Instant Messaging." *Research in the Teaching of English* 45 (2011): 378–404. Print.

Haas, Christina, Brandon Carr, and Pamela Takayoshi. "Building and Maintaining Contexts in Interactive Networked Writing: An Examination of Deixis and Intertextuality in Instant Messaging." *Journal of Business and Technical Communication* 25 (2011): 276–98. Print.

Haswell, Richard H. "NCTE/CCCC's Recent War on Scholarship." *Written Communication* 22.2 (2005): 198–223. Print.

Heath, Shirley Brice. *Ways with Words: Language, Life, and Work in Communities and Classrooms.* Cambridge: Cambridge UP, 1984. Print.

Jacobs, Gloria. "Complicating Contexts: Issues of Methodology in Researching the Language and Literacies of Instant Messaging." *Reading Research Quarterly* 39 (2004): 394–406. Print.

———. "Fast Times and Digital Literacy: Participation Roles and Portfolio Construction within Instant Messaging." *Journal of Literacy Research* 38 (2006): 171–96. Print.

Lee, Carmen. "Affordances and Text-Making Practices in Online Instant Messaging." *Written Communication* 24.3 (2007): 223–49. Print.

Lewis, Cynthia, and Bettina Fabos. "Instant Messaging, Literacies, and Social Identities." *Reading Research Quarterly* 40 (2005): 470–501. Print.

Lincoln, Yvonna S. "The Making of a Constructivist." *The Paradigm Dialog.* Ed. E. Guba. Newbury Park: Sage, 1990. 46–66. Print.

MacDonald, Susan P. "The Language of Journalism in Treatments of Hormone Replacement News." *Written Communication* 22.3 (2005): 275–97. Print.

Nardi, Bonnie A., Steve Whittaker, and Erin Bradner. "Interaction and Outeraction: Instant Messaging in Action." *Proc Conf on Computer Supported Collaborative Work CSCW* (2000): 79–88. Print.

Nastri, J., J. Pena, and J. Hancock. "The Construction of Away Messages: A Speech Act Analysis." *Journal of Computer-Mediated Communication* 11 (2006): 1025–45. Print.

Swales, John M. *Genre Analysis: English in Academic and Research Settings.* Cambridge: Cambridge UP, 1990. Print.

5.

A Complicated Geometry: Triangulating Feminism, Activism, and Technological Literacy

Kristine L. Blair

Researcher Patti Lather has defined *empowering feminist research* as a method for counteracting the invisibility and distortion of women's experience, a type of long-standing patriarchal exclusion that for Patricia Sullivan extends to the academy. Indeed, Sullivan contends that academic discourse communities have been male dominated, focusing on mastery models and modes of discourse that "women had little voice in shaping" (39–40) but that they must adapt to in order to succeed. These mastery models have applied to technological literacy acquisition as well, with the larger cultural understanding of computer literacy all too often being perceived as a male domain (Kramarae; Stabile; Wajcman). Many computers and writing specialists have theorized digital identity development in a range of technological spaces and have questioned the role that the composition curriculum can play in fostering identity construction within the academy and beyond it. In the process, they have countered some of the presumptions about who has access to technology, noting that as writing and communication technologies become increasingly digital, it is vital that we pay attention to the cultural, political, and material conditions that impact access to these technologies.

While recent data from the PEW Research Center for Internet and American Life can quantify the changing demographics of online life, the continuing work of Gail Hawisher and Cynthia Selfe (*Literate Lives*) has chronicled in narrative form the technological literacy development of women faculty and students from diverse cultural backgrounds, grounding that acquisition in equally diverse day-to-day contexts. Hawisher and Selfe privilege stories of women's technological access in part because they are strikingly similar to our own literacy narratives as feminist teacher-researchers (*Literate Lives* 646). Inevitably, such stories represent a triangulation of feminist theory and action research, along with the materiality of technological literacy. As the title of this chapter suggests, such triangulation is a complicated process that defies a linear progression of more objectivist data collection and representation strategies.

This chapter emphasizes the importance of deploying feminist theory and method in digital spaces through "technofeminist research," which Judy Wajcman defines as a "scholarly activity that redefines the problem of the exclusion of groups of people from technological domains and activities" ("Feminist Theories"). Not unlike feminist research, technofeminist research intertwines the personal and the political, situating technological literacy in a range of familial, educational, and professional contexts that have often marginalized women's voices. Writing of the constructed nature of both technology and gender, Wajcman asserts that technofeminism represents "a coming together of many diverse voices engaged in dialogue, influencing each other and each being modified in the process" (*Technofeminism* 8). Because of the emphasis on diverse voices, a significant component of both feminist and technofeminist research is the role of narrative as a powerful method for women and girls to articulate their relationships to technology within academic and social spaces and "to render the complexities of individual and social experience" (Journet, current volume, 14). Furthermore, such methodological articulation involves the development of activist projects and pedagogies that foster safe havens for all students to experiment with technologies in ways that establish reciprocal mentoring models among student participants and between participants and teacher-scholars. Given these components, I trace the relationship between feminism and technology, outlining questions and methods that lead to a materialist, activist approach to researching digital literacy practices. Finally, I profile an ongoing action research project, the Digital Mirror Computer Camp, to document the way these goals and methods can lead to community action on behalf of women and girls and ultimately foster a community of technofeminist researchers devoted to this goal.

From Feminism to Technofeminism

Sullivan relies heavily on Sandra Harding's characterizations of feminist research, including (1) acknowledging women's experiences as a starting point for (2) providing women researchers and subjects the explanation of social phenomena with a theoretical framework of gender and power and (3) doing so in a way that equally acknowledges the positionality of the researcher and the cultural assumptions he or she brings to data collection and representation. More recently, Nancy Naples confirms that feminist research has concerned itself with method and politics, attending to the social relations manifest in everyday activities and lived experiences (94). In an era in which women's literacy experiences are as much online as offline, migrating these goals and the methods accompanying them into virtual spaces is a priority for technofeminist rhetoricians seeking to make online spaces hospitable to women's social, professional, and political goals. Notably, scholars that include Wajcman, Carole Stabile, and Cheris Kramarae have explored the ways in which technological spaces are gendered domains that have impacted access, equity, and empowerment for women across cultures. And certainly, composition scholars such as Selfe, Hawisher, and Katrina Powell and Pamela Takayoshi, among others, have called for further research about the literate practices of women and girls as a cultural class of individuals for whom technological access and experience have been constrained by gender bias.

Despite these intersections between feminism and technology, Faith Wilding asserts that feminists must learn to deploy an activist politics that can address issues of identity, representation, and empowerment in a digital age (9). For technofeminist rhetoricians, such activism must also acknowledge technological literacy acquisition and the role gender plays in that acquisition, not as an essentialist, biological variable but as a materialist, cultural one. Thus, the questions for technofeminist researchers, including those working in rhetoric and composition, must address (1) how and why women access technology in their daily lives, (2) what larger material constraints impact that access, and (3) what methods best enable opportunities for women to make their lived experiences with technology more visible. Given these questions, a large component of technofeminist work across the disciplines has relied upon more-qualitative methods, particularly narrative, as a way of generating knowledge about how and why women use and are used by a range of technologies within the classroom and the larger culture. Significant examples include Flis Henwood, Helen Kennedy, and Nod Miller's *Cyborg Lives: Women's Technobiographies*, a compilation of women's accounts of their relationship to everyday technologies, a project similar to Kramarae's earlier *Technology and Women's Voices: Keeping in Touch*. In her foreword to the Henwood, Kennedy, Miller collection, Wajcman contends that "presenting a diversity of narratives . . . enables us to transcend once and for all the traditional dichotomy of technology as either empowering or disempowering for women" (8). Equally important is Wajcman's emphasis on biography as a method for grounding experience through cultural differences that include age, race and ethnicity, class, and sexuality.

This reliance on narrative within technofeminist research meshes with a range of theoretical frameworks and pedagogical strategies essential to rhetoric and composition studies as well as computers and writing studies, including technological literacy narratives. Emphasizing narrative as a methodology in their own interview-based research, Hawisher and Selfe further assert that technological literacy narratives contextualized within historical, political, economic, and ideological movements foster a multidimensional understanding of the influences on women's literacy histories ("Women and the Global Ecology"). As I have discussed with former students and colleagues Angela Haas and Christine Tulley, women with limited access to technology can often view a lack of technological knowledge as an innate inability to use computers. Hence, a focus on women's literacy narratives can help them theorize their computer histories within similar structures of difference that, as Wajcman and Hawisher and Selfe consistently stress. can potentially empower students through shifts in technological attitude and aptitude.

With the goal of empowerment in mind, technofeminist research has often combined articulation of women's online experiences with a political activism that rejects any definition of research that presumes neutrality. Instead, feminist researchers often aim to describe and ideally transform the conditions of those individuals and groups studied. In contrast to the paradigm that presumes objectivity on the part of the researcher, technofeminist researchers are often personally and politically connected to the groups they study, balancing their joint status as insiders and outsiders (Naples 49) in ways that are consistent with participant-observer methods. Moreover, the personal narratives of researchers and subjects "are radical for many because they are still being written against older, more-established genres" (Journet, current volume, 21), including, I would add, larger cultural narratives about who uses technology and how. As the next section outlines, however, these research methods are not without critics.

From Essentialism to Materialism

Technofeminists are as obligated as any other group of scholars to interrogate their ideological assumptions about the need to empower women. Failure to do so risks reinscribing the very gendered categories they hope to subvert by characterizing their goals and methods as biased and essentialist. As a feminist, I became personally aware of this obligation when reading Thomas Skeen's "Constructing Essentialism: *Computers and Composition* and the 'Risk of Essence,'" an article that responded to my coauthored piece with Haas and Tulley on women's online writing spaces. In his review, Skeen concludes that such technofeminist research and its focus on gendered differences among technology users may risk essentializing the women and girls we study. In this instance, Skeen focuses on our discussion of the Cybergrrl Project, which Tulley and I developed in 1999 as an after-school computer class for adolescent girls. For Skeen, because such research focuses on women's ways of negotiating technological access, it may inadvertently essentialize their online identifies and inhibit the relationship between theory and practice as well as the potential for political action by portraying women's technological experiences in limiting rather than liberating ways.

Admittedly, Skeen is correct in one particular respect: Technofeminist theory must translate into technofeminist practice. Wilding asserts that success in subverting "the male order of things" (9) in online environments is dependent on feminists' ability to align theory and practice. In the case of composition studies, this alignment first involves questioning the extent to which digital discourse communities allow women and girls to develop professional and personal identities within those communities. In the spirit of technofeminism, however, we must also heed Wilding's call by questioning how a range of transformative pedagogies, rhetorical choices, and literacy practices works to subvert existing gendered hierarchies in these spaces.

In crafting "Response," my own published response to Skeen, I noted that rather than viewing the emphasis on women-centered spaces and experiences with technology as essentialist, <u>feminist theory and method call for a materialist approach that questions how political, social, and economic conditions impact women as a class of individuals.</u> Equally important is the need to question how existing inequities can and should be transformed through feminist action. In this way, such research has as its goal to create gains not just for women but for any group for whom technological literacy acquisition is mediated through inequitable social and educational frameworks. Rather than presume that all technofeminist educators need to do is provide learning spaces for girls in order for literacy and resulting empowerment to occur, what such experiences can do is help participants develop a shared understanding of the role of technology in their own lives and articulate those experiences through digital composing processes. These processes have the potential to move women from the position of users of technological spaces to designers of them, a shift that meshes with Wajcman's "imperative that women

materialist approach

are involved throughout the processes and practices of technological innovation" ("Feminist Theories").

Skeen's analysis and critique of my work with former graduate students on the Cybergrrl Project struck a personal note about the need to articulate what I do as a researcher and why it is important. I view myself as a member of a community of technofeminist researchers within computers and writing studies, a community whose goals have been twofold: (1) to research the extent electronic spaces have been hospitable to individuals from diverse backgrounds and (2) to provide spaces in our teaching and scholarship where these diverse groups have more of a role in shaping our critical understanding of technology's possibilities and constraints. For me, although Skeen makes an important point about our need for articulation, he relies on too narrow a set of articles to make that point and does not acknowledge the ongoing research questions we have asked and the research methods we have used to address them. Perhaps most problematic is that Skeen does not sufficiently account for the larger historical context surrounding women's access to literacy and communication that drives our questions and methods. But just as Skeen is obligated to make this acknowledgment, so, too, are technofeminist researchers obligated to articulate our research questions and methods to newer members of the community, notably our graduate students as future teacher-scholars. Inevitably, the story of technofeminist work is much more robust in theory and practice because of a complicated triangulation of voices to articulate the role of technology in women's and girls' lived experiences, including our own experiences as teachers and researchers.

From Theory to Practice to Action

The emphasis on narratives of lived experience across media genres is not only a necessary methodological approach but also a potentially powerful form of technofeminist, activist research. Sharing our stories allows us to articulate our research questions, our methods of investigation, and finally our political and pedagogical goals, complicated though this articulation may be. For instance, in her study of the literacy organization GirlZone, Mary P. Sheridan-Rabideau chronicles how "one grassroots feminist organization used texts both to construct meaning and to construct themselves as meaningful in their everyday lives" (2). Although Sheridan-Rabideau's study of GirlZone profiles a range of literate practices from creative writing to radio broadcasting, deploying similar feminist pedagogies and political activism through community outreach can apply to technological literacy as well.

As an example of such activist outreach, my most recent technological literacy project is a three-day residential computer camp for middle-school girls titled the Digital Mirror Computer Camp, a space in which girls develop skills in blogging, web authoring, digital imaging, and video and audio editing. In addition to functional literacy skills, the girls receive opportunities to reflect on the role of these and other communication technologies in school and family life, creating a personal portfolio that documents technological growth and reflects—via the genre of a video literacy narrative—the ways technology helps maintain connections with family and friends.

Now in its fifth year, the camp has developed into two separate tracks, one for new girls and one for returning girls to sustain the interest level and the skills set obtained the previous year in a team-development model. Returning girls have developed a professional web presence for the camp itself, conducting interviews and writing for various audiences about elements of the camp, including safety concerns as well as curricular benefits and social opportunities. Ultimately, the significance of the Digital Mirror Computer Camp is in its status as a qualitative, activist response to statistical data from the American Association of University Women (AAUW) documenting that the numbers of women choosing technological majors and resulting careers for women are limited ("Position on Science"). With these limits in mind, the camp balances functional literacy with more critical and rhetorical literacies, as Stuart Selber advocates in his book *Multiliteracies for a Digital Age*. Accordingly, we have been conscious of the activist goal of expanding the limited view of women and girls as mere consumers or operators of particular technologies (i.e., copy machines, printers, word-processing software) in professional or scholastic settings. Moving beyond a functional view of technological literacy aligns technology with rhetoric to foster a critical citizenry who access information and communicate in a range of media. In the case of the camp, technology also allows participants to deploy narrative, biography, and other genres to critically and rhetorically explore identity and the role that various tools play in shaping that identity. Our overall goal has been to allow our participants, as Stabile originally suggested, to harness technology for their own personal, social, and professional purposes, to tell their own stories about the role technology plays in their lives, and to validate women's literacy practices.

Rather than view the development and delivery of a computer camp for girls as an essentialist enterprise that somehow presumes innate qualities on the part of women, the goals of the Digital Mirror Computer Camp have

not just consumers or operators

been more materialist, making technological opportunities more accessible to girls from a range of sociocultural backgrounds. This distinction allows technofeminist researchers to engage in activities that responsibly blend theory and practice to benefit the populations we serve. A major goal of a community action project like the Digital Mirror Computer Camp is to move girls from the role of uncritical users of today's latest communication technologies and to help them gain more rhetorical control of the digital spaces in which they represent themselves. This goal is consistent with Wajcman's assertion that such ownership can better equalize both gender and power relations, leveling the technological playing field.

Conclusion: From Mastering to Mentoring

The technofeminist goals of the Digital Mirror Computer Camp and projects like it are closely tied to Sullivan's original call to question the role that gender plays in our understanding of composing and to avoid privileging male perspectives as universal. Returning to Sullivan's early work confirms that "emergent forms of teacher research are helping researchers learn more about women's and men's different experiences in which they compose, about the cultural differences among individual writers in these contexts" (58). As technofeminist teacher-scholars, my collaborators and I viewed it as our responsibility to develop a project like the Digital Mirror Computer Camp that allows researchers, participants, and even parents to question to what extent technological literacy acquisition is a gender-fair process. In this sense, we collectively advance work by the AAUW by collecting more data that address how individual attitudes and larger cultural assumptions about women and technology are changing. Similar to the original Cybergrrl Project Tulley and I have discussed in several venues, we have functioned as mentors, coaches, and models of women using technology, working closely with the girls as they developed their projects in ways that mesh with a feminist ethic of care that enable, rather than constrain, the integrity of our research methods and objectives.

Nevertheless, Skeen's article is an important reminder for feminist researchers in digital spaces of the need to not presume our goals, our methods, and our outcomes are easily understood and do not require continued articulation of the powerful, yet complicated triangulation of feminist methodology, political action, and technological literacy. Fostering a positive and sustainable relationship between technological literacy and identity construction invariably calls for reciprocal mentoring models between researchers and their subjects and among researchers themselves.

I have attempted to stress this reciprocity with women graduate students working on the Digital Mirror Computer Camp as a collaborative team of teacher-scholars who will continue to contribute to technofeminist research in their own academic careers. Such reciprocal models connect to the support I myself received from Hawisher and Selfe, scholars whose technofeminist collaborations have defined a method privileging the voices of women and others often disenfranchised from the male-dominated technoculture in which we live and work. Their efforts have also helped to create a community of researchers committed to making literacy acquisition a lifelong process for students and citizens, regardless of gender.

As an example of the technofeminist methods and goals outlined throughout this chapter, the Digital Mirror Computer Camp fosters the technological literacy development of women and girls and emphasizes narrative and action research as core technofeminist methods for articulating the experiences, values, and material conditions that define and delimit the role of technology in their lives. These narratives are inextricably tied to our own technological histories as women and as teacher-scholars. In these roles, we must negotiate our multiple identities in ways that openly acknowledge the personal and political goal of making our research benefit women as a diverse group across cultures who have individual technological stories to be researched and shared. Such a qualitative, materialist emphasis in data collection and representation is vital to maintaining gender equity as part of our current understanding of what it means to be technologically literate. Thus, technofeminists must continue to provide important mentoring opportunities for women and girls to sustain these literacies and for current and future technofeminist researchers to study and learn from them.

Works Cited

American Association of University Women. "Position on Science, Technology, Engineering and Mathematics (STEM) Education." *American Association of University Women.* May 2010. Web. 10 Jan. 2011. <http://www.aauw.org/advocacy/issue_advocacy/actionpages/STEM.cfm>.

———. *Tech Savvy: Educating Girls in the New Computer Age.* New York: AAUW, 2000. Print.

Blair, Kristine. "Response to Thomas Skeen's 'Constructing Essentialism: *Computers and Composition* and the 'Risk of Essence.'" *Computers and Composition* 25 (2008): 130–33. Print.

Blair, Kristine, and Christine Tulley. "Whose Research Is It Anyway? The Challenge of Deploying Feminist Methodology in Technological Spaces." *Digital Writing Research: Technologies, Methodologies, and Ethical Issues.* Ed. Dànielle DeVoss and Heidi McKee. Cresskill: Hampton, 2007. 303–17. Print.

Haas, Angela, Christine Tulley, and Kristine Blair. "Mentors versus Masters: Women's and Girls' Narratives of (Re)Negotiation in Web-based Writing Spaces." *Computers and Composition* 19 (2002): 231–49. Print.

Harding, Sandra. "Is There a Feminist Method?" *Feminism and Methodology*. Ed. Sandra Harding. Bloomington: Indiana UP, 1987. 1–14. Print.

Hawisher, Gail, and Cynthia Selfe. "Women and the Global Ecology of Digital Literacies." *Women and Literacy: Local and Global Inquiries for a New Century*. Ed. Beth Daniell and Peter Mortensen. New York: Erlbaum, 2007. 207–28. Print.

Henwood, Flis, Helen Kennedy, and Nod Miller, eds. *Cyborg Lives: Women's Technobiographies*. York, UK: Raw Nerve, 2001. Print.

Kramarae, Cheris. *Technology and Women's Voices: Keeping in Touch*. New York: Routledge, 1988. Print.

Lather, Patti. "Feminist Perspective on Empowering Research Methodologies." *Women's Studies International Forum* 11 (1988): 569–81. Print.

Naples, Nancy. *Feminism and Method: Ethnography, Discourse Analysis, and Activist Research*. New York: Routledge, 2003. Print.

Powell, Katrina, and Pamela Takayoshi. "Accepting Roles Created for Us: The Ethics of Reciprocity." *College Composition and Communication* 54.3 (2003): 394–422. Print.

Selber, Stuart. *Multiliteracies for a Digital Age*. Carbondale: Southern Illinois UP, 2004. Print.

Selfe, Cynthia, and Gail Hawisher. *Literate Lives in the Information Age: Narratives of Literacy from the United States*. Mahwah: Erlbaum, 2004. Print.

Sheridan-Rabideau, Mary P. *Girls, Feminism, and Grassroots Literacies: Activism in the GirlZone*. Albany: State U of New York, 2008. Print.

Skeen, Thomas J. "Constructing Essentialism: *Computers and Composition* and the 'Risk of Essence.'" *Computers and Composition* 24.2 (2007): 198–213. Print.

Stabile, Carole. *Feminism and the Technological Fix*. New York: Manchester UP, 1994. Print.

Sullivan, Patricia A. "Feminism and Methodology in Composition Studies." *Methods and Methodologies in Composition Research*. Ed. Gesa Kirsch and Sullivan. Carbondale: Southern Illinois UP, 1992. 37–61. Print.

Wajcman, Judy. "Feminist Theories of Technology." *Cambridge Journal of Economics*. 2009. Web. 10 Jan. 2011. <http://cje.oxfordjournals.org/cgi/content/abstract/ben057v1>.

——. Foreword. Henwood, Kennedy, and Miller, *Cyborg Lives* 7–8.

——. *TechnoFeminism*. Cambridge: Polity, 2003. Print.

Wilding, Faith. "Where Is the Feminism in Cyberfeminsm?" *n. paradoxa* 2 (1998): 6–12. Print.

method
vs.
methodology

6.

Making Ethnography Our Own: Why and How Writing Studies Must Redefine Core Research Practices

Mary P. Sheridan

Some questions take a long time to figure out, requiring multiple angles of analysis and, at times, years of situated study. Literature reviews provide important background information; surveys offer useful lay-of-the-lands; interviews and case studies go nicely in-depth, generally with a few people for a short period of time. And yet, to understand the perspectives and contexts of those we study across long periods of time and space, ethnography proves uniquely useful as a method (specific practices or ways of doing research) and a methodology (specific justifications for why we do research).

Like all research, ethnography is highly responsive to the situation at hand, applying particular methods to specific issues or problems. Yet, what is distinctive about ethnography is its orientation to understanding the rich visible and seemingly invisible networks influencing the participants in the study. Through long-term research, ethnography highlights the impact of these networks; in the process, ethnography examines perspectives that are often misunderstood, underdeveloped, or occluded in popular understandings of an issue, thereby informing policies and practices that both affect the participants and inform the much-larger networks and structures in which these participants are located.

Especially since the late 1980s, increasing numbers of writing studies scholars have conducted ethnographies or used ethnographically informed methods to examine the connections between everyday language practices—whether in homes, workplaces, civic spaces, communities, and/or classrooms—and larger cultural issues, such as those dealing with education or activism. And yet, even as we writing studies scholars expand what we study, where we study, and why we study, we are still negotiating what it means to do ethnographic research. This chapter examines this dynamic, evolving methodology and argues that writing studies scholars need to define how ethnography works for us. Consequently, after describing ethnography's history and practices, this chapter turns to how writing studies researchers have taken it up and ends by arguing that, as a field, we need to responsively develop our own ethnographic practices as we investigate what it means to research composing today.

A Brief History

Before writing studies scholars can define our uptake of ethnographic research, we need to understand the history of this research tradition—a history that shows that ethnography has always been a dynamic methodology responsive to the issues, opportunities, and sponsorships at hand.

Ethnography emerged primarily out of anthropology, as practiced by different schools in different countries. The British ethnographic tradition, for example, traces back to Bronislaw Malinowski, often seen as the father of anthropology. Although he originally went to the Tribriand Islands to conduct conventional social survey, World War I delayed his return, giving him extended time to research *with* the participants of the study in order to learn how participants define what is (as opposed to what is lacking). After returning to England, Malinowski eventually landed a job at the London School of Economics, mentoring students to "grasp the native's point of view, *his* [*sic*] relation to life, to realize *his* [*sic*] vision of his world" (25); in time, many of Malinowski's students would teach at leading institutions (e.g., Oxford, Cambridge, Manchester), establishing this tradition of British social anthropology.

In the U.S. tradition, Franz Boas is the founding figure, and he, too, adapted traditional methods from diverse fields. Adopting many of Malinowski's insights into his work with American Indians, Boas combined anthropology and linguistics in an effort to save languages and knowledge from dying out. In doing so, he forwarded an investment in social action as opposed to merely reporting supposedly objective facts. His students continued to spread these engaged, activist anthropological practices, making them commonplace today.[1]

Ethnographers modified these methods by studying closer to home, working to make the familiar (the known or assumed ways of acting or being) strange (a distanced view on how these are constructed). For those interested in language and culture, these ethnographies generally focus on what Dell Hymes calls an "ethnography of communication," by offering what Clifford Geertz calls a "thick description," a detailed, in-depth look *autonomous vs. ideological* [handwritten annotation]

at local practices from multiple angles. One such ethnography is Shirley Brice Heath's *Ways with Words* in which Health documents the complex literacy practices of those in the Piedmont Carolinas, communities whose literacy practices are often unacknowledged and undervalued by city-based, middle-class educators. By analyzing how members of different groups meet and defy hidden and overt cultural expectations, Heath encouraged mainstream academic readers to understand the construction of their own literacy practices just as they understand those of marginalized groups. In this way, Heath called ethnographers to move away from what Brian Street calls "autonomous" views of literacy (i.e., arguments where literacy *in itself* can effect other social and cognitive practices) and toward "ideological" views of literacy (i.e., arguments where literacy is a socially situated practice with multiple components—aural, visual, performance, multimodal—that work with and against a range of other social and cognitive practices). Ethnographers working in this ideological tradition expose the hidden political and economic consequences of prevalent views of literacy with the hopes of fostering more-just practices.

In their uptake of ethnography, writing studies scholars have simultaneously embraced ethnography and struggled to make this methodology their own. Wendy Bishop, for example, reported that she felt she was almost "inventing ethnography" within our field in the sense that her main resources in the mid-1980s were documents "written for social scientists and anthropologists" (quoted in Mortensen and Kirsch, xix). The difficulty in working with documents whose focus was not on the issues of language and learning so central to the field of writing studies prompted scholars to adapt ethnography's situated, ongoing, emic focus on the complex networks that intersect at the nexus between language (particularly composing) and culture, facilitating an increase of ethnographic research within writing studies. Just a few years after Bishop's above lament there emerged several models (Bishop; Chiseri-Strater; Doheny-Farina), practical guides (Bleich; Brodkey; Chin; Herndl; Moss), and eventually awards for ethnographic research in our field (e.g., Doheny-Farina's NCTE Excellence in Technical and Scientific Writing Award; Cushman's Braddock Award; Sohn's Dissertation of the Year; Sheridan-Rabideau's Book of the Year on Civic Engagement from *Reflections* and Outstanding Book award from the Coalition of Women Scholars in Rhetoric and Composition). These works illustrate how current writing studies researchers are adapting ethnographic methods to study the ways writing mediates the lives of everyday people, whether these people are negotiating governmental services, life in Appalachia, or girl-focused activism in small-town America. The goal of this work is to extend previous activist ethnographic research so that a researcher can be, to paraphrase Ellen Cushman's award-winning article, "an Agent of Social Change."

Recursive Stages in Making Ethnography Our Own

Despite the blossoming of recent work, there is still much to accomplish to make ethnography our own. First, we need to understand common ethnographic practices, and then we need to figure out how to make these commonalities useful for those of us in writing studies.

Although ethnographic research needs to be continuously revisited and adjusted to fit the research questions at hand, there are some general stages. The first stage is often a "preresearch" stage where ethnographers gain a deep understanding of issues they think will be most salient. In addition to reviewing earlier studies on relevant methods and topics—activities that may continue throughout the project—ethnographers may work out the project's logistics. For example, ethnographers might negotiate with participants and institutional review boards (IRBs) about everything from what and who will be studied to how the data will be represented. In the second stage, ethnographers gather extensive qualitative and quantitative data from multiple perspectives via practices as diverse as writing field notes, activity logs, or maps (of space or interaction clusters); collecting artifacts, histories, and statistics; engaging in informal conversations, formal interviews, and focus groups; conducting surveys; making recordings (photos, video, audio). Cross-checking their observations through a process called "triangulation," ethnographers continue to review and code the information gathered, researching for patterns to guide their ongoing research.[2] The third stage, the writing-it-up stage, is often the most challenging. Even when ethnographers know their audience, the story to tell, and the participants to include, ethnographies are no longer considered scientifically objective documents that transparently describe a culture; rather, ethnographies require researchers to draw upon highly rhetorical moves to persuade readers that the researcher has truly "been there" and gotten it right (Geertz).

Despite this tidy, three-part framework, ethnography is highly recursive and very messy, and ethnographers' acceptance of that messiness reflects an important distinction between *doing* ethnography and *being* an ethnographer. Being an ethnographer is about developing habits of seeing and ways of being that make sense of cultural practices from within the culture being studied. Although ethnographers' commitment to understand the complexity of people and practices from an emic perspective remains firm, they must be flexible in their responses to the unexpected; in practice, ethnographers do not follow a predetermined, three-stage framework but rather adapt long-standing methodological traditions to fit the current opportunities and challenges they face as they crack open the complexities of contemporary questions.

This need for such suppleness was certainly apparent in my ethnographic research. I started with the questions of whether preteen girls were losing their sense of confidence and curiosity and, if so, what people can to do help. Already volunteering at GirlZone—a local community organization offering girls weekly workshops on activities ranging from creative writing to skateboarding, from cooking to car mechanics—I wanted to put my academic training into action. Since I started this research in the 1990s, when postmodern theories about how the play of language can help people carve a space for imagining new ways to understand themselves as political agents,[3] I began looking at how literate activities at GirlZone did, and did not, provide a space for girls to work out some of their anxieties and imagine possibilities for a greater range of options than girls generally see available to them in the media.

Over the course of the next six years, I examined the composing practices of the GirlZone girls and organizers, which eventually led me to study the texts of local and national funding organizations, constructions of girl culture in popular media, feminist manifestos of different waves, and grassroots activists of various sorts. Throughout this research, I engaged in what I consider typical ethnographic practices such as living in the messy reality that challenges the idea that "typical practices" can address highly contextualized questions.

Although I started my preresearch strategies with broad but seemingly defined boundaries, I quickly expanded these boundaries. Beyond reading literature reviews on girl culture and on community literacy, I engaged with the literature on the national and international funding climate for nonprofit organizations, on the "youthquake" of grassroots activism, on fourth-wave feminism, and on the visual culture prevalent in punk zine movements, to name just a few areas. Similarly, I extended my initial analysis of GirlZone workshops, fund-raisers, and community events to include systematic research of GirlZone participants far beyond GirlZone itself (e.g., meetings with funders, the city council, the National Organization of Women), requiring me to examine the many ways texts mediate how people come to understand themselves.

Throughout this research were many, many negotiations. With my own institution, I had to balance the IRB's ominous-sounding informed-consent form and the welcoming tone that defined GirlZone projects; this balance needed renegotiation when I moved to a different university. With my participants, my initial agreement to be an extra pair of hands at workshops and to provide an archive of GirlZone's history changed when my extended ethnographic research allowed me detailed access to a range of participants in roles that shifted over time. For example, when I became pregnant with my daughter during my research, mothers of GirlZone girls often felt more comfortable in talking about the dilemmas they faced raising girls when they knew that I, too, would be struggling with these issues with my own daughter. Even the girls felt more comfortable including me in on "secrets every mom should know about how to raise a girl and tween." When triangulating my data (e.g., field notes, interviews, videos of public performances, documents about or by GirlZone participants, research on national activist trends or girl culture, community literacy practices), I realized that this information would not have been forthcoming if I had not had long-term engagement, in a variety of roles, that allowed me to earn participants' trust. Ethnographic research made these important but often obscured perspectives visible in ways other methods would not have.

Because of this access, I felt obligated to give back to the people and organization of GirlZone in ways I had not anticipated when my research started, a move similar to some doing applied anthropological research where cataloging exotic cultures has given way to arguing for the benefit of those studied (see Conquergood). At times, this giving back was easy; as an academic, I gave clout to GirlZone participants' work and was asked to speak to the press as a sort of credentializing agent, and as a long-term participant, I happily became a sounding board, a board member, and a quasi-consultant who could speak to funding agencies. At other times, my desire for reciprocity brought unanticipated conflicts, something every ethnographer will need to face during the course of study. For example, grassroots organizations are often made up of tight-knit groups of people who share important laughs and feel rifts acutely. This was clearly the case at GirlZone, so when the founding organizers had a falling out, I had to negotiate how to honor my relationships with these people through the prism of my multiple roles at GirlZone (as a researcher, as a participant, as a friend). Although I couldn't anticipate the many contingencies that inevitably occurred, having extensive up-front conversations about reciprocity, exit plans, and people's roles before, during, and after the research minimized hurt feelings and complicated entanglements and helped me handle the fuzziness of the hallmark ethnographic term *participant-observer*, where I both engaged in and studied the activities of the group.

Despite these ongoing negotiations, my write-up of this research reflected common anxieties about ethnography in the 1990s. Agreeing with Sancho Panza's argument that "those who turn other people's lives into texts hold real power" (paraphrased in Newkirk 14) and that this power comes with political and ethical consequences,[4] I turned to research in the field for guidance on how to mitigate what Norman K. Denzin and Yvonna S. Lincoln, among others, called "the crises of representation." Some researchers who similarly struggled with the question of how to write for others called on ethnographers to abandon this methodology. Yet, as Gesa E. Kirsch argues, this is no option, particularly for historically marginalized groups who may acutely feel the dangers of others representing them. Instead, Kirsch suggests that ethnographic research should continue to give voice to the pressing problems that are too often unexamined ("Ethics" xiii). In other words, rather than abandon a method because some challenge it, we should find ways of better using ethnographic methods for ends that are, in Kirsch's terms, more equitable and socially justified. In short, ethnographers, like all researchers, should be aware of a methodology's limitations, make explicit our practices and stance, and work to redress trouble spots as best we can, in part by adapting our research methods to the issues at hand.

With this advice in mind, I started to incorporate James Clifford's call to move from "paradigms of experience and interpretation" to "discursive paradigms of dialogue and polyphony" (41) where many voices share the telling of the narrative. At times, I enacted this discursive paradigm by noting in the text where my views differed from my participants' (Sheridan-Rabideau). Others have chosen different tactics, such as showing different angles of data via field notes (Chiseri-Strater) or by presenting field notes, creative writing, and ethnographic versions of the data (Wolf). Despite such democratic possibilities, it is not always easy to include multiple voices legitimately; participants may have a different vision or merely not want to spend the time it takes to create meaningful dialogue about an academic text beyond their interests (Kirsch, "Ethics"), ultimately leaving researchers to make the final edits. Consequently, ethnographers need to disclose in the final written document their positionality and the decisions they make. Such practices not only allow readers to understand what and how conclusions were made but also expose the messiness of these research stages, reinforcing ethnographers' need to adopt recursive rather than static methods if they are to answer the most pressing questions that emerge during their research.

Methods of Our Own

As the previous sections foreground, we in writing studies need to adapt existing research practices for our own purposes even as we draw upon, *in informed ways*, the dominant ethnographic paradigms, historically set out by anthropologists. These paradigms are shaped by many factors, such as the purpose/questions asked, the data collected, and the audience expectations for such research, but what most ethnographies share is long-term participation with information gathered through multiple methods in order both to understand various participants' perspectives and to locate these perspectives within larger social, economic, and political forces.

Writing studies research often focuses on educational contexts with the goal of offering policy. Although such educational settings sometimes limit researchers' ability to meet the practices that may traditionally comprise a full-on ethnography, J. Green and David Bloome offer a spectrum of labels that define diverse ethnographic practices for researchers who focus on educational settings:

1. Doing ethnography includes "the framing, conceptualizing, conducting, interpreting, writing, and reporting associated with a broad in-depth, and long-term study of a social or cultural group, meeting the criteria for doing ethnography as framed within a discipline of field."

2. Adopting an ethnographic perspective means "that it is possible to take a more focused approach (i.e., do less than a comprehensive ethnography) to study particular aspects of everyday life and cultural practices of a social group. Central to an ethnography perspective is the use of theories of culture and inquiry practices derived from anthropology or sociology to guide the research."

3. Using ethnographic tools, such as interview, time-activity charts, document content analysis, and digital sound recording, allows for "the use of methods and techniques usually associated with fieldwork. These methods may or may not be guided by cultural theories of questions about the social life of group members" (quoted in Heath and Street, 121).

Green and Bloome's distinctions among doing ethnography, adopting ethnographic perspectives, and using ethnographically informed tools can help researchers articulate both what they are doing and why they are doing it.

Many writing studies scholars would quickly agree with Green and Bloome's categorizations. As noted above, much writing studies research would fall comfortably under ethnographic research as traditionally defined; Cushman's research with inner-city residents, Sohn's with Appalachian women, and mine with central Illinois' girls and women all meet more traditional goals of long-term, participant-observation to gather participants' perspectives and to uncover the larger structural forces shaping the language and cultural practices of a particular group of people. Such writing studies research examines how culture and language practices intersect across the life span in a variety of extra- and noncurricular settings in ways that read intelligibly to most people doing ethnography. Similarly, many writing studies scholars openly acknowledge that they do not conduct what anthropologists may consider "true ethnographies," but rather they adopt ethnographic perspectives or use ethnographic tools. In such work, researchers generally privilege at least one aspect in their "ethnographically informed" research, such as "ethnographic narratives" (Brodkey), "ethnographic interviews" (Chin), or "ethno-oriented case studies" (Brueggemann).

And yet, there is a tension between traditional ethnographers and some writing studies scholars about who gets to define what is and is not an ethnography. Some traditionally trained ethnographers, such as Heath and Brian V. Street, are troubled when researchers (and not just in writing studies) cherry pick from ethnography—taking the promise of ethnographic methods without doing the background research to understand the historical and theoretical underpinnings of this research practice, thus diluting and even distorting its potential. Many writing studies scholars agree with this critique. For Keith Rhodes, classroom-based research, a staple in our field, does not qualify as ethnography since he believes classroom sites are not legitimate, sustained "cultures" and since this research privileges academic theories, not the theories of student cultures. Moreover, Rhodes argues that too often, educational "ethnographies" focus on deficiencies of students, offering moralistic evaluations instead of descriptive assessments. These "simpler, hypothesis-testing 'qualitative research'" are not true ethnographies (28). Although Rhodes argues that writing studies scholars should not give up on ethnography nor necessarily throw out their current practices, they should accurately describe what they do and embrace their qualitative research for what it is (see Nickoson, current volume, for more on teacher research).

On key points, I agree with the above critiques. For example, I agree that we must be deeply grounded in the research methods we choose, and we must define what we mean when we say we are doing ethnography. These are good practices for any research. And yet, writing studies scholars can certainly tap the promise of ethnographic research without being locked into seemingly static anthropological traditions, for these traditions are themselves changing (remember the earlier history section) and varied (see Cintron for an account of how different leading ethnographers out of the anthropological tradition can be). Because methods are not rigid things written about in books but flexible practices meant to be understood and adapted for present needs, we in writing studies should learn the histories of the methods we adopt, but we should also feel confident to adapt these methods so they are appropriate to our forums, uses, and practices.

For those of us in writing studies, this research may include classrooms, though likely as one site of participants' language and cultural practices. For example, following Katherine Schultz's call to research across multiple sites for an extended period in order to better understand participants' perspectives, researchers like Kevin Roozen investigate how hobbies from years earlier shape current student practices or how classroom activities can inform students' rich literate activities years later in spaces far removed from the classroom.

As we define our research agenda as informed by but not entirely beholden to a seemingly static ethnographic tradition, we continue to define the value of doing ethnographic work in ways that respond to contemporary conditions, such as those afforded by digital technologies (B. Smith) or those demanded by the increased ways institutions mediate our lives (D. Smith). These new conditions ask researchers to draw upon methodologies not as fixed, acontextual practices that any one field can own but rather as orientations that help us examine situated practices through a variety of methods. Ethnography can provide researchers with ways to pursue the questions we find most pressing, especially those that connect everyday language use with larger cultural practices.

There is a high cost in doing ethnographic research: the extended time, the personal entanglements, the sheer messiness. Even so, the rewards are great, most notably gaining emic perspectives that support, challenge, or most likely complicate public pedagogies about language and culture in telling ways. Few other methodologies provide such benefits, benefits that can help our field learn about the people and literacy practices we hope to engage. To reap these benefits, writing studies scholars need to continue to define and develop our own ethnographic research tradition.

Notes

1. The academy wasn't the only sponsor of anthropological research; governmental sponsorship was also important in both the U.K. and the U.S. traditions. After World War II and during the Cold War, governments continued the practice of learning about cultures from "natives" themselves (an emic perspective), largely in order to better influence governmental practices and policies around the world.

2. This practice is much like grounded theory, a methodology that emphasizes in situ, field-based, and context-driven studies of human activity. Researchers develop categories that emerge from the ground up (as opposed to top-down analyses) through iterative, recursive constructions of theories about the people and practices researchers study.

3. See Probyn; Butler.

4. Some went further. Patricia Sullivan argues, "The question is not whether the ethnographer has gotten the other right, and hence has produced an account that can be taken as authoritative, but whether the ethnographer has a right to appropriate an other for the sake of knowledge and can 'speak for' another without compromising the other's own powers of representation" (103). These representational critiques came from many sources that began to congeal in poststructuralist analyses of narrative, where critics wonder who is telling the story (e.g., the cultural tropes? the data? the ethnographer?) and whose story it is to tell.

Works Cited

Bishop, Wendy. *Ethnographic Writing Research: Writing it Down, Writing It Up, and Reading It.* Boston: Boynton/Cook, 1999. Print.

Bleich, David. "Ethnography and the Study of Literacy: Prospects for Socially Generous Research." *Into the Field: Sites of Composition Studies.* Ed. Anne Ruggles Gere. New York: MLA, 1993. 176–92. Print.

Brodkey, Linda. "Writing Ethnographic Narratives." *Written Communication* 4.1 (1987): 25–50. Print.

Brueggemann, Brenda J. "Still-Life: Representations and Silences." Mortensen and Kirsch, *Ethics and Representation* 17–39.

Butler, Judith. *Gender Trouble: Feminism and the Subversion of Identity.* New York: Routledge, 1990. Print.

Chin, Elaine. "Redefining 'Context' in Research on Writing." *Written Communication* 11.4 (1994): 445–82. Print.

Chiseri-Strater, Elizabeth. *Academic Literacies: The Public and Private Discourse of College Students.* Portsmouth: Boynton/Cook, 1991. Print.

Cintron, Ralph. "Wearing a Pith Helmet at a Sly Angle: Or, Can Writing Researchers Do Ethnography in a Postmodern Era?" *Written Communication* 10.3 (1993): 371–412. Print.

Clifford, James, "On Ethnographic Authority." *The Predicament of Culture: Twentieth Century Ethnography, Literature, and Art.* Cambridge: Harvard UP, 1988. 21–54. Print.

Conquergood, Dwight. "Performing as a Moral Act: Ethical Dimensions of the Ethnography of Performance." *Literature in Performance* 5 (1985): 1–13. Print.

Cushman, Ellen. "The Rhetorician as an Agent of Social Change." *College Composition and Communication* 47.1 (1996): 7–28. Print.

Denzin, Norman K., and Yvonna S. Lincoln, eds. *Handbook of Qualitative Research.* Thousand Oaks: Sage, 1994. Print.

Doheny-Farina, Stephen. "Writing in an Emerging Organization: An Ethnographic Study." *Written Communication* 3.2 (1986): 158–85. Print.

Geertz, Clifford. *Works and Lives: The Anthropologist as Author.* Stanford: Stanford UP, 1988. Print.

Green, Judith, and David Bloome. "Ethnography and Ethnographers of and in Education: A Situated Perspective." *Handbook of Research on Teaching Literacy through the Communicative and Visual Arts.* Ed. James Flood, Shirley Brice Heath, and Diane Lapp. New York: Macmillan, 1997. 181–202. Print.

Heath, Shirley Brice, and Brian V. Street, with Molly Mills. *On Ethnography: Approaches to Language and Literacy.* New York: Teachers College P, 2008. Print.

Herndl, C. "Writing Ethnography: Representation, Rhetoric, and Institutional Practices." *College English* 53.3 (1991): 320–32. Print.

Hymes, Dell. "Models of the Interaction of Language and Social Life." *Directions in Sociolinguistics: The Ethnography of Communication.* Ed. John J. Gumperz and Dell Hymes. New York: Holt, 1972. 35–71. Print.

Kirsch, Gesa E. *Ethical Dilemmas in Feminist Research.* Albany: State U of New York P, 1999. Print.

———. "Ethics and the Future of Composition." *Composition Studies in the New Millennium: Rereading the Past, Rewriting the Future.* Ed. Lynn Z. Bloom, Donald A. Daiker, and Edward E. White. Carbondale: Southern Illinois UP, 2003. 129–41. Print.

Malinowski, Bronislaw. *Argonauts of the Western Pacific.* 1922. New York: Dutton, 1961. Print.

Mortensen, Peter, and Gesa E. Kirsch, eds. *Ethics and Representation in Qualitative Studies of Literacy.* Urbana: NCTE, 1996. Print.

Moss, Beverly. "Ethnography and Composition: Studying Language at Home." *Methods and Methodology in Composition Research.* Ed. Gesa Kirsch and Patricia A. Sullivan. Carbondale: Southern Illinois UP, 1992. 153–71. Print.

Newkirk, Thomas. "Seduction and Betrayal in Qualitative Research." Mortensen and Kirsch, *Ethics and Representation* 3–16.

Probyn, Elsbyth. *Sexing the Self: Gendered Positions in Cultural Studies.* London: Routledge, 1993. Print.

Rhodes, Keith. "Ethnography of Psychography? The Evolution and Ethics of a New Genre in Composition." *Visions and Voices: Refiguring Ethnography in Composition.* Ed. Cristina Kirklighter, Cloe Vincent, and Joseph M. Moxley. Portsmouth: Boynton/Cook, 1997. 24–36. Print.

Roozen, Kevin. "The 'Poetry Slam,' Mathemagicians, and Middle-School Math: Tracing Trajectories of Actors and Artifacts." *Exploring Semiotic Remediation as Discourse Practice.* Ed. Paul Prior and Julie Hengst. New York: Palgrave, 2010. 124–59. Print.

Schultz, Katherine. "Looking across Space and Time: Reconceptualizing Literacy Learning in and out of School." *RTE* 36 (2002): 356–89. Print.

Sheridan-Rabideau, Mary P. *Girls, Feminism, and Grassroots Literacies: Activism in the GirlZone.* Albany: State U of New York P, 2008. Print.

Smith, Beatrice. "Researching Hybrid Literacies: Methodological Explorations of 'Ethnography' and the Practices of the Cybertariat." *Digital Writing Research: Technologies, Methodologies, and Ethical Issues.* Ed. Heidi A. McKee and Dànielle Nicole DeVoss. Cresskill: Hampton, 2007. 127–52. Print.

Smith, Dorothy. *Institutional Ethnography: A Sociology for People.* Lanham: AltaMira, 2005. Print.

Sohn, Katherine. *Whistlin' and Crowin' Women of Appalachia: Literacy Practices since College.* Carbondale: Southern Illinois UP, 2006. Print.

Street, Brian. *Literacy in Theory and Practice.* London: Routledge, 1984. Print.

Sullivan, Patricia A. "Ethnography and the Problem of the 'Other.'" Mortensen and Kirsch, *Ethics and Representation* 97–114.

Wolf, Margery. *A Thrice Told Tale: Feminism, Postmodernism, and Ethnographic Responsibility.* Stanford: Stanford UP, 1992. Print.

7.

Reclaiming the Mind: Eco-Cognitive Research in Writing Studies

Kristie Fleckenstein

Like a typical first day in any composition class, two students meet and seek to establish shared ground. "Hey, Drajha," says one. "Hi, Isabella," responds the other, and they are off. At the same time, the instructor, Professor Plum, talks over them, providing her students with information they'll need to participate. "Okay," she tells her class of twelve, "I think this is a pretty simple interface." However, unique to this situation is that the entire exchange takes place in FirstClass's virtual classroom; thus, both social interactions and teacher information are mediated solely through a textual interface that unfolds synchronously in a narrow band of white at the bottom of the individual student's computer screen. How did students and teacher read the real-time online text that served not only as their gateway into the virtual class but also as the class itself?

This question arose in response to data collected in 2002 as part of an ethnographic study of virtual community building.[1] While the dynamic by which strangers coalesced as a community in a virtual space served as the original impetus for the study, when I recently returned to the videos, classroom discourse, and interviews, the phenomenon that piqued my interest had less to do with community and more to do with cognition. So, to pursue my question concerning the *processes* of online reading, I needed a cognitive paradigm, which enables the researcher to investigate the individual mind in action. Unfortunately, research shaped by a cognitive orientation had virtually disappeared from writing studies. Dominant during the late 1970s and early 1980s, a cognitive orientation contributed significantly to the twentieth-century renascence of writing studies, providing a conceptual framework and a set of analytical tools designed to help a researcher explore writing and reading as forms of thinking. Scholars relied on a cognitive orientation to discern the mental activities involved in writing (Emig; Flower and Hayes), revision (Sommers), reading (Haas and Flower), and other thinking processes intrinsic to creating meaning. Thus, to satisfy my curiosity about the *how* of online reading, a process central to both online writing and online community building, I first had to recuperate a cognitive paradigm for writing studies.

This chapter argues that <u>Gregory Bateson's ecological cybernetics offers a valuable framework for resuscitating cognitive research</u>. As a zoologically trained anthropologist who contributed crucial insights to early systems theory (cybernetics), psychology (addiction and family therapy), evolution, and communication, Bateson developed a theory of the individual mind as shaping and shaped by the larger systemic Mind within which it is networked. Thus, while Bateson is rarely cited as a direct progenitor of cognitive psychology, he contributed substantially to the network of concepts that served as the foundation for the cognitive revolution. His concept of an "ecology of mind" offers a particularly robust starting point for reenergizing cognitive research in writing studies. To demonstrate the potential of an *eco-cognitive* paradigm, I divide this chapter in three parts. I begin by reviewing two key controversial precepts underlying cognitive psychology: information processing and artificial intelligence. I then reanimate cognitive research for writing studies by reconfiguring both, offering *difference processing* and *contextual intelligence* as useful alternatives. The last section demonstrates an eco-cognitive paradigm in action.

The Computer in the Mind

In a 1986 review of research in writing, Marlene Scardamalia and Carl Bereiter claim that the cognitive-science framework provides "pretty much 'the only paradigm in town' for investigating complex mental processes" (779). The drive to investigate thinking in writing and reading derives from the influence of cognitive psychology, a mid-twentieth-century phenomenon that seeks to provide insight into the operations of human memory, perception, learning, and problem-solving (Anderson 2). This section provides a snapshot of early cognitive research in writing studies, beginning first with two key cognitive precepts and illustrating each through Linda S. Flower and John R. Hayes's cognitive process model of writing. I choose this work because it was "the most widely cited model" of the composing process, one that fixed "the vocabulary people use in talking about the composing process" (Scardamalia and Bereiter 781). The section concludes with disciplinary criticism of cognitive research and the shift to a sociocultural perspective.

The emergence of cognitive psychology in the late 1950s can be traced to a groundswell of forces circulating prior to World War II and culminating in the post–World War II Macy Conferences on cybernetics. As John R. Anderson explains, modern cognitive psychology draws from two key precepts: information processing and computer science, particularly artificial intelligence. The first principle underlying cognitive psychology concerns information processing, which Allen Newell and Herbert A. Simon anchor in topics such as control theory, information theory, and game theory. Information processing, they explain, attends to the flow or sequence of mental operations in the performance of a cognitive task (4), such as looking for a matching pair of socks. As Anderson describes it, *information* consists of the various mental constructs used by the individual, ranging from questions (Where's the matching blue sock?) to memory (When did I last see it?), to plans (Look in the laundry room), to task representation (Find the sock so I can get to work). In addition, information also refers to the end result of the entire activity: the location of the lost sock. Finally, the *process* part of information processing concerns the sequence of cognitive operations, such as defining the problem, marshaling memory, developing a plan, changing the plan, and so forth. Thus, key elements of information processing direct attention to naming mental constructs, identifying mental activities operating on those constructs, determining the serial order of those activities, and accounting for the end knowledge resulting from the activities and constructs (11–12).

Information processing plays a vital role in writing research framed by a cognitive orientation, as Flower and Hayes's work illustrates. Following in the steps of Newell and Simon, Flower and Hayes approach writing as a "problem" to be solved ("Problem-Solving"). The goal of writing research, like that of cognitive research, is to identify all the basic activities and information constructs used in solving the problem posed by writing. Flower and Hayes describe the act of writing as a "set of distinctive thinking processes," directly tying their work with the principle of information processing ("Cognitive" 366). They identify specific mental activities (planning, translating, and reviewing) and determine the sequence in which those processes unfold (hierarchically organized and embedded within one another) (367; 375–77). In addition, they highlight information, or mental constructs such as goals, that drive the mental activities (367; 377–79). Writers' goals consist of both high-level and supporting subgoals, an insight that places creativity "in the hand of the working, thinking writer" (381) or, more accurately, in the mind of the working, thinking writer. Thus, the identification of cognitive activities, description of the organization of those activities, and account of the end result all reflect the influence of information processing.

The second key precept undergirding cognitive psychology involves the privileging of artificial intelligence and computer modeling, both of which are linked to the belief that the human brain functions like a digital computer. Early cognitive psychology borrowed a number of concepts from systems theory but particularly those associated with machine intelligence. Newell and Simon serve as key informants of this cross-over between human intelligence and artificial intelligence. For them, the computer-mind analogy constitutes a tool to think with (What have we learned from programming computers, and how might we use that knowledge to understand human cognition?) and a means to assess the rigor of that thinking (How does this model of human thinking map onto a computer program?). As they explain, a model of human thinking should possess sufficient detail and accuracy that a computer can be programmed to perform the target behavior. The reciprocity between artificial intelligence and the human constitutes a central feature of cognitive psychology in the 1970s and 1980s.

Artificial intelligence circulates through the cognitive process model of writing. While Flower and Hayes do not explicitly link their model to computer programming, they do present their theory in the form of a flow chart that describes the "flow of *information* from one box or process to another" (386n11, original emphasis). Reminiscent of the sequential breakdown and organization of a computer program, the cognitive-process model also constitutes a response to a "problem in design," the researchers claim, that again resonates with artificial intelligence. Flower and Hayes suggest that the cognitive-process model serves as an account of "an imaginary, working 'Writer'"; thus, their description of the functional system accounts for the way in which this fictitious writer would perform in the real world. While Flower and Hayes refer to the model as a "metaphor," not a program, it is a metaphor that can be used to foster the transformation of poor writers into good writers (368), implicitly suggesting the influence of artificial intelligence in their modeling.

Although cognitive research in writing studies was initially popular, not everyone joined the revolution. Criticism of the cognitive-process model of writing and cognitive psychology in general swirled around two objections. First, critics questioned the foundational premises of the model: Is writing a species of problem solving? Ann E. Berthoff charged that a problem-solving approach strips away from writing the formative power of imagination, reducing writing to manipulation, rather than creation, of information. Second, critics pointed to what the cognitive orientation left out: emotions, bodies, and other elements of the non-verbal (Brand). Gradually, interest in and attention to cognitive research waned as disciplinary attention shifted away from questions about the individual writer to questions about the culture within which the individual writes. As a result of this concatenation of philosophical and methodological criticism, research inspirited by a cognitive orientation virtually disappeared in writing studies. However, we are now at a moment when a variety of issues central to our disciplinary agenda, ranging from the impact of technologies on cognition (Hayles) to learning transfer (Beaufort), invites a reclamation of a cognitive orientation, especially one informed by the insights of its critics. Bateson's ecological cybernetics offers a powerful template for just such a shift.

An Ecology of Mind

In 1990, Jerome Bruner, a key contributor to the cognitive revolution, noted with disappointment the wrong turn taken by cognitive psychology. Echoing criticism voiced by Berthoff and other writing scholars, Bruner contends that the initial aim of discovering and describing "the meanings that human beings created out of their encounters with the world" had been derailed by the dominance of artificial intelligence, which had replaced meaning with information (2, 4). How, then, might we revise cognitive psychology to refocus on meaning rather than information manipulation, the motive that impelled the emergence of the field in the first place? My goal in this section is to answer that question by drawing on Bateson's ecology of mind, which transforms information processing into *difference processing* and artificial intelligence into *contextual intelligence*.

Bateson's ecology of mind reconfigures the individualist orientation of traditional cognitive psychology, yielding an eco-cognitive, rather than a cognitive, paradigm. For cognitive science, the human mind operates like a computer program, separate from its environment. However, for Bateson, a mind does not exist locked out of the bone house (separate from the neurology of the brain) or locked in the bone house (separate from the external environment). Rather, "the individual mind is . . . immanent also in pathways and messages outside the body" (467). Therefore, how we define or parse off the individual mind—and, thus, individual cognition—depends on something more than isolated, discrete information constructs and processes potentially code-able in the zeroes and ones of computer language. It depends on internal and external linkages constituting the mind in action at any one point. The object of study, then, in

[handwritten marginal note: refocus on meaning rather than information]

an eco-cognitive paradigm is the mind as it materializes from an array of message pathways.

The first important shift from a cognitive to an eco-cognitive orientation concerns information processing. For Flower and Hayes, the mind is analogous to a central processing unit that deploys discrete mental activities in the service of a set of dynamic goals and subgoals. However, for Bateson, there is no central processing unit; there is only the distributed intelligence of an ecology of mind formed by an assemblage of "differences that make a difference" (459). As Bateson's elementary unit of information, difference is the result of a disparity that has significance (458). An infinite number of differences exist within any phenomenon, impossible for any individual to perceive. What becomes information is that which is important for the individual at that moment. For instance, in my search for the lost sock, information in the ecology of mind that we might call "Kris-finding-the-lost-sock" results from my recognition of other elements in my environment that affect finding the sock. As a result, I do not "see" the breakfast dishes in the sink because they are not a difference that makes a difference. However, the pile of unfolded laundry has consequence for the "finding-the-sock" pattern and my identity as "sock finder (or sock loser)" in that ecology of mind. The laundry is information, but it remains information only as long as the pattern created by the circulation of that difference exists. Once the lost sock is found, the pile of laundry ceases to be a difference that matters, and the "Kris-finding-the-lost-sock" ceases to be an ecology of mind.

News of difference combines to privilege context, challenging the second precept of traditional cognitive psychology: artificial intelligence. Mid-century cognitive psychology operated on the premise that the individual mind functioned in isolation like the software of a computer program, an aspect replicated in Flower and Hayes's cognitive-process model. Where the writer is composing, with what tools, and in what physical condition are questions that have no bearing on the cognitive-process model. However, bracketing off the material results in what Bateson calls a serious epistemological error because the individual mind doesn't think—the context thinks. Writer plus room plus tools plus body provides the matrix from which emerges an ecology of mind. Bateson illustrates this contextual versus artificial intelligence with an example drawn from evolution. Like Darwinian evolution, cognitive psychology errs in conceiving of the individual organism (or, in the case of evolution, a homogenous set of organisms) as the unit of survival and change (457). However, Bateson explains, "the unit of survival is not the breeding

the context thinks

organism, or the family line, or the society"; instead, the unit of survival is the "flexible organism-in-its-environment" (457). In other words, the context—organism plus environment—survives. Thus, the modern horse did not evolve *on* the grassy plain, Bateson claims. Rather, the proto-horse evolved *with* the proto–grassy plain. They coevolved in dialogue with the minute changes—differences that made a difference—in each other. Ergo, to understand human behavior, "you are always dealing with total circuits, completed circuits. This is the elementary cybernetic thought" (465). To comprehend the mind as it creates meaning rather than manipulates information, we have to consider the entire context because it is the context—the ecology of mind—that thinks, reads, and writes.

Eco-Cognition and Reading Bodies

Mind as an ecology rather than a computing machine transforms two key concepts from mid-twentieth-century cognitive psychology. Information processing becomes *difference processing,* and artificial intelligence becomes *contextual intelligence.* Both changes invite renewed attention to questions of cognition or, perhaps more accurately, questions of eco-cognition. This final section illustrates the possibilities of an eco-cognitive paradigm by returning to Isabella, Drajha, and Professor Plum. First is a brief description of online reading as a kinetic process. Second, I add detail to that description by exploring the influence of eco-cognition on three aspects of my research: the definition of the phenomenon, selection of a data set, and development of an analytical lens to examine the data. Questions in the conclusion offer further directions for eco-cognitive research.

The phenomenon of kinetic reading offers a tentative and partial answer to my research question. I define *kinetic reading* as a physical engagement with and negotiation of symbol systems. The physical component involves more than a hand turning a page or clicking a mouse. Kinetic reading relies on and integrates an element of physical action within the construal of linguistic/imagistic meaning. Thus, central to kinetic reading is the somatic interface of the body. In addition, my preliminary work suggests that *juggling*—the physical, mental, and emotional movement among competing texts and images—constitutes a key strategy in kinetic reading. To arrive at both definition and strategy, I relied on an eco-cognitive orientation to define my phenomenon of study.

My focus on the kinetic aspects of online reading grew out of the principle of contextual intelligence. To understand a particular ecology of mind, we have to include all the relevant pathways. "The way to delineate a system [an ecology of mind] is to draw the limiting line in such a way that you do not cut any of these pathways in ways which leave things inexplicable," Bateson counsels (465). But all pathways are not relevant all the time. For instance, Bateson explains that if we want to understand a blind man walking, then the ecology of mind includes the blind man's cane through which information (differences that make a difference) is communicated throughout the entire system. However, if we want to understand the blind man eating at the dinner table, then the cane is no longer relevant. This was a particularly potent insight for me because it directed my attention to the *physiological* aspects of reading: the messy concerns of bodies, emotions, and environments. As a product of a "thinking context," reading relies on and integrates physical action within the interpretation of (or response to) linguistic/imagistic meaning.

The physiotextual juggling evident in figure 7.1 illustrates the importance of physiological pathways in kinetic reading. To begin, students actively employed eyes and hands to juggle texts, assigning variable attention to different portions of the units in circulation. In one three-way conversation, each participant copes with the unfolding text with varying degrees of meaningfulness. First, the teacher lectures, in the midst of which two students strike up a dialogue unrelated to the teacher's information. When Isabella in line 8 contributes a piece of metadiscourse— "this is kinda weird to me"—commenting on the virtual experience, teacher and student juggling collide. In the middle of an overview of the technological interface that she began in line 5, Professor Plum interprets Isabella's "kinda weird" comment as an extension of her own discussion of technology. So she provides a pragmatic solution to the "strangeness" of the situation—increasing the amount of white space within which students type their contributions—that she expects Isabella to read as part of the technology lecture. Isabella juggles her conversation with Drajha to attend to the teacher's addition, responding with what she hopes is a suitably respectful comment: "oh thats better, thanks." Then Isabella juggles again, by putting aside Professor Plum's unfolding text and asking Drajha about the presence of other members of their small group. In the meantime, Professor Plum is doing her own juggling. She intervenes, almost scrambling to catch up with the rapidly deployed textual turns, to provide some technical information that will enable Isabella to track who is and is not present.

As an instance of contextual intelligence, this brief snippet reveals the extent to which kinetic reading engages the hand and eye through textual juggling. The unfolding textual interactions consist of multiple points of contact among the three active participants. Each point of contact

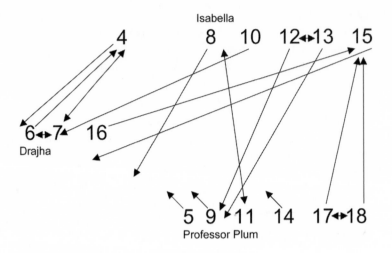

Fig. 7.1. Diagram of interactions, lines 4–18.

Line	Writer	Text
4	ISABELLA:	hey Drajha
5	PROFESSOR PLUM:	Okay, well I think this is a pretty simple interface
6	DRAJHA:	hi Isabella
7	DRAJHA:	Isabella is my mom's name
8	ISABELLA:	this is kinda weird to me, being in here
9	PROFESSOR PLUM:	You can adjust the whiteboard above the group window by dragging the edge of it
10	ISABELLA:	Drajha is not my mom's name
11	PROFESSOR PLUM:	Yes, it's a little strange
12	ISABELLA:	o thats better
13	ISABELLA:	thanks
14	PROFESSOR PLUM:	So you can see more of the text
15	ISABELLA:	is anyone else here?
16	DRAJHA:	All of us are here.
17	PROFESSOR PLUM:	Isabella, you can see a list of people by clicking on the card file icon
18	PROFESSOR PLUM:	It shows you a list of the people in the room

requires contributors to use eyes and hands to cope with the constantly generated lines of texts, sifting mentally and physically what is worthy of attention, what is worthy of a specific kind of attention, and what can be ignored. Such textual juggling increases in speed, selectivity, and somatic stress as lurkers become participants, adding their posts and thus adding to the pool of what must be juggled. It intensifies as new pathways of information expand the ecology of thinking-reading mind.

The second contribution of an eco-cognitive paradigm to this project concerns the selection of relevant data, particularly the decision to integrate visual and verbal records. Focused on identifying information processes, traditional cognitive research collected and parsed data primarily through protocol analysis or verbal reports generated by a research subject speaking aloud during the performance of a task. The researcher recorded this thinking out loud, separated the text into units, and analyzed it for patterns. Flower and Hayes built their cognitive-process model out of five years of verbal protocol collection and analysis ("Cognitive" 366). However, Bateson's eco-cognition directs attention to the feedback and feedforward loops of *difference* processing. So to attend to the relevant physiological "differences that make a difference" in kinetic reading, I needed to expand my data set to include both verbal and physical performances as well as the sites vital to both. Two examples illustrate the salience of such data for understanding the somatic difference processing in kinetic reading.

How students designed environments for their computers—their gateway into their class—aligned with how they juggled their online texts. For example, Katya and Maddie Star created very different environments for their computers. Katya situated her computer in the left-hand corner of her room directly next to her roommate's workspace so that they could talk as they studied. In addition, she frequently turned away from her computer to share face-to-face conversations with friends who wandered into her dorm room through the door she habitually left open. Throughout the semester, Katya showed a high tolerance for juggling texts, remaining one of the few students in the study who enjoyed the class just as much at the end as she did at the beginning of the semester. Maddie Star's environment and attitude to the juggling contrasted considerably. She designed an intensely private space, nesting her computer under her elevated bunk bed, buttressing it in with walls of milk-crate bookcases filled with books and school supplies. She sought to control her physical space to minimize interruptions; the computer served as her predominant focal point. Similarly, Maddie Star sought to control her virtual space, displaying limited patience with the textual chaos of twelve people trying to maintain multiple conversations simultaneously. For Maddie Star, the textual juggling required by kinetic reading in a virtual-classroom situation was frustrating rather than enjoyable. Attention to visual as well as verbal data provided these important insights into the physiological difference processing essential to kinetic reading.

Finally, the third impact of eco-cognition on this inquiry into online reading concerns the analytical lens I developed to examine my data. Data are not meaningful until interpreted, so the lens a researcher creates to discern patterns in those data is crucially important. The complementarity of contextual intelligence and difference processing provides useful guidelines for contriving just such a lens. To illustrate, because an ecology of mind (the thinking-reading context) emerges from differences that make a difference, an analytical lens must direct attention to critical feedback-feedforward loops of differences. For my work, three crucial loops consisted of somatic engagement, paralinguistic responses to the textual interface, and emotional response to the discourse, each of which is evident in the various accounts of juggling offered above.[2] For instance, the textual juggling represented in figure 7.1 reflects how two students and one teacher perceive and perform a text somatically: with eyes, hands, and bodies. A second significant difference concerns paralinguistic responses to the tool(s) by which we create a text, a factor reflected in the environments Katya and Maddie Star created for their computers. Finally, the third difference that makes a difference in kinetic reading involves the range of emotional responses readers have to the evolving online text, which Maddie Star found frustrating and Katya pleasurable. Influenced by an eco-cognitive paradigm, I was able to design an analytical lens that helped me tease out the various physiological differences intrinsic to the ecology of thinking-reading mind.

This one small glimpse of kinetic reading hints at the possibilities of an eco-cognitive paradigm. An enriched eco-cognitive orientation invites us to recommit to research on the individual mind in action, one shaped not by information processing but by difference processing, not by artificial intelligence but by contextual intelligence. It leads us to think in new ways and to ask new questions. I pose a few eco-cognitive questions for further investigation. For instance, if the context—the ecology—thinks, reads, and writes, then are the insights of kinetic reading applicable beyond the assemblage of relationships that exists within any one moment? Or, if pathways of difference processing connect thinking contexts (which Bateson believes), then what news of difference crosses from one ecology of mind to another? In other words, what is transferred, and how is that transferred difference reconfigured in the new ecology of mind? These questions merely scratch the surface of eco-cognitive questions, leading us into new avenues of research and new insights into literacy. Bateson asserts that "the most important task today is, perhaps, to learn to think in the new [ecological] way" (468). Perhaps this is the most important task for twenty-first-century writing studies scholarship.

Notes

1. This study, which I codirected with Carole Clark Papper, was supported by grants from the Spencer Foundation and NCTE Research Foundation.

2. Mark Amsler's work with affective literacy was particularly helpful in defining these three key differences.

Works Cited

Amsler, Mark. "Affective Literacy: Gestures of Reading in the Later Middle Ages." *Essays in Medieval Studies* 18 (2001): 83–109. Print.

Anderson, John R. *Cognitive Psychology and Its Implications.* 2nd ed. New York: Freeman, 1985. Print.

Bateson, Gregory. *Steps to an Ecology of the Mind: Collected Essays in Anthropology, Psychiatry, Evolution, and Epistemology.* Northvale: Aronson, 1987. Print.

Beaufort, Anne. *College Writing and Beyond: A New Framework for University Writing Instruction.* Logan: Utah State UP, 2007. Print.

Berthoff, Ann E. "From Problem-Solving to a Theory of the Imagination." *College English* 33.6 (1972): 636–49. Print.

Brand, Alice G. "The Why of Cognition: Emotions and the Writing Process." *College Composition and Communication* 38.4 (1987): 436–43. Print.

Bruner, Jerome. *Acts of Meaning: Four Lectures on Mind and Culture.* Cambridge: Harvard UP, 1990.

Emig, Janet. *The Composing Processes of Twelfth Graders.* Urbana: NCTE, 1971. Print.

Flower, Linda S., and John R. Hayes. "A Cognitive Process Theory of Writing." *College Composition and Communication* 32.4 (1981): 365–87. Print.

———. "Problem-Solving Strategies and the Writing Process." *College English* 39.4 (1977): 449–61. Print.

Haas, Christina, and Linda Flower. "Rhetorical Reading Strategies and the Construction of Meaning." *College Composition and Communication* 39.2 (1988): 167–83. Print.

Hayles, N. Katherine. "Hyper and Deep Attention: The Generational Divide in Cognitive Modes." *Profession* (2007): 187–99. Print.

Newell, Allen, and Herbert A. Simon. *Human Problem Solving.* Englewood Cliffs: Prentice-Hall, 1972. Print.

Scardamalia, Marlene, and Carl Bereiter. "Research on Written Composition." *Handbook on Research in Education.* 3rd. ed. Ed. M. C. Wittrock. New York: Macmillan, 1986. 778–803. Print.

Sommers, Nancy. "Revision Strategies of Student Writers and Experienced Adult Writers." *College Composition and Communication* 31.4 (1980): 378–88. Print.

PART TWO

Revisioning Research in Composition

8.

Revisiting Teacher Research

Lee Nickoson

What is teacher research, exactly? Who conducts teacher research, and when, why, and for what purposes? What distinguishes teacher research from other forms of writing research? Answers to these questions might seem obvious enough: Teacher research is the study of a writing class conducted by one who teaches it with the ultimate purpose of improving classroom practice. It may surprise readers, however, that long-standing epistemological disagreements—differences of opinion on what teacher research *is* and *does*—abound. Noted teacher-research scholars Stephen Fishman and Lucille McCarthy's description of teacher research as "highly amorphous" and with "audiences, settings, methods, and purposes [that] vary markedly," for example, is much more expansive than the definition I supply earlier. Just as competing understandings of teacher research as a methodology exist, so, too, are there multiple perspectives on the role and purview of the researcher. Some see teacher researchers as those who study their own classes, while others posit the role of the teacher researcher more broadly. For instance, Colin Lankshear and Michele Knobel, new-media literacy and literacy-education scholars, respectively, posit teacher researchers as "classroom practitioners at any level, preschool to tertiary, who are involved individually or collaboratively in self-motivated and self-generated systematic and informed inquiry undertaken with a view to enhancing their vocation as professional educators" (9).

Taking up the seemingly obvious questions that begin this chapter, the following discussion explores the complexities of teacher research as an approach to the study of writing. I begin by offering a brief historical overview of teacher research in the field of composition before turning to a more detailed discussion of the powerful symbiotic relationship between teaching and researching identities that is at the center of teacher research. To illustrate the unique opportunities such work provides us as compositionists, I draw upon my own experiences with teacher research and illustrate those unique opportunities and use those experiences to posit multimethodological study as a next step for teacher researchers. The essay concludes with possibilities that readers interested in establishing or growing such a research agenda might pursue.

A Brief History

In her 1997 essay, "On *Reading* Teacher Research," Susan Lytle lists no fewer than fifteen synonyms for teacher research: "teacher inquiry, practitioner research, practitioner inquiry, qualitative practitioner research, action research, critical action research, collaborative action research, participatory action research, emancipatory research, practice-as-inquiry, reflective practice, educative research, classroom inquiry, researcher-in-practice, inquiry-based professional development." Teacher. Practitioner. Research. Inquiry. Understanding teacher research as subject matter thus includes unique challenges because of the multiple methods in which it is identified and practiced. Ruth E. Ray forwards the predominant vision of teacher research espoused by compositionists: "What distinguishes teacher research from other composition research is its collaborative spirit, its emphasis on the interrelationships between theory and practice, and its interest in bringing about change—in the teacher, the student, the school system, the teaching profession, the file of study, and the practice of research—*from within the classroom*" ("Composition" 183). Both the complexity and the dynamicism of teacher research stem from the multiple ways in which key terminology Ray articulates—concepts of collaboration, the theory/practice relationship, and inquiry as change agent—are taken up. To be sure, teacher research can represent many things to many people.

Any history of teacher research as understood and practiced in composition grows from Lawrence Stenhouse and Ann Berthoff and the traditions each scholar has come to represent. Stenhouse, a British historian and educational theorist-practitioner, is credited with introducing the term *teacher research* in his influential 1975 book, *An Introduction to Curriculum Research and Development*. Stenhouse conceived of teacher research as rigorous, systematic, and reflective inquiry grounded in comparative case studies, urging teacher researchers to conduct case studies of their own students and, in close partnership with other practitioners, to compare findings to explore predetermined research questions. A primary goal for teacher research, Stenhouse forwards, is to amass an ever-developing clearinghouse in order to enhance pedagogy and research practices.[1]

Stenhouse vs. Berthoff — insider, outsider, empirical, reflective 103

Stenhouse's idea of teacher research indeed represents an objectivist, positivist approach to inquiry and thus was strongly critiqued by lead teacher-research scholars working in the 1980s and 1990s. The Stenhousian approach, as it came to be known, was viewed by many as, in fact, working in direct opposition to an understanding of teacher research as invested in and, in fact, growing out of deeply held notions of teachers as experiential experts, most notably linked to the argument Berthoff makes in "The Teacher as Researcher." Unlike Stenhouse, who promoted teacher inquiry as an effort at objective renderings of student learning, Berthoff defines teacher research as a professional enterprise in which the role of teacher as expert insider is privileged, and the teacher's anecdotal knowledge, or lore, is valued.[2] Moreover, whereas Stenhouse promoted empirical, naturalistic, and observational methods of inquiry in which the classroom functioned as a site for systematic data collection, Berthoff envisioned teacher research as practitioners calling upon extant knowledge based on recollections of and reflections on teachers' experiences in their classrooms and situating that knowledge among new scholarly conversations. Berthoff thus posited the teacher, rather than any outside researcher, as expert and, in fact, often epistemologically at odds with external academic researchers. In a second seminal disciplinary essay on teacher research, "Composition from the Teacher Researcher Point of View," Ray articulates her approach to teacher research as a feminist enterprise, systematic and collaborative, a dialectic form of inquiry, an approach that stems directly from "*within the classroom*" (emphasis added) and that has increased teaching effectiveness as its explicit goal. In the tradition of Berthoff and Dixie Goswami and Peter Stillman, Ray positions teacher research in direct contrast to quantitative study, arguing that "knowledge and truth in education are not so much found through objective inquiry as socially constructed through collaboration among students, teachers, and researchers" (175).[3] Whereas Stenhouse lauded actively involving outsider (i.e., distanced, objective) perspective with the inclusion of fellow teachers, co-researchers Berthoff and Goswami and Stillman, Ray, and other lead teacher researchers in composition privilege insider perspectives (i.e., local, subjective).

More recently, discussions of teacher research as methodology suggest the benefits of a hybrid approach to practitioner inquiry. For example, Fishman and McCarthy's *Unplayed Tapes: A Personal History of Collaborative Teacher Research* (2000) borrows from both the Stenhouse and Berthoff traditions to cast teacher research in a new light. Fishman and McCarthy draw on their twenty years' experience with teacher research (the "unplayed tapes" created in support of their collaborative work), skill-fully placing personal experience in relationship to various theoretical debates. Conceiving of teacher-researcher as participant-observation research, they argue that while we cannot—indeed, as teacher-scholars we should not—remove classroom as a site of our study, our inquiries, nevertheless, benefit from the additional, "outsider" teacher-researcher perspective a co-researcher brings to any project. Whereas Ray locates collaboration between a teacher researcher and her students, Fishman and McCarthy shift the focus of collaboration to the dynamics of teacher-researcher partnerships.

Heavily influenced by Fishman and McCarthy, Lankshear and Knobel persuasively argue for yet another reconceptualizing of teacher research. In their book *Handbook for Teacher Research: From Design to Imple-mentation* (2004), Lankshear and Knobel recast several leading tenets of teacher research. Teacher research, they argue, would benefit from embracing quantitative methods of study as a complement to more natu-ralistic forms of inquiry and need not be limited to "direct or immediate research of classrooms."

> Although the ultimate point of impact sought from teacher research is on what occurs *in* classrooms, it does not follow that this end is best served solely through direct empirical study *of* classrooms. Teachers may learn much of value for informing and guiding their current practice by investigating historical, anthropological, so-ciological or psychological studies and theoretical work conducted in other places or at other times. These could be studies of policy, communities, social class, the work world, non-standard language varieties, and so on. (7; original emphasis)

Stenhouse, Berthoff, Fishman and McCarthy, and Lankshear and Knobel have as common ground a concept of teacher inquiry as an intellectual and professional endeavor that grows out of that teacher's questions, con-cerns, and/or curiosities. All of these scholars likewise conceive of and practice teacher research as a form of action research, the goal of which is improved teaching effectiveness that, in turn, leads to the development of the teacher-researcher as pedagogue and investigator. Lankshear and Knobel, however, widen—or scope out—the purview of teacher research in ways that include sites beyond that of the classroom, as well as quan-titative and qualitative methods of study.

Most instances of published research with the explicit label of *teacher research* follow the Berthoff model of inquiry and are likely to be either a

[margin annotations, handwritten: "studies of classrooms"; "need not be studies of be to have doesn't + have"; "teacher research as action research"]

case study (such as Janet Emig's canonical *Composing Processes of Twelfth-Graders*) or classroom ethnography (such as Elizabeth Chiseri-Strater's *Academic Literacies*). Yet, by adopting Lankshear and Knobel's concept of teacher-researcher, we expand the models of teacher-researcher available to include historical studies, interview and survey research, and discourse analysis, among others.[4]

Teacher-Researcher, Researcher-Teacher

Fishman is eloquent in describing the almost symbiotic relationship between his professional identities of teacher and researcher eloquently: "[T]he greatest power teacher research has given me is the ability to unify my life" (274). "Teacher" and "researcher" identities are difficult if not impossible to separate, and my experience bears this out. But again, as my experience shows, the closeness between these identities has several advantages: a flexibility in both pedagogical and scholarly focus, a source of intellectual and professional excitement, and an opening up to collaboration in ways that researchers otherwise are not likely to experience. Teacher research has offered ways for me to unify my teacherly and researcherly selves; it has also served as an ongoing catalyst for my pedagogical and scholarly development. Specifically, rather than happening in isolation or as discrete phenomena, my scholarly wonderings happen precisely at the point where my teacherly and scholarly selves intersect.

To give a bit more detail, I regularly teach courses on composition pedagogy, writing assessment, and methods of studying writing to undergraduate and graduate students alike, and the scholarship that most captures my interest is research on composition and composition pedagogy, writing assessment, and feminist understandings of composition. As someone who is deeply invested in issues of composition pedagogy and research, I find that teacher research provides opportunities to explore the questions that rise directly out of my "teacherly" activities (e.g., classroom practice, conferencing with students outside of class, my participation on dissertation committees) in systematic and productive ways. I am also equally drawn to teacher research because it allows me to engage with and contribute to scholarly conversations about students' literacy development and ways I, as their instructor, might support that development. Cathy Fleischer comments on fluidity that teacher inquiry provides practitioner scholars in her book-length autobiographical narrative, *Composing Teacher-Research: A Prosaic History*: "As teacher-researcher, I read theoretical texts from a practical perspective; as a reader of theoretical texts, I practiced teacher-research from a theoretical perspective" (5). It is that constant interplay between teaching and research as recursive activities that keeps me curious and continues to leave me energized.

Teacher research, as Fishman and McCarthy describe it, is powerfully amorphous and includes a vast array of studies, efforts that span the rhetorical spectrums of audience, purpose and occasion, from informal, instructor-generated surveys of students' experiences with a particular assignment to a formal, ethnographically informed study of a particular classroom community that will ultimately appear in a scholarly journal. I offer a few of my own experiences with teacher research as examples of how, why, and to what end compositionists engage such work.

My scholarly introduction to teacher research included reading and immediately connecting with Ray's essay "Composition from the Teacher Researcher Point of View," assigned reading for a research methods seminar. Finding myself drawn to research teacher research because of, as Ray so aptly describes it, its uniquely "collaborative spirit, its emphasis on the interrelationships between theory and practice, and its interest in bringing about change—in the teacher, the student, the school system, the teaching profession, the field of study, and the practice of research—*from within the classroom*" (183; original emphasis), I quickly became invested in exploring possibilities for how teacher research might help me better understand and affect students' learning experiences my classes. And so I read, spending time reading the work of Ray, Berthoff, Lytle, Patricia Lambert Stock, Fleischer, and other esteemed composition teacher researchers in order to become versed in the conversation. My first practical introduction to teacher research as systematic study (i.e., sustained inquiry intended for a public audience beyond that of the classroom studied) was no less than my dissertation, for which I relied on descriptive, observational methods in my effort to "tell the story" of the classroom community as I, acting in the dual capacity of teacher and researcher for the study, interpreted it. I consider the dissertation to have been a deeply meaningful experience. First and foremost, a completed and successful (i.e., defended) dissertation research project allowed me to formally transition from graduate student to rhetoric and composition faculty. It continued to serve me in productive ways as a researcher, too, as I revisited and expanded particular arguments from the dissertation for numerous conference presentations and publications on classroom-based writing assessment.[5]

My experience writing the dissertation impacted my research interests in other, less visible but more personally meaningful ways as well. My interest in collaborative and feminist approaches to composition pedagogy *and* research, for example, is the direct result of the fieldwork I undertook for the dissertation. Having made my project—the initial research questions and guiding interests for study—public to my student-participants, I was surprised when, as a group, my students would regularly volunteer suggestions or insights, at times interrupting class discussions with, "Hey, you should write this down" or "This might be something important for your study," and other gentle (and not-so gentle) reminders that I came to understand as representative of the students' own investment in my telling the story of *our* classroom community. I remembered Ray's cautionary call that we take seriously the ethical dimension of teacher research when it involves students: "Students are not merely subjects whom the teacher researcher instructs and assesses; they are co-researchers, sources of knowledge whose insights helps focus and provide new directions for the study" ("Composition" 175–76). The realization that students are, in fact, active participants rather than distanced subjects of my research project—and all the ethical complexities imbedded in such a relationship between teacher-researcher and student-participants—led me to seek additional opportunities to study and enact both feminist pedagogy and methodologies of research. I subsequently coedited *Feminism and Composition: A Critical Sourcebook*, a collection that grew directly from our shared experiences in a graduate seminar on feminism theory in composition. And, perhaps less publicly visible is the sustained influence the experience I enjoyed with the student–research participants continues to have on my classroom practice: I strive to enact some form of sustained, systematic, collaborative research with my students in courses I teach.

What I hope is clear from this brief personal narrative is that my orientation to teacher research has shifted in the years since my dissertation work. Echoing Lankshear and Knobel, teacher research, for me, has come to include various other forms of research, projects often located beyond the space of the classroom but that continue to have direct import on my teaching. What has remained a constant, though, is the mutually informing relationship between scholarship and pedagogy.

Extending Teacher Research as Collaborative, Multimethodological Inquiry

Just as teacher research remains central to our work as compositionists, it also remains ripe with possibilities for future study. As described earlier, both Fishman and McCarthy and Lankshear and Knobel advance compelling arguments for extending teacher research in ways that involve multiple methods and researcher perspectives. For Fishman and McCarthy, this "integrative approach" might include pairing with another teacher researcher who functions as a participant-observer of the co-researcher's class in order to gather empirical and narrative-based data for study. For Lankshear and Knobel, reimagining teacher research includes expanding both the methods and the sites for study. I believe, as do many of my co-contributors to the current collection,[6] writing researchers, in this case teacher-researchers, would do well to pursue multimethodological, robustly collaborative inquiry.

What might such an approach include? Look like? Various researchers who share an interest in investigating a particular location or phenomena would assemble to create a team that in turn would bring various methodological skill sets, experiences, and perspectives to the study at hand. Research teams might look and function quite differently, depending on the project identified. For example, teams might consist of a small group of faculty from the same department who, along with their writing-program administrator, share an interest in exploring how their majors understand the purposes of writing at the end of their undergraduate experience. Faculty would bring particular expertise and/or interests to the study: a compositionist experienced in interview research, a literary scholar skilled at performing content analysis, and a writing program administrator who is familiar with institutional archives. Each researcher would contribute unique skills, histories, and perspectives to his or her investigation. Additionally, each researcher would bring a particular motivation to the study. While an administrator could be motivated to learn about how the writing program might better support student writers, literature faculty might be motivated by a desire to study what critical reading skills transfer to other contexts, and a teacher researcher would be motivated by an investment in advancing her understanding of student literacy practices, and, in turn, improving classroom practice. But, of course, this is one of many possibilities for realizing research teams. Teams could include faculty and students alike, or skilled mentor-researchers and novice mentee-researchers, and so on. Teams might be cross-disciplinary; they could pull from writing researchers from discrete subfields . . . the possibilities are many. And, of course, just as research team members could include any number of constituencies, the studies themselves could be located either inside or beyond the space of the classroom. Thus, multimethodological research once again involves a reconceptualization of how teacher researchers understand inquiry as a collaboration so that though it very well may include a teacher's study of her own classroom (as it is traditionally conceived), it perhaps includes fellow teacher researchers (in the traditions of Stenhouse and Fishman and McCarthy) and is not limited to the classroom as the site of inquiry (Lankshear and Knobel) but rather explodes possibilities for how, with whom, and for what reason we engage the work of research.

Developing as a Teacher-Researcher

As with any inquiry-based project, teacher research presents the researcher with numerous logistical and ethical challenges. Much of the important work of the teacher-researcher needs to take place long *before* he or she enters the site. Foundational concerns include strategies for negotiating and publicly performing not only the teacher researcher's dual roles but also those of the student-participants, co-researchers, or other primary audiences involved. Power differences between and among researchers and participants; differing levels of involvement or passion various stakeholders are likely to bring to the project; how the project is articulated and roles identified; the methods by data will be gathered, coded, and interpreted—all of these and other attendant ethical considerations demand the teacher-researcher's attention before he or she enters the field. Recognizing that this decision-making process can seem arduous if not overwhelming, I offer the following suggestions to helpful resources available to most if not all compositionists:

- Read. Read much, often, and from a range of forums *as a teacher-researcher.* As is true for any researcher, teacher-researchers benefit from reading in composition and rhetoric and beyond. Devote time to reading article- and book-length examples of teacher research. Look at practical how-to guides that help the researcher better conceptualize studies.[7] Journals such as *Composition Studies, English Education, Pedagogy,* and *Research in the Teaching of English* serve as good starting points, though we would do well to read beyond the discipline as well.[8]

- Use local resources. Writing program administrators can make wonderful resources for anyone considering undertaking teacher research. WPAs are likely to have a running list of needed practitioner-based research projects. They are also very likely to know of previous studies that might be of help to plan, organize, conduct, write up, and present the project. Members of the institution's internal review board (IRB) are also important resources for any researcher. Does the school have an office dedicated to supporting teaching excellence (such offices are often identified as centers of teaching and learning or centers for teaching excellence)? If so, get to know the faculty and staff. Do they have learning communities for those interested in teaching effectiveness? Teacher research? If so, consider participating. Membership in such groups can provide opportunities for beginning researchers to learn from and work with other new and more experienced teacher researchers from across campus. Involvement in such groups can also serve as an invaluable support for researchers engaged in a live project.

• Take full advantage of professional communities. Department and cross-disciplinary discussion or research groups; larger professional organizations such as the National Writing Project (NWP), National Council for Teachers of English (NCTE), or the Council of Writing Program Administrators (WPA) can all be tremendously supportive communities for teacher-researchers. The Research Network Forum, Qualitative Research Network, and Computers and Writing Graduate Network Forum are just a few of the many examples of excellent one-day professional workshops designed specifically to support development of in-process research. Start by asking colleagues and mentors to visit your classes, and reciprocate.

• Develop your range of methodological experience. Consider taking coursework on or otherwise exposing yourself to various methods and methodologies, both from within your field and from other disciplines (education, psychology, sociology, mathematics and statistics, communications; see Haswell, current volume). If the opportunity arises, volunteer to collaborate in a supporting role with colleagues more experienced in teacher research.

• Go public. Present your findings in public venues: participate in (or establish!) department colloquia series, or consider submitting your research to institution teaching and/or research fairs. Seek out regional as well as national and international conferences as venues to present your work.

Taking advantage of these and other opportunities provides new teacher researchers ways in to understanding the pragmatics involved with conducting teacher research. Such efforts also serve to help us become familiar with the curiosities and conversations that drive such inquiry.

Teaching remains at the heart of what, as *compositionists*, we are about. To be sure, teacher research is a recursive, collaborative, and explicitly change-based scholarly endeavor. As with any approach to research, it is important both for those who are new(er) to methodological discussions of teacher research and those of us who have been at this work for a while to consider carefully what it is we want our research to do. By examining and engaging teacher research in the ways suggested here, we can put ourselves in a position to effectively learn not only *about* our students but also—and crucially—*from* them. We will be in the position to understand how they write and why, how they learn, and what their educational and literate goals are. The aim of teacher-researchers is a deeper understanding of student writers. Building our disciplinary knowledge, teacher research can aid us in simultaneously developing a deeper understanding of *our students as writers*, building our abilities to reach them and make a positive difference in their literate lives.

Notes

1. Stenhouse's conceptualization of teacher inquiry reads as a precursor to what Richard Haswell terms RAD (replicable, aggregable, data-driven) research.

2. For examples of other foundational work in the same tradition as Berthoff, see Goswami and Stillman; Bissex and Bullock; Lather; Cochran-Smith and Lytle; and Fleischer.

3. Ray expounds on teacher research as uniquely situated in *The Practice of Theory: Teacher Research in Composition* (1993), a tremendously useful introduction to the theory and practice on teacher research and a must-read for all interested in teacher-research scholarship. "Toward a Teacher Research Approach to Graduate Studies" (chapter 5) provides beginning teacher-scholars particularly useful introductory discussions of theoretical and practical considerations commonly involved with teacher research.

4. See, in the current volume, Rohan and Lamos for historical studies; Selfe and Hawisher and Inoue for interview and survey research; and Haas, Takayoshi, and Carr for discourse analysis.

5. For more on these, see Nickoson-Massey, "Rethinking Approaches to Writing Assessment" and "(Re)Imagining Writing Assessment as a 'New' Literacy."

6. For example, see Broad; Grabill; Haswell; Hesse; and Selfe and Hawisher.

7. For examples of methods, see Bissex and Bullock; Chiseri-Strater and Sunstein; Daiker and Morenberg; Fleischer; Freeman; Lankshear and Knobel; and Ritchie and Wilson.

8. Research on the Teaching of English publishes a very useful annual bibliography of teacher-research studies each November.

Works Cited

Berthoff, Ann. "The Teacher as Researcher." Goswami and Stillman, *Reclaiming the Classroom* 28–39.

Bissex, Glenda, and Richard H. Bullock, eds. *Seeing for Ourselves: Case Study Research by Teachers of Writing.* Portsmouth: Heinemann, 1987. Print.

Chiseri-Strater, Elizabeth, and Bonnie S. Sunstein. *What Works? A Practical Guide for Teacher Research.* Portsmouth: Heinemann, 2006. Print.

Cochran-Smith, M., and Susan Lytle. *Inquiry as Stance: Practitioner Research for the Next Generation*. New York: New York Teachers College P, 2009. Print.

———. *Inside/Outside: Teacher Research and Knowledge*. New York: Teachers College P, 1993. Print.

Daiker, Donald A., and Max Morenberg, eds. *The Writing Teacher Researcher: Essays in the Theory and Practice of Class-Based Research*. Portsmouth: Boynton/ Cook, 1990. Print.

Fishman, Stephen, and Lucille McCarthy. *Unplayed Tapes: A Personal History of Collaborative Teacher Research*. New York: Teachers College P, 2000. Print.

Fleischer, Cathy. *Composing Teacher-Research: A Prosaic History*. Albany: State U of New York P, 1995. Print.

Freeman, Donald. *Doing Teacher Research: From Inquiry to Understanding*. New York: Heinle, 1998. Print.

Goswami, Dixie, and Peter R. Stillman, eds. *Reclaiming the Classroom: Teacher Research as an Agency for Change*. Portsmouth: Boynton/Cook, 1987. Print.

Haswell, Richard H. "NCTE/CCCC's Recent War on Scholarship." *Written Communication* 22.2 (2005): 198–223. Print.

Lankshear, Colin, and Michele Knobel. *Handbook for Teacher Research: From Design to Implementation*. Maidenhead: Open University, 2004. Print.

Lather, Patti. *Getting Smart: Feminist Theory and Pedagogy within/in the Postmodern*. New York: Routledge, 1991. Print.

Lytle, Susan L. "On Reading Teacher Research." *Focus on Basics: Connecting Research and Practice. National Center for the Study of Adult Learning and Literacy* 1.A. 1997. Web. 27 July 2007. <http://www.ncsall.net/?id=480>.

Nickoson-Massey, Lee. "(Not) Breaking the Rules: A Situated Inquiry of Response, Assessment, and Agency in a College Composition Class." Diss. Illinois State U, 2003. Print.

———. "(Re)Imagining Writing Assessment as a 'New' Literacy." *Engaging Audience: Theory and Practice*. Ed. Brian Fehler, Elizabeth Weiser, and Angela Gonzales. Urbana: NCTE, 2009. 235–43. Print.

———. "Rethinking Approaches to Writing Assessment." *Practice in Context: Situating the Work of Writing Teachers*. Ed. Peggy O'Neill and Cindy Moore. Urbana: NCTE, 2003. 235–43. Print.

Ray, Ruth E. "Afterword: Ethics and Representation in Teacher Research." *Ethics and Representation in Qualitative Studies of Literacy*. Ed. Peter Mortensen and Gesa E. Kirsch. Urbana: NCTE, 287–300. Print.

———. "Composition from the Teacher Researcher Point of View." *Methods and Methodology in Composition Research*. Ed. Gesa E. Kirsch and Patricia A. Sullivan. Carbondale: Southern Illinois UP, 1992. 172–89. Print.

———. *The Practice of Theory: Teacher Research in Composition*. Urbana: NCTE, 1993. Print.

Ritchie, Joy, and David Wilson. *Teacher Narrative as Critical Inquiry: Rewriting the Script*. New York: Teachers College P, 2000. Print.

Stenhouse, Lawrence. *Research as a Basis for Teaching: Readings from the Work of Lawrence Stenhouse*. London: Heinemann, 1985. Print.

———. *An Introduction to Curriculum Research and Development*. London: Heinemann, 1975. Print.

9.

Autoethnography in the Study of Multilingual Writers

A. Suresh Canagarajah

The best way to define autoethnography is through the three words that make it up—that is, auto, ethno, graphy. *Auto*: The research is conducted and represented from the point of view of the self, whether studying one's own experiences or those of one's community. *Ethno*: The objective of the research and writing is to bring out how culture shapes and is shaped by the personal. *Graphy*: Writing is not only the main means of generating, analyzing, and recording data; there is an emphasis on the creative resources of writing, especially narrative, for accomplishing the social and scholarly objectives of this research. The triad of requirements will help us distinguish between many other forms of writing that are similar to autoethnography and treated as synonymous with it in some circles.

Carolyn S. Ellis and Arthur P. Bochner list thirty-nine labels ranging from autobiographical ethnography to writing stories that share similarities with autoethnography ("Autoethnography" 739–40). To take genres familiar in our field, literacy autobiographies are often based on the personal and feature narrative writing. However, the extent to which the authors consider their literacy trajectory and practices in relation to social and cultural influences will help us decide if they are autoethnography. The same consideration applies to creative nonfiction, which may adopt creative writing and personal voice. At the other extreme, certain forms of qualitative research, such as case studies, narrative studies, and action research, may feature the researcher in some level of interaction with the subjects to present cultural practices. However, the extent to which the self is the basis for interpretation and analysis will help determine if it is autoethnography. Many forms of writing, such as ethnographic memoir, ethnographic poetics, indigenous ethnography, narrative ethnography,

113

native ethnography, and reflexive ethnography, often succeed in maintaining the balance among the self, culture, and narrative writing.

This chapter first discusses the epistemological assumptions shaping autoethnography, then the significance of this approach for the study of multilingual writing, especially from non-Western communities, and, next, the methods typically employed in this research approach through three different projects I have conducted. The conclusion presents some of the challenges in writing autoethnography and claiming significance for the knowledge constructed.

The Approach

Autoethnography is committed to developing an emic and holistic perspective on socially situated practices, similar to ethnography. That is, autoethnographers aim to represent the insider perspective on an experience or a culture (emic). They also keep all the variables and contextual conditions intact in their analysis and representation (holistic). To this end, autoethnography may use some of the forms of data elicitation adopted by ethnography to study culture, that is, participation, observation, interviews, and artifacts. The researchers also theorize ground up, developing the relevant constructs from their observations, without imposing etic (outsider) constructs from their field. Like ethnographers, they may also triangulate multiple sources of data to arrive at reliable findings. Despite these similarities, however, the researcher/subject roles are fused in autoethnography. The researchers study the practices of a community of which they are members, and they are visible in the research. In this sense, autoethnography is different from ethnography (at least in the dominant modernist tradition) where the ethnographer is detached from the community studied and is hidden in the text as he/she adopts "realist" descriptive techniques in deference to an objective representation and analysis of the culture.

Autoethnography is oppositional to the research approaches in both the quantitative and qualitative traditions that are informed by modernist principles of objectivity, empiricism, rational analysis. Though there are differences in emphases, autoethnographers at the most radical end of the epistemological spectrum (e.g., Ellis and Bochner) emphasize the following aspects:

- The self as the basis for knowledge. Along with traditions such as phenomenology and symbolic interactionism, autoethnographers believe that the self is dynamically involved in constructing reality and co-constructing experiences with others. To leave out the personal is to miss significant aspects of the experiences being studied.

evocative

- **The role of narrative in constructing knowledge.** Autoethnographers foreground the narrative as the focus of description and tool for analysis. They feel that explicit analysis filters out important dimensions of the experience. The most radical practitioners desist from even adding a separate analytical or theoretical discussion separate from the narrative (for an example, see Ellis, *Revision*). Readers are expected to engage with the narrative to experience the analysis and theory embedded in the story.

- **Learning from emotions.** Autoethnographers believe that positivistic academic inquiry has demoted the place of emotions in understanding experiences and subjects. Feelings and emotions are treated as important dimensions of social experience and a key to knowledge.

- **The validity of constructivism.** For the above reasons, autoethnographers employ writing that is frankly evocative. They adopt literary devices (i.e., of poetry and fiction) and other performative techniques (i.e., theatrical renditions and dialogue) to describe the experience with textural richness and immediacy. They believe that description reconstructs the experience in significant ways, and it is impossible for anyone to claim that their rendition is free of values or perspectives. Some may claim, ironically, that their evocative description is more real than reality—as it gets to the essence of the experience more effectively.

- **The objective of social change.** While modernist inquiry aims for detached inquiry free of ideological influences and treats the construction of knowledge as an end in itself, autoethnographers believe in research that is politically committed and disturbs the status quo. They take pride in writing that moves readers to critique and change social conditions.

In adopting these orientations, the use of autoethnography enables marginalized communities to publish their own culture and experiences in their own voices, resisting the knowledge constructed about them. Considering the history of ethnography where marginalized communities have been studied, described, and theorized by researchers from privileged communities, autoethnography enables them to counter such unfair and distorted representation. It is this function that Mary Louise Pratt celebrates in her description of autoethnography as a literate art of the contact zone. She defines autoethnographic writing as "a text in

Pratt

which people undertake to describe themselves in ways that engage with representations others have made of them. Thus if ethnographic texts are those in which European metropolitan subjects represent to themselves their others (usually their conquered others), autoethnographic texts are representations that the so-defined others construct *in response to* or in dialogue with those texts" (35). As Pratt implies, to be effective in this mission, subalterns have to engage with metropolitan knowledge. For this reason, autoethnographic texts are multivocal. The voices of the marginalized are not pure; they are articulated in relation to the knowledge constructed by others, although with an objective of resistance.

Despite the somewhat European epistemological framing above, I find autoethnography resonating well with the South Asian background I come from. In the Hindu oral culture, there is an appreciation of narrative as knowledge.

Significance for Multilingual Writing

Though autoethnography has implications for the exploration of diverse themes and contexts in composition, I see a special role for this approach in understanding multilingual writing, given the current needs and priorities in our field. Composition theory and pedagogy have experienced a global spread and relevance. As other communities adopt composition, we are required to know their writing practices and teaching traditions. If not, composition would become a colonizing movement. Furthermore, migration has introduced American classrooms to multilingual students, making the need to understand multilingual writing practices more urgent. More important, writing is increasingly becoming multilingual for everyone (including native English speakers) in the context of Internet and digital literacy.

Despite the motivation and need to learn the composing practices of multilingual writers, the knowledge produced on this subject is limited because of the methods adopted. Textual analyses or observations of large student groups miss the subtle negotiations that take place as multilingual writers shuttle between languages. Though ethnographies have been conducted on multilingual writing, they have been done mostly by researchers who are not multilingual themselves. These ethnographers do not come from the community inhabited by the writer, and they do not draw their subjects directly into the study and reporting of the findings. As a result, even ethnographies have unwittingly adopted "native speaker" norms in descriptions of multilingual writing. Such studies have distorted the competencies of multilingual persons and led to the perception that multilingual writing is deficient. If we are to construct new paradigms that do justice to the strengths and resources multilingual writers bring to writing, we have to gain access to insider perspectives on multilingual composing. Autoethnography enables multilingual writers to describe their writing practices in all their contextual specificity and cultural uniqueness, helping metropolitan scholars to develop cross-cultural understanding.

There are important reasons why multilingual writers should themselves talk about multilingual communication. Research in applied linguistics shows that those who are multilingual adopt unique strategies to communicate with each other in intercultural situations (Firth and Wagner; Canagarajah, "Lingua"). For example, they co-construct grammars from their different varieties of English or their vernaculars. Meaning for them is an intersubjective construct. As such, it is difficult for those outside the interaction, let alone native speakers who do not adopt such strategies, to describe their communicative practices. I find that multilingual students adopt such negotiation strategies in writing classrooms. Letting multilingual writers themselves describe their literacy trajectories and negotiation strategies provides a more insightful research approach (as I have recently done through the literacy narrative of a Saudi Arabian student in "Multilingual").

Autoethnography enables us to develop knowledge on the literacies of multilingual students in different parts of the world without depending on researchers from the center. Multilingual students and scholars will find autoethnography "researcher friendly" (Chang 52). They do not need a huge budget, sophisticated instruments, hundreds of subjects, and limitless time to do this form of research. In fact, "researchers" (who do not necessarily have to be academics) are studying and describing the experiences they are already invested in. Furthermore, scholars from marginalized communities do not need access to the latest literature on rhetoric and composition in order to publish their experiences. We do not hear of literacy experiences from the periphery because local scholars are not familiar with composition theory in order to frame their experiences with relevance to our journals. Even those multilingual scholars without a background in rhetoric and composition are able to present their writing practices through their reflections and narratives. Publications such as Diane Belcher and Ulla Connor's *Reflections on Multiliterate Lives* and Christine Pearson Casanave and Stephanie Vandrick's *Writing for Scholarly Publication* have enabled multilingual scholars from diverse disciplines to reflect on their writing and/or publishing practices and describe their resources and constraints in English writing. The narratives may serve as "data" that enable interpretation from multiple theoretical angles.

Autoethnography is also reader friendly. Because literacy bears immense significance for social and educational opportunities today, it is important for those outside the academy to also understand its problems and prospects. Also, multilingual students and scholars from the periphery can read, analyze, and theorize literacy via autoethnography, without scholarly apparatus. Furthermore, scholars outside composition also need to understand the implications of writing for their knowledge-production activity. The most gratifying experience of publishing my literacy narratives from the periphery (*Geopolitics of Academic Writing*) was the e-mails I received from scholars in agriculture, pharmaceuticals, political science, and history on the way my argument resonated with their experiences in their own fields.

Methods

Different research methods are used in different types of autoethnography: self-in-the-collective, interactive, and self-reflective. In the first, the author/researcher describes a collective experience as an insider to the community. Though autoethnographers are visible in the research and may adopt a personal orientation to the experience described, they are mindful of representing the experiences of the group. Interactive autoethnography is constructed when two or more subjects each become researcher-cum-subject as they interview each other to co-construct the experience. The third approach approximates autobiography as the authors reflect on their own experience, in the light of social and cultural life, to represent their perspectives. Each of these approaches requires slightly different research methods. I illustrate them in relation to my own studies.

Self-in-the-Collective

This mode of autoethnography approximates traditional ethnography and adopts well-known fieldwork methods. In modernist ethnography, there are cases where ethnographers have reflected on their experiences and perceptions during the research process. In this sense, they have adopted a reflexive orientation and represented themselves in their research. The difference in autoethnography is that the researchers are also members of the community studied. My study of the writing/publishing practices in my native academic community in Sri Lanka falls into this genre (*Geopolitics*). In this project, I studied how my colleagues and I in Sri Lanka wrote for academic publications from a context of poverty, war, and the resulting lack of resources. There were many advantages in adopting an autoethnographic approach. As I was myself experiencing the same difficulties in writing and publishing that my colleagues were experiencing, I knew what to look for and what to ask. Furthermore, I had myself adopted some of the coping strategies local scholars use to overcome the difficulties they face. Given these strategies' unorthodox nature, they are not easily divulged to outsiders. Furthermore, I could evoke with poignancy the frustrations and struggles involved in writing from Sri Lanka, which my colleagues may not have had the time or interest in articulating. My access to closed faculty meetings, academic committees, and administrative channels would not also have been available to an outside researcher. Similarly, I had access to academic literacy events in informal contexts, as in tea rooms and houses of colleagues, which are rarely available to outsiders.

To study the local writing and academic culture, I adopted many traditional methods: taking field notes on literacy events, recording interactions in academic gatherings, collecting samples of writings by colleagues for close analysis, interviewing colleagues on their reading/writing practices, and documenting policies on publishing and scholarship. What made this research different from traditional ethnography was the attitude and perspectives I brought to bear on all this data. The interpretive perspective shaped by my own feeling of exclusion from publishing circles in the West shone a critical light on all this data. Therefore, the writing of this research shuttled between the personal voice and analysis of objective data. However, the diversity of data sources enabled me to triangulate the findings to some extent and provided readers ways of gaining additional perspectives on the local academic culture to complicate or contradict my claims.

Interactive

I adopted this approach to analyze the mentoring of a novice multilingual scholar, Ena Lee, into academic publishing. When her submission to *TESOL Quarterly* (*TQ*) was rejected, I (as the editor of *TQ*) mentored her to revise the article for another independent review. This was part of an initiative to apprentice novice multilingual authors into publishing. Though the article was accepted for publication after multiple rounds of revision, the author decided not to send the final version for publication. It was during a chance face-to-face meeting some time after this incident that Ena and I realized that the apprenticeship had not gone the way we thought it would. There were many cases of misunderstanding and miscommunication in the experience, which revealed certain unacknowledged tensions and conflicts. After this epiphany, Ena and I discussed the possibility of studying this apprenticeship experience to figure out what went wrong. We wrote interview questions for each other, focusing on our attitudes and expectations at every stage of the publishing process. What is called "the interactive interview" is a popular technique used in other autoethnographies of this nature (Ellis, *Ethnographic I*). Based on these questions, Ena and I journaled our reflections and reflected on issues of socialization into academic literacy in the context of the multiple artifacts of this experience—such as drafts of the article, correspondence, and referee comments. Putting these forms of data together, we co-constructed our narrative. True to the research method, we presented the study as a dialogue in a conference presentation.[1] We read our lines successively to piece together our experience. The dialogue dramatized the tensions, misunderstandings, and epiphanies we ourselves experienced.

The autoethnography complicated scholarship on academic literacy socialization in insightful ways. The research process made Ena and me keenly aware of the tensions and misunderstandings that can occur between mentors and apprentices. Other ethnographies on literacy socialization have not been able to bring out such tensions, as the novice authors were observed objectively and their successful publishing outcome was taken as evidence of the effectiveness of the mentoring experience.[2] Our study raised the possibility that even in cases of successful mentoring, it is possible that novice authors feel pressured to accommodate the expectations of the gatekeepers in order to ensure publication. The autoethnography also revealed the idiosyncrasies of uptake (with diverse motivations for adopting or rejecting feedback), revision strategies of authors, and the negotiation strategies around a submission. Such details do not emerge easily in studies that adopt objective research methodologies.

Self-Reflective

I adopted this approach to explore my literacy trajectory as I shuttled between my native community and the United States for education and employment. I initially learned writing in Tamil in Sri Lanka, before moving to the United States for graduate studies and learning English academic writing according to the expectations here. Then I moved to Sri Lanka after my doctorate to teach there, negotiating bilingual writing at that time. Later, I fled the fighting in the country to teach and write in the United States.[3] While the Tamil oral communication strategies that structured my academic articles were not appreciated in the American context, the formal and calculated structure of American academic writing sounded too self-conscious and condescending to my Tamil colleagues and students. In writing these tensions and the ways I negotiated them, I moved beyond simply recording experiences to gaining a new understanding of ways to reconcile these tensions. Though some of the early drafts represented a crisis narrative, subsequent drafts developed a hybrid orientation. Such autoethnographies have helped multilingual authors develop a self-awareness of their writing challenges and resolve some of the struggles deriving from textual conflicts.[4]

To write this autoethnography, I journaled my memories of learning writing in formal educational contexts in Sri Lanka and the United States, and of composing and publishing in transnational contexts. I also looked at some of my writing samples from different points of my writing/publishing trajectory. These artifacts helped jog my memory and brought into relief new details about my writing experience. Reading other multilingual scholars' literacy biographies (cited above) also helped me reflect on how my trajectory and experiences were similar or different. Additionally, the questions Belcher and Connor suggested to me served as a heuristic to elicit and analyze my experiences.[5] Other autoethnographers have adopted diverse techniques for introspection and memory analysis, such as self-observational data, including systematic self-observation that involves keeping a record of one's own activities, trajectories, and changes; and interactive self-observation that makes one's experiences explicit in working with a few others who are involved in a similar project (see Chang 89–95). Self-reflective data includes using field notes to record the researcher's private and personal thoughts and feelings and reading the self-narratives of others to bring out comparisons. Methods for collecting personal memory data include writing an autobiographical timeline; "inventorying self," which means not only collecting information but also evaluating and organizing it; and "visualizing self," which includes drawing kinship diagrams, free drawing of people, self, places and events to generate thought, and reflecting on photographs or video to externalize submerged thoughts and feelings (Chang 71–88).

Multilingual students can adopt these strategies to generate thoughts and feelings about their writing in different genres and languages and about learning writing under different pedagogical approaches, contexts, and teachers. I have also provided prompts to students to help them construct their literacy autoethnographies. An analysis of one such narrative produces useful insights into ways in which multilingual writers employ their repertoire to construct multimodal texts ("Multilingual Strategies").

Challenges

It is important to consider ways of writing a balanced narrative that keeps issues of collective life, disciplinary concerns, and analysis in focus. It is easy to take things to an extreme and end up navel gazing, leading to the cynicism among researchers that autoethnography is not research but "me-search." Autoethnographies that conduct a tangled introspective analysis or celebration of personal feelings ignore their larger cultural and social implications or their scholarly significance. (I find some of the writing in Ellis's *Revision* leaning in that direction). This approach has been called *evocative* autoethnography by Leon Anderson (373), who calls for an *analytical* autoethnography that shows the theoretical and analytical implications of the narratives. Ellis and Bochner in "Analyzing Analytic" reject this dichotomy and accuse Anderson of reducing the critical edge of autoethnography and attempting to make compromises with traditional ethnography. They argue that narratives are powerful enough to construct knowledge without a distinct analysis. Though I understand the need to give primacy to the self and the narrative, I believe that it is possible to embed analysis and theorization of relative effectiveness in one's narrative.

There are also ethical considerations in writing about others in one's autoethnography. Our real-life stories involve other people. Though our identities are necessarily explicit, one should decide how to identify others. There could be painful experiences others may not want to revisit. Some references could be perceived as denigrating. Many autoethnographers consider it important to get consent from those who are featured in one's narrative. In *Geopolitics of Academic Writing*, my colleagues were identified by their real names, as their published work was discussed in my manuscript. I made certain to send the prepublication draft for a "member check." Significant changes were made in the final draft, based on their feedback. Even then, the published version created some displeasure. Some colleagues felt that comparing them with Western scholars and their publishing standards and finding them wanting were insulting.

In addition to the practical problems in framing one's story appropriately and deciding how to represent the characters, there are epistemological questions on the research-worthiness of the autoethnography. First of all, there are questions on the truth value of a narrative based on the self. Is the knowledge gained from autoethnography more reliable as it derives from personal experience? Poststructuralists would argue that the self that grounds the narrative is not whole or unmediated. It is important, therefore, not to get carried away by the power of the personal for giving truth value to experiences.

me-search

A related concern is the value that should be given to the cultural descriptions simply because they are narrated by insiders. As Clifford Geertz in *Local Knowledge* points out, there are also advantages from the "experience far" perspective, especially in its ability to defamiliarize social life for different insights. Insiders have their own blinders that might prevent them from providing a fair account. Furthermore, it is important to realize that no one is ever a complete insider, I had to acknowledge in *Geopolitics* that my status as a bilingual and U.S.-trained scholar separated me from my colleagues. I considered how I could triangulate my "experience near" and "experience far" perspectives for deeper insights.

Generalizing from the personal narrative of a single person (the "*N* of one") is also questionable. Can one person's experiences of a culture serve as a reliable perspective on the community? Furthermore, how far can we generalize from a single case? How can we be sure that the experiences are even true to that one person's life? To what extent are the autoethnographic accounts based on selective memory? Though the autoethnography provides a case among cases, there are benefits from getting this very concrete and intense focus of a single person. Just as there is value from scope, there is value from depth. While objective descriptions that come from interviews or surveys with numerous subjects provide one kind of perspective, the descriptions of a single subject provide a different insight into cultural life. Scholars would argue that how a culture is "experienced" in the inner life is as or more important than how it is perceived from outside (Marcus and Fischer 45–76).

From the above perspective, the more autoethnographies we have the better. If all knowledge is local and personal, we must all become storytell- ers—both inside and outside the academy. Let a thousand flowers bloom.

Notes

1. See Canagarajah and Lee.
2. See Belcher; Flowerdew.
3. See Canagarajah, "Fortunate Traveler."
4. See Li, "Writing"; Shen, "Classroom."
5. For the list of questions, see Belcher and Connor, *Reflections*, 209–11.

Works Cited

Anderson, Leon. "Analytic Autoethnography." *Journal of Contemporary Ethnography* 35.4 (2006): 373–95. Print.

Belcher, Diane. "Seeking Acceptance in an English-Only Research World." *Journal of Second Language Writing* 16 (2007): 1–22. Print.

Belcher, Diane, and Ulla Connor, eds. *Reflections on Multiliterate Lives.* Clevedon, England: Multilingual Matters, 2001. Print.

Canagarajah, A. Suresh. "The Fortunate Traveler: Shuttling between Communities and Literacies by Economy Class." Belcher and Connor, *Reflections on Multiliterate Lives* 23–37.

——. *A Geopolitics of Academic Writing.* Pittsburgh: U of Pittsburgh P, 2002. Print.

——. "Lingua Franca English, Multilingual Communities, and Language Acquisition." *Modern Language Journal* 91.5 (2007): 921–37. Print.

——. "Multilingual Strategies of Negotiating English: From Conversation to Writing." *Journal of Advanced Composition* 29 (2009): 711–43. Print.

——. "Non-Discursive Requirements in Academic Publishing, Material Resources of Periphery Scholars, and the Politics of Knowledge Production." *Written Communication* 13.4 (1996): 435–72. Print.

Canagarajah, A. Suresh, and Ena Lee. "Periphery Scholars Publishing in Professional Journals." TESOL Convention, Tempe, Florida. 17 Mar. 2006. Presentation.

Casanave, Christine Pearson, and Stephanie Vandrick, eds. *Writing for Scholarly Publication: Behind the Scenes in Language Education.* Mahwah: Erlbaum, 2003. Print.

Chang, Heewon. *Autoethnography as Method.* Walnut Creek: Left Coast, 2008. Print.

Ellis, Carolyn S. *The Ethnographic I: A Methodological Novel about Autoethnography.* Walnut Creek: Altamira, 2004. Print.

——. *Revision: Autoethnographic Reflections on Life and Work.* Walnut Creek: Left Coast, 2009. Print.

Ellis, Carolyn S., and Arthur P. Bochner. "Analyzing Analytic Autoethnography: An Autopsy." *Journal of Contemporary Ethnography* 35.4 (2006): 429–49. Print.

——. "Autoethnography, Personal Narrative, Reflexivity: Researcher as Subject." *Handbook of Qualitative Research.* Ed. Norman K. Denzin and Yvonna S. Lincoln. Thousand Oaks: Sage, 2000. 733–68. Print.

Firth, Alan, and Johannes Wagner. "Second/Foreign Language Learning as a Social Accomplishment: Elaborations on a Reconceptualized SLA." *Modern Language Journal* 91 (2007): 798–817. Print.

Flowerdew, John. "Discourse Community, Legitimate Peripheral Participation, and the Nonnative-English-Speaking Scholars." *TESOL Quarterly* 34 (2000): 127–50. Print.

Geertz, Clifford. *Local Knowledge: Further Essays in Interpretive Anthropology.* New York: Basic Books, 1983. Print.

Li, Xiao-Ming. "Writing from the Vantage Point of an Outsider/Insider." *Non-Native Educators in English Language Teaching.* Ed. George Braine. Mahwah: LEA, 1999. 43–56. Print.

Marcus, George, and Michael M. J. Fischer. *Anthropology as Cultural Critique: An Experimental Moment in the Human Sciences.* Chicago: U of Chicago P, 1986. Print.

Pratt, Mary Louise. "Arts of the Contact Zone." *Profession 91.* New York: MLA, 1991. 33–40. Print.

Shen, Fan. "The Classroom and the Wider Culture: Identity as a Key to Learning English Composition." *College Composition and Communication* 40.4 (1989): 459–66. Print.

10.

Racial Methodologies for Composition Studies: Reflecting on Theories of Race in Writing Assessment Research

Asao B. Inoue

We need, I argue, *racial methodologies* for our research in composition studies but more particularly writing assessment. An attention to the ways race functions in and is produced by our research methods is absent in most of the published research in writing assessment. To illustrate, I compare three writing assessment research projects, an early quantitative one on writing placement scores by Edward M. White and Leon Thomas that considers race, a recent qualitative project by Cathy Spidell and William H. Thelin that considers student reactions to grading contracts, and the quantitative portion of a research project I currently conduct on grading contracts. Then I suggest ways that racial methodologies are needed and may be used in future research.

In 1989, Samuel Messick, a leading validity expert, argued that "testing serves multiple ends inherently entangled with contending or conflicting social values. As a consequence, the interpretations and uses of tests need to be justified not only in scientific and professional forums, but in the public arena as well" (91). Messick calls for ethical research methodologies that account for all stakeholders in an assessment. Validation research can do this since it is research that inquires into what a test says it is assessing—that is, validation is research on an assessment that eventually argues the degree to which the assessment's decisions are okay or adequate. In other words, validity (or the outcome of validation research) is a set of arguments, or "an integrated evaluative judgment of the degree to which empirical evidence and theoretical rationales support the *adequacy* and *appropriateness* of *inferences* and actions based on test scores or other modes of assessment" (Messick 13; original emphasis).

validation
research

To make these validity arguments, a researcher must account for all stake-holders in the assessment.

In 2002, Brian Huot refined Messick's call: "Since affirmative action is increasingly under fire, it is time we visited fully the impact of assessments upon minorities, so that instead of adjusting test results, we could use tests that are fair to all" (*(Re)Articulating* 9). Huot gestures more strongly to inequities of race, gender, class, sexual preference, and ability produced by writing assessments. He suggests that fully equitable writing assessments involve more than getting "minorities" to perform like mainstream (white) students; they involve rethinking methods, both in assessment design and validation research. More recently, I theorize directly racial validation, offering a racial validity heuristic that accounts for the power relations of an assessment, the parts that make up the test, and the purposes agents endorse for a writing assessment ("Technology" 113). Since racial formations construct at least the power relations and parts of an assessment, racism may occur even without expressed racist purposes by agents. Thus I call for racial validity.

Messick, Huot, and I are not the first to make such calls in writing-assessment circles or see the importance of considering race in writing-assessment methods. In 1986, Roscoe Brown called for research on the effects of African American English in writing proficiency exams. In 1992 and 1993, Geneva Smitherman analyzed NAEP scores from 1969 to 1979, looking at correlations between tests scores and African American English (AAE). In 1996, Sandra Kamusikiri argued for an "Afrocentric assessment method" that accounts for an historically produced AAE (189).

Additionally, there has been research that demonstrates racist outcomes in assessments, usually through validation research and arguments.[1] In 2004, Hunter Breland, Melvin Y. Kubota, Kristine Nickerson, Catherine Trapani, and Michael Walker found that the average SAT essay scores for black and Latino/a test-takers were lower than whites' and Asian Pacific Islanders' average essay scores (5). Arnetha Ball investigated the ways European-American teachers scored essays hierarchically along racial lines, with white students receiving the highest scores (178). In a study of teacher commenting practices at California State University, Fresno, researchers found that teachers marked errors on papers from black, Asian Pacific Islander (mostly Hmong), and Latino/a students (mostly Mexican American) more copiously than on the papers from white students, causing very different social effects that could be traced along student racial formations (Bulinski et al.).

In Great Britain, David Gillborn discusses a U.K. school assessment, the Foundation Stage Assessment (FSP), that was created by the government in response to an independent, national research collaboration (Gillborn and Mirza). Results showed that when black Caribbean and black African U.K. students start school, they generally perform higher on tests than their white peers (Gillborn 100); however, once the FSP was instituted, black Caribbean and black African students were assessed into the lowest-performing categories (104–6). Gillborn's research argues that the socioeconomic status of black Caribbean and black African students could not account for their poor test results since they began school with higher test results than their wealthier, white peers. It was the FSP itself that created the black Caribbean and black African failure, which disregarded race in its methods and procedures, as well as disregarded the findings of the previous Gillborn and Mirza report.

In 1998, Catherine Prendergast argued that composition studies has lacked any consistent treatment of race or investigations of racism. She calls this lack of treatment of race an "absent presence" in the literature, making the study of racism an "absent *absence*" (36; original emphasis). She says that we must consider what Victor Villanueva asks of us, that is, to examine the "*colonial sensibility* within both national and composition communities" (37; original emphasis). Some progress has been made to alleviate this problem, as suggested in my brief review above. However, it is still difficult to find consistent research methodologies that incorporate informed notions of race and racial formations in the work of writing-assessment specialists, WPAs, and compositionists who attempt to understand their programs, classrooms, and students.

Let me be clear: Writing assessment as a field has yet to address explicitly and consistently "race" as a theoretical concept or racial formations in and around specific writing assessments, thus the field has not addressed racism as potentially structural and status quo.[2] My claim, then, is one about methodology as much as it is about the kinds of inquiries the writing-assessment community takes up and the assumptions we hold as we inquire. If we do not construct methods of research that are reflective of the racial formations that surround our assessments (our civic communities) and make up our classrooms, then we risk (re)producing racism from our assessments and perhaps even from our pedagogies. We will never address directly the structural problems that cause the SAT test gaps in African Americans and Latinos/as or the unintentional adverse effects of teacher commentary as found at CSU, Fresno, or the unintentional failure of black Caribbean and black African students in the UK's

Foundation Stage Assessment. As the last two sections in this chapter suggest, conscientious teacher-researchers (like White and Thomas and Spidell and Thelin) may unintentionally miss different effects of assessments on different racial formations if they are not looking for them, even though they are attempting to understand the effects of those very assessments. Students are never just "students." They are classed, gendered, and raced (among other dimensions), so our research methods must account for these dimensions.

Racial Formation Theory

A few words on my terms. When I say "racial methodologies," I mean research methodologies that use informed theories of race and account for racial formations in collecting data, forming hypotheses, making observations, and drawing conclusions. Although racial theories in racial methodologies do not have to be based on racial formation theory, I draw upon racial formation theory to understand race and racism.

Racial formation theory, developed by ethnic studies scholar Michael Omi and sociologist Howard Winant, attempts to account for previous ethnicity-based, class-based, and nation-based theories of race. Omi and Winant explain "racial formation":

> The theory of racial formation suggests that society is suffused with racial projects, large and small, to which all are subjected. This racial "subjection" is quintessentially ideological. . . . Race becomes "common sense"—a way of comprehending, explaining, and acting in the world. A vast web of racial projects mediates between the discursive or representational means in which race is identified and signified on the one hand, and the institutional and organizational forms in which it is routinized and standardized on the other. (60)

Racial formation, in short, is a set of social and historical processes, or products of "racial projects" (55–56), that (re)create and transform racial categories in society, which often represents and organizes bodies in essentialized and unequal ways. Racial formations are also (re)created through routines, structures, and institutions, thus making them common sense and a part of everyday experience. Writing assessments and the research done on them, then, are "racial projects," producing and drawing on racial formations in the classroom, academy, and society. Omi and Winant explain that a racial project that is racist "creates or reproduces structures of domination based on essentialist categories of race" (71). This means that if a writing assessment is racist, it is not because the motives of individual teachers or WPAs are biased or prejudiced, but because the assessment (re)produces particular "structures of domination based on essentialist categories of race" or by the way the assessment consistently arranges unevenly (unfairly) particular bodies—the way it routinizes social formations or naturalizes certain social arrangements (e.g., black student failure in schools).

In short, racial formation theory asks us to consider a few methodological questions: How are racial formations accounted for in a writing assessment? What relation to the writing construct do the various racial formations have to it?[3] What kinds of data are worth gathering in order to validate an assessment's decisions along racial formations? What possible racialized hypotheses and conclusions can one draw from any data gathered? How might any observations or conclusions already be racialized?

Racism as an "Absent Presence"

One notable early attempt to understand racism as an "absent presence" in a test is White and Thomas's 1981 investigation of the "effect of different kinds of testing upon the distribution of scores for racial minorities" (276). They compared the scores of students on two college-entrance writing tests, the Test of Standard Written English (TSWE) and the English Placement Test (EPT), which the California State University system designed and used with the Educational Testing Service (ETS) for determining "general skill in reading and written communication" and providing a "brief description" of strengths and weaknesses (277). They found that the TSWE and the essay portion of the EPT distributed scores toward the lower end for students of color, particularly black students on the TSWE. White and Thomas cannot explain the different distribution of scores but eliminate "bias towards these students" on the part of readers (raters). Readers, they explain, were carefully trained on the construct and didn't know the identity of any student-writers (280). The more likely cause, they claim, "has to do with the significance of a usage test for determining the writing ability of black students" (280). It is not clear what their explanation means. White and Thomas say nothing else except that the test is not "biased" in the conventional sense. Their methods only allow them to investigate consistency in ratings (reliability) as a source of the skewed ratings.

Their explanation also reveals a methodological problem: One cannot find racism in the EPT or TSWE if one does not have a robust definition for it. Their research methods, ones based on decontextualized notions of interrater reliability (e.g., Do raters rate black student writing differently than white student writing?) with no regard for who those raters are (i.e., most likely predominantly white, middle-class teachers),[4] do not allow conclusions about racial formations constructed by the results of either test, even though they clearly see a problem in the results. Their methods look to reliability, or consistency in ratings (consistency of raters' judgments), and training on the writing construct (the writing proficiency the tests assess), which is based on a white, middle-class discourse; thus, inquiring into reliability will not say much about any racism. White and Thomas associate racism with "bias" in readers, and since there is no reader bias according to traditional standards, they eliminate racism as a product of either test (or eliminate it as a reason for the skewed distributions of students of color). Thus, they seemingly deny racism without inquiring into racial formations of students and raters or into the whiteness of the writing construct itself.

Despite these methodological flaws, it is important to recognize White and Thomas's laudable and early attempt to understand writing assessment's production of racial formations and racism through the distribution of test scores, and their hinting at the lack of sufficient validity of the writing construct for decisions about black students' writing abilities—all before Omi and Winant ever published on racial formations. The lesson we learn perhaps is that just because we break up our data racially, it does not mean our methods for analyzing and understanding that data are informed by a robust theory of race, one that allows us to inquire appropriately into racism. For White and Thomas, my guess is that it might have helped to have some theory that linked their writing construct to whiteness or at least a way methodologically to account for the racialized, reader-dispositions raters used to make judgments. In short, their good work demonstrates the "absent presence" of racism in writing assessment research.

Race as an "Absent Presence"

More recent research on grading contracts illustrate race as an "absent presence." In 2006, Spidell and Thelin report on a study of "student reaction to contract grading" in two college composition courses (taught by Spidell) at "a mid-western four-year university campus" (36, 38). As they explain, student voices have not been a part of the research on grading contracts. Their goal was "to learn more about how students experience grading contracts" (36).

However, Spidell and Thelin's methodology is raceless, thus it can draw no conclusions about the way racial formations may react differently to grading contracts. Their methods do not define, attempt to gather, differentiate, or report along any racial formations that occur in their classrooms or because of the grading contract. In their methods section, they make one mention of students as racialized bodies in classrooms: "We used purposeful sampling . . . to align ethnically with classroom demographics. For example, one student participant came from a middle-eastern background and another self-identified as African-American" (39). While I acknowledge that given the way they were able to sample (from only two courses taught by one teacher) and given their likely mostly white student enrollment at their university, they probably could not sample a statistically significant population of black or Latino/a students, let alone Asian Pacific Islanders or Native Americans.[5] This would make it difficult to draw any conclusions about students other than white students, but they do not say this. Their description suggests that one Middle Eastern student (who may be an international student or a U.S. Asian Pacific Islander student, but they do not say) and one black student are adequate for sampling their classrooms. Statistically, however, one student representing the sentiments of a particular group is never adequate. It would seem that they are not concerned about the way grading contracts may create racial formations or how black or Middle Eastern American students feel about contracts.

The rest of their sample is racially unmarked, presumably white. Why racially mark these two students and not the others? The literature on whiteness explains part of the answer: Whiteness, as a racial category, as a social structure that groups people, and as an organizing principle, is always unnamed and unmarked (Chambers 192; Kennedy, Middleton, and Krista Ratcliffe 365). Students are first assumed to be white, then they are racialized, goes the logic, which means only students of color get raced, and without them, "race" becomes unimportant in the research. Not only is the majority of Spidell and Thelin's respondents unraced, in all their discussions of student voices, even cursory self-identifications of race are absent. Students are just "students," and race is an "absent presence." And this absence occurs not because Spidell and Thelin do not see racial formations in their classrooms but because their methodology does not accommodate racial formations explicitly. Their methods do not assume a need to investigate whiteness in their classrooms or grading contract. A racial methodology, however, would have to call this sample white and thus would draw conclusions that explicitly mark these student reactions as white student reactions from the upper Midwest and more likely Ohio.[6] This means that their conclusions, as interesting and important as they are, may not apply so well to the black students or Latino/a students in their classrooms or in mine at CSUF.

One Attempted Racial Methodology

In order to see what is gained when a racial methodology is used, consider the research on grading contracts that I do at CSUF as a part of our program-assessment efforts. I do not attempt in this brief example to provide a full accounting of my methods, findings, or conclusions, and I simply point to a few differences in methods and what they mean to the observations a researcher can make. Our student population is approximately 31 percent Latino/a (mostly of Mexican descent), 18 percent Asian Pacific Islander (mostly of Hmong descent), 7 percent black, and 32 percent white.[7] The diversity of our students is perhaps one benefit that Spidell and Thelin did not have at their research site, but diversity in student populations studied does not mean one cannot study racial formations in those same populations (whites are raced, too). Additionally, at CSUF, many of our teachers voluntarily use grading contracts (similar to Peter Elbow's contract for a "B"; see Danielewicz and Elbow), and we use a midpoint and endpoint online survey of all students in all writing courses that gathers reactions to grading contracts, among other things. Students self-identify their gender, race, and languages spoken in the home. These data allow us to make observations about racial formations.

One observation that Spidell and Thelin make is that students resist grading contracts because contracts "did not quantify their efforts," meaning since assignments did not have points or grades assigned to them, students did not know how they were doing in their classes (41). At CSUF, I ask four questions that get at similar resistances to grading contracts, each of which use Likert-type scales (four statements that roughly identify the student's feelings):

- How effective overall do (did) you find the grading contract to be in your writing class?

- Did the grading contract help you write better?

- How happy are (were) you with the grading contract as a student in the class?

- Do you prefer a grading contract over traditional grading systems (where grades are placed on each assignment) in courses like this one?

In our English 5B and 10 courses (the two exit points of our FYW program), our spring 2009 students provided the responses summarized in table 10.1. For the question concerning happiness with the contract, more white students were happy or very happy with the contract (66 percent) than black students (60 percent for 5B), but Asian Pacific Islander (Hmong) students were most happy as a formation (73.8 percent for 5B; 66.7 percent for 10). However, in the one-semester course, Engl 10, black students were happier with the contract (75 percent), which could be a function of the blacks who sign up for the accelerated course. In the final preference question, again, Asian Pacific Islanders prefer the contract over traditional grading (81.5 percent in 5B), and they remain the formation with the most positive responses to the contract. Meanwhile, white students prefer contracts in the fewest numbers. It would appear that whites could be more resistant to contracts than their peers of color, especially their Asian Pacific Islander (Hmong) peers at CSUF, who tend to be closest generationally to their families' immigration experiences (most often occurring in the late 1970s and 1980s). Some might call our Hmong formation as Generation 1.5.[8] If happiness with and resistance to contracts have an inverse relationship, then these findings agree with Spidell and Thelin's but only for white students.

And what about that resistance to contracts based on grades and not knowing where you stand in a course? As one might expect, white students pass 5B and 10 courses at the highest rates, and spring 2009 was no exception. In 5B, 95.4 percent of all white students passed the course, while 86.3 percent passed in 10. Of all white 5B students, 85.9 percent got As or Bs; 75.2 percent got the same two grades in 10. Black students, who tended to be less happy about contracts in 5B than black students in 10, passed 5B in the lowest numbers (87.4 percent) and received fewer As and Bs (76.9 percent). Black students in 10 passed at an even-lower rate (85.8 percent) and received even fewer As and Bs (57 percent), yet they were happier with the contract. One could make an argument that grades and passing rates affect the way these racial formations feel about contracts in different ways or that each racial formation may form different connections between grades and passing rates and their feelings for grading contracts.

Interestingly, Asian Pacific Islanders received only marginally better grades than blacks and passed at lower rates in 10 than blacks in 10. Asian Pacific Islanders passed 5B at 90.3 percent and in 10 at a rate of 84.6 percent. About 80.1 percent of their grades were As and Bs in 5B, and 67.9 percent of their grades were As and Bs in 10. So while Asian Pacific Islanders were happiest with the contract, preferred it, and found it most effective, they didn't receive the highest grades or pass in the highest numbers. Since lower grades and passing rates do not explain why the Asian Pacific Islanders had higher levels of happiness and preference with grading

Table 10.1

Exit-survey results on grading contracts in FYW courses, California State University, Fresno, spring 2009

	Race of students (%)														
	All[1]	Black	Latino/a	White	Asian PI	All	Black	Latino/a	White	Asian PI	All	Black	Latino/a	White	Asian PI
Helpful[2]	No					Yes					Not sure				
ENGL 5B	17.6	22.7	11.3	30.7	11.1	43.6	40.9	45.9	29.7	58.0	38.7	36.4	42.9	39.6	30.9
ENGL 10	18.3	0.0	35.0	18.0	7.7	40.9	62.5	30.0	42.0	38.5	40.9	37.5	35.0	40.0	53.8
Effectiveness[3]	Somewhat or not effective					Effective or very effective									
ENGL 5B	21.0	27.3	18.9	25.3	18.5	79.0	72.7	81.1	74.7	81.5					
ENGL 10	27.2	25.0	31.6	28.0	23.1	72.8	75.0	68.4	72.0	76.9					
Happiness[4]	Somewhat or not happy					Happy or very happy									
ENGL 5B	27.5	40.0	35.0	34.0	26.3	72.5	60.0	65.0	66.0	73.8					
ENGL 10	32.6	25.0	35.0	34.0	33.3	67.4	75.0	65.0	66.0	66.7					
Preference[5]	I prefer traditional grading.					I prefer a grading contract.									
ENGL 5B	26.2	27.3	26.9	31.7	18.5	73.8	72.7	73.1	68.3	81.5					
ENGL 10	37.4	25.0	42.1	40.0	33.3	62.6	75.0	57.9	60.0	66.7					

Notes: 1. All numbers on all four questions in the spring 2009 survey matched closely the numbers of the fall 2008 survey. In general, the longer students at California State University Fresno were exposed to contracts, the more they found them effective, were happy with them, and preferred them (all ENGL 5B). Students of color found the contracts more effective and preferred them to traditional grading, especially by the end of the stretch program (ENGL 5A/5B). Asian Pacific Americans, who are mostly Hmong and often generation 1.5 language users, offered the most positive responses to contracts, and in most cases, were above the overall percentages as well in each category. In ENGL 5B, all students numbered 432; black students, 27; Latino/a, 186; white, 118; and Asian Pacific Islands, 100. In ENGL 10, all students numbered 139; black students, 9, Latino/a, 78, white, 32, and Asian Pacific Islands, 18.

2. Helpful: The longer students were exposed to contracts, the more they found them helpful in their writing; however, the results were mixed across the board. Interestingly, more black students in ENGL 10 than in any other group or course

found their contracts helping them write better, with Asian Pacific Americans in 5A coming close in numbers.

3. Effectiveness: Fresno State's Asian Pacific American population (who are mostly Hmong) found grading contracts effective in higher numbers than all other groups. Latinos/as (mostly Mexican American) in 5B (2nd semester with contracts) found contracts effective, but fewer did so in ENGL 10.

4. Happiness: More Asian Pacific Americans in 5B than any other group, except for black students in 10, were most happy with their contracts. Most groups in both 5B and 10 were similarly happy with their contracts.

5. Preference: The majority of all students preferred the grading contract, especially in the second semester of using it (5B). More Asian Pacific American students in both 5A and 10 preferred the grading contract than any other group. In ENGL 5B, all students of color preferred the grading contract over their white peers by a small but noticeable margin. In ENGL 10, more Asian Pacific Americans and black students preferred contracts than their white and Latino/a peers.

contracts (thus, low levels of resistance), they suggest that grades may not tell much of the story behind Asian Pacific Islander student acceptance of grading contracts, even when most students themselves argue that grades are important. I suspect that historical relations with schools, teachers, and grading mechanisms are affecting differently racial formations, and their choices in our directed self-placement seem to influence each racial formation's resistance to the contract differently. It would appear, at least at CSUF that student resistance to grading contracts is not as simple as Spidell and Thelin's research suggests.

My initial findings, then, suggest that not only do different racial formations react differently to grading contracts, thus showing a need to make observations by race in future research, but that grading contracts do not change dramatically the lower (than white peers) passing rates and lower course grades of students of color, at least at CSUF. It does appear that for whites, the better the grade, the higher the preference (and the less resistance), but this is not the case for Asian Pacific Islanders at CSUF and only marginally so for blacks. For these formations of color, preference and perceived effectiveness of contracts have less to do with their passing rates or course grades. While I cannot speak directly to students' sense of knowing where they stand in a course, it stands to reason that confusion about where students stand in a course does not occur evenly across racial formations at CSUF since the results in table 1 are strikingly similar to the midterm survey responses (same questions) and results from both Fall 2008 and 2009.

Finally, if my methodology only allowed me to look at the overall percentages on the survey, in passing rates, or in grade distributions, then I would lose the nuances mentioned above, lose the unevenness and differences by racial formation. Additionally, I would miss the way contracts, at least at CSUF, seem to work better for students of color. In short, to coin a phrase by Cornel West, "race matters" in research methodologies in composition studies.

It is hard to fault White and Thomas or Spidell and Thelin completely. What I am arguing is a paradigm shift in the methodologies of the field. However, it is time to consider the ways we conceive of race and use racial formations in and through our methodologies. Even when our universities serve mostly white, middle-class students, we have an obligation to understand these racial formations as such. More important, we have an obligation to understand why some students are not making it in or through college successfully. How do we do this? A few initial ideas:

- Formulate well-theorized and robust concepts of "race," each racial formation, and "racism." Beyond racial formation theory, consider whiteness studies, critical race theory, and postcolonial theory.

- Collect racial data on students that can be linked to other data.

- Consider racializing your hypotheses, thus your conclusions. For instance, if your conclusions are about how well students reflect on their revision practices, then consider in what ways those students and their teachers are racialized and the ways that the construct measured ("reflection") is also racialized.

- Consider the broad racial categories you intend to employ and their nuances at your site, in your research, and in what kinds of arguments you plan to make. For instance, the category "Latino/a" is very broad and may not be similar to the Latino/a groups at other sites. It may mean Chicano or Mexican descent at your school but Puerto Rican at another. White groups, Asian Pacific Islander groups, and Native American groups have this issue, too.

- Be cautious when cutting data by race after you have already analyzed it for other criteria, such as passing rates. This will not give you the same picture of racial formations that you would get if you first cut by race, then by other criteria.

- Be ready to explain to teachers and students why you are gathering racial data. Many will view gathering this data as a racist project itself.

Notes

1. It should be noted that *racist* and *racism* do not refer to the attitudes, behaviors, or intentions of agents around assessments. The terms refer to the social outcomes and arrangements from assessments and/or the methods used to produce assessment results and decisions.

2. I use the term *race* to identify the theoretical concept of the historical grouping of bodies, not a static essence of any particular group of bodies. It should be emphasized that investigating "race" and "racism" in assessments are not the same thing.

3. A *writing construct* is used as one criterion to validate a writing assessment's decisions. A writing construct is the theoretical psychological dimension an assessment is purporting to measure in order to make valid enough decisions, for instance, "writing proficiency" or passing a first-year-writing course.

4. The Office of the Chancellor at California State University reports that in 1985, only 14 percent of all CSU faculty were of color, and this percentage grew to 24 percent by 2002 (Chancellor's Office 1). This figure appears to have increased to 27 percent by 2007 (California State University). My guess is, because of California's severe budget crisis, furloughing, and hiring freezes, this number has dropped since then.

5. Since they do not say what "mid-western four-year university" the students come from and since both researchers are from the University of Akron, one might assume that Akron is the university these students come from. If so, and this is not certain, then the student enrollment for Fall 2008 was mostly white (77.6 percent), with the next largest formation being black (11.5 percent). University of Akron, "Quick Facts and Figures," <http://www.uakron.edu/about_ua/quick_facts.dot>.

6. The University of Akron website states that of the total 20,058 FTE (full-time equivalent) in Fall 2008, 18,805 were in-state FTE, meaning most students were from Ohio.

7. For a precise breakdown of all racial formations (as identified by the university) and language spoken by students in the first-year writing program, see my article "Self-Assessment as Programmatic Center." CSUF's student populations are quite complex, arguably more complex in their racial formations than the University of Akron.

8. See Harklau, Losey, and Siegal for definitions of Generation 1.5 students. Christina Ortmeier-Hooper describes "Generation 1.5" students as "U.S. resident ESL students who had completed at least some of their secondary schooling in the United States" but quickly complicates these distinctions in U.S.-born students who speak other languages at home (390).

Works Cited

Ball, Arnetha F. "Expanding the Dialogue on Culture as a Critical Component When Assessing Writing." *Assessing Writing* 4.2 (1997): 169–202. Print.

Breland, Hunter, Melvin Y. Kubota, Kristine Nickerson, Catherine Trapani, and Michael Walker. *New SAT Writing Prompt Study: Analyses of Group Impact and Reliability.* New York: College Entrance Examination Board, 2004. Print.

Brown, Roscoe C., Jr. "Testing Black Student Writers." *Writing Assessment: Issues and Strategies.* Ed. Karen L. Greenberg, Harvey S. Wiener, and Richard A. Donovan. New York: Longman, 1986. 98–108. Print.

Bulinski, Meredith, Andrew Dominguez, Asao B. Inoue, Maryam Jamali, Megan McKnight, Holly Riding, Sharla Seidel, and Jocelyn Stott. "'Shit-Plus,' 'AWK,' 'Frag,' and 'Huh?': An Empirical Look at a Writing Program's Commenting Practices." Conference on College Composition and Communication, San Francisco, California. 22 Mar. 2009. Presentation.

California State University. "Profile of CSU Employees 2007: Gender and Ethnicity." *California State University.* 28 Apr. 2009. Web. 9 Jan. 2010. <http://www.calstate.edu/hr/employee-profile/2007/faculty/gender-ethnicity.shtml>.

Chambers, Ross. "The Unexamined." *Whiteness: A Critical Reader.* Ed. Mike Hill. New York: New York UP, 1997. 187–203. Print.

Chancellor's Office. "Faculty Gender and Ethnicity in the CSU: 1985 to 2002." *California State University.* Aug. 2003. Web. 9 Jan. 2010. <http://www.calstate.edu/HR/FacDemoStudy1985_2002.pdf>.

Cohen, Geoffrey L., Claude M. Steele, and Lee D. Ross. "The Mentor's Dilemma: Providing Critical Feedback across the Racial Divide." *Personality and Social Psychology Bulletin* 25.10 (1999): 1302–18. Print.

Danielewicz, Jane, and Peter Elbow. "A Unilateral Grading Contract to Improve Learning and Teaching." *College Composition and Communication* 61.2 (2009): 244–68. Print.

Davidson, Marcia, Kenneth W. Howell, and Patty Hoekema. "Effects of Ethnicity and Violent Content on Rubric Scores in Writing Samples." *Journal of Educational Research* 93.6 (2000): 367–73. Print.

Gillborn, David. *Racism and Education: Coincidence or Conspiracy?* New York: Routledge, 2008. Print.

Gillborn, David, and Heidi S. Mirza. *Educational Inequality: Mapping Race, Class and Gender—A Synthesis of Research Evidence.* Report HMI 232. London: Office for Standards in Education, 2000. Print.

Hamp-Lyons, Liz, and Bonnie Wen Xia Zhang. "World Englishes: Issues in and from Academic Writing Assessment." *Research Perspective on English for Academic Purposes.* Ed. J. Flowerdew and M. Peacock. Cambridge: Cambridge UP, 2001. 101–16. Print.

Harklau, Linda, Kay M. Losey, and Meryl Siegal, eds. *Generation 1.5 Meets College Composition: Issues in the Teaching of Writing to U.S.-Educated Learners of ESL.* Mahwah: Erlbaum, 1999. Print.

Huot, Brian. *(Re)Articulating Writing Assessment for Teaching and Learning.* Logan: Utah State UP, 2002. Print.

———. "Reliability, Validity, and Holistic Scoring: What We Know and What We Need to Know." *College Composition and Communication* 41.2 (1990): 201–13. Print.

Inoue, Asao B. "Self-Assessment as Programmatic Center: The First Year Writing Program and Its Assessment at California State University, Fresno." *Composition Forum* 20 (Summer 2009). Web. 15 Nov. 2009. <http://compositionforum.com/issue/20/calstate-fresno.php>.

———. "The Technology of Writing Assessment and Racial Validity." *Handbook of Research on Assessment Technologies, Methods, and Applications in Higher Education.* Ed. Christopher Schreiner. Hershey: IGI Global, 2009. 97–120. Print.

Kamusikiri, Sandra. "African American English and Writing Assessment: An Afrocentric Approach." White, Lutz, and Kamusikiri, *Assessment of Writing* 187–203.

Kennedy, Tammie M., Joyce Irene Middleton, and Krista Ratcliffe. "Whiteness Studies." *Rhetoric Review* 24.4 (2005): 359–402. Print.

McLeod, Susan, Heather Horn, and Richard H. Haswell. "Accelerated Classes and the Writers at the Bottom: A Local Assessment Story." *College Composition and Communication* 56.4 (2005): 556–80. Print.

Messick, Samuel. "Validity." *Educational Measurement.* Ed. Robert L. Linn. 3rd ed. New York: Amer. Council on Educ., 1989. 13–103. Print.

Omi, Michael, and Howard Winant. *Racial Formations in the United States: From the 1960s to the 1990s.* 2nd ed. New York: Routledge, 1994. Print.

Ortmeier-Hooper, Christina. "English May Be My Second Language, But I'm Not 'ESL.'" *College Composition and Communication* 59.3 (2008): 389–419. Print.

Prendergast, Catherine. "Race: The Absent Presence in Composition Studies." *College Composition and Communication* 50.1 (1998): 36–53. Print.

Rubin, Donald, and Melanie Williams-James. "The Impact of Writer Nationality on Mainstream Teachers' Judgments of Composition Quality." *Journal of Second Language Writing* 6.2 (1997): 139–53. Print.

Smitherman, Geneva. "Black English, Diverging or Converging? The View from the National Assessment of Educational Progress." *Language and Education* 6.1 (1992): 47–61. Print.

———. "'The Blacker the Berry, the Sweeter the Juice': African American Student Writers and the National Assessment of Educational Progress." Annual Meeting of the National Council of Teachers of English. Pittsburgh, Pennsylvania. 17–22 Nov. 1993. Paper.

Spidell, Cathy, and William H. Thelin. "Not Ready to Let Go: A Study of Resistance to Grading Contracts." *Composition Studies* 34.1 (2006): 35–68. Print.

Sternglass, Marilyn. *Time to Know Them: A Longitudinal Study of Writing and Learning at the College Level.* Mahwah: Erlbaum, 1998. Print.

Villanueva, Victor. *Bootstraps: From an American Academic of Color.* Urbana: NCTE, 1993. Print.

———. "Maybe A Colony: And Still Another Critique of the Composition Community." *JAC* 17 (1997): 83–190. Rpt. in *The Norton Book of Composition Studies.* Ed. Susan Miller. New York: Norton, 2009. 991–98. Print.

White, Edward. M., and Leon Thomas. "Racial Minorities and Writing Skills Assessment in the California State University and Colleges." *College English* 43.3 (1981): 276–83. Print.

White, Edward M., William D. Lutz, and Sandra Kamusikiri, eds. *Assessment of Writing: Politics, Policies, and Practices.* New York: MLA, 1996. Print.

Young, Morris. *Minor RE/Visions: Asian American Literacy Narratives as a Rhetoric of Citizenship.* Carbondale: Southern Illinois UP, 2004. Print.

11.

Writing Program Research: Three Analytic Axes

Douglas Hesse

The bylaws of the Council of Writing Program Administrators (WPA), adopted December 29, 1977, stipulate that membership in the organization should include no one "other than program directors and former directors" or people "designated by their departments or colleges as holding administrative responsibility" (14). Over thirty years later, the directive is politely ignored. WPA has a graduate student category and welcomes any faculty member with professional interests in program administration. An organization spawned to serve the needs of a fairly narrow group of faculty thus now invites a broader membership.

Paralleling the organization's shifting membership, writing program research has similarly evolved over the decades. Those same founding bylaws outlined a mission "to establish a clearinghouse of research on writing program administration," with its newsletter (the predecessor of *WPA: Writing Program Administration*) charged to "report programmatic research" (Council 14–15). The nature of such research was reasonably defined twenty years later by Shirley Rose and Irwin Weiser as "theoretically-informed, systematic, principled inquiry for the purpose of developing, sustaining, and leading a sound, yet dynamic, writing program" (ix). Making such a definitional distinction (cleaving program research from other kinds of scholarship in writing studies) is more than homage to Aristotelian categorization. It's a legitimization gesture, a move to claim a body of knowledge and practice as sufficiently unique as to merit particular recognition, perhaps even credentialing for its practitioners. It marks program research as applied but grounded, legitimate as Research, capital R, even if it seems servile to administrative (the pejorative adjective would be "bureaucratic") ends. The definition is fine, but it doesn't explicitly account for the now-origami-ed nature of writing-program research. My purpose in this chapter is to unfold this field of practices along three analytic axes: purpose, audience, and act.

My design is not to focus on method or research tradition per se. Writing-program researchers variously employ the full panoply of methodologies, from experimental to ethnographic, empirical to hermeneutic, survey to history, linguistic to theoretical, and all points between. Which methodology best applies is a function of the purpose, audience, and research act at hand. Historically, certain situations have occasioned more of some types of studies than others (with assessment, for example, rhetorical success usually depends on empirical measures), but there's no signature method of writing-program research.

Rather, its most distinguishing feature is its setting, as research done "about" or "within the context of" a program. The distinction is meaningful. "Research about" takes features of the program as the objects of study for direct programmatic ends; "research within" might do so, too—but it also might not. Researchers might instead use the program as a vehicle to study artifacts or practices outside the program's specific purview, for reasons at best related only indirectly to it. As a research setting, a writing program means a network of subsites (for example, all sections of a particular course, rather than a single class), unified by common goals ("learn how to shape writing for different audiences"), requirements ("at least twenty-five pages of writing in at least four different papers"), student populations ("all first-year students except those who have scored 5 on the AP Language and Composition exam"), and so on. The setting includes relationships among faculty who are obliged at some level both to one another and, generally, to a director or chair with agency, authority, and responsibility to organize and speak for the program. It invokes, furthermore, the relationships of these features and people, taken as a whole, to larger institutional structures that house them. As a result, "program research" entails a different order of complexity than does, say, classroom research. (Think of the difference between saying how well a particular class is working and saying how well the program as a whole is working.) However, the program's complexity may often carry resource advantages that other research scenes do not. For example, a writing-program researcher, especially one sanctioned by the program's leader, can more easily gather data from dozens or hundreds of students than can a researcher operating outside such structures. Programs frequently have some operational resources, too (from photocopying to record keeping), however modest these might be in tight budget times.

It's time for less abstraction. Consider two sets of potential research questions, each more complexly broad than politely manageable:

Set A

1. How well do students write after taking course X?
2. What writing attitudes and beliefs do students have as a result of taking course X?
3. What teaching practices result in the highest course evaluations among our WAC classes?
4. Do the pedagogies followed by course X faculty reflect current theories and research?

Set B

1. What is the relationship between the kinds of writing students do in high school and the kinds they do in college?
2. What kinds of self-sponsored writing do students do, writing not obliged by school or work situations?
3. How well do twenty-year-olds recognize irony in writing?
4. What do writing faculty most reward in student writing?

Set A reflects the kinds of questions most commonly associated with research *about* the writing program, yielding findings (one hopes) directly applicable to administrative efforts. Set B is different. Certainly, its answers may shape teaching practices and course/program designs, but I suggest these questions lead to more "basic" research. They inquire not about "our" students in our specific instructional setting but about students generally. For example, the knowledge generated by B.2 (about kinds of self-sponsored writing) little applies, at least on the surface, to administering a specific program.

While it's difficult to see the A questions addressed outside the context of a writing program, it's relatively easy to imagine that happening with B, whose pursuits don't need programmatic imprimaturs and may, in fact, benefit from their absence. Still, there are advantages in pursuing Set B through a program's apparatus, with its access to students, its channels for communication, and even its built-in clerical help, communication structures, and physical presence.

Furthermore, set B research can serve the purpose of "developing, sustaining, and leading a sound, yet dynamic, writing program," not in the direct/applied sense of generating evidence for program-specific arguments but in a more indirect/strategic one. If a writing program is recognized as a place where research happens, never minding the particular nature of that research, the program has constructed a stronger ethos. As the program advocates for particular resources or requirements, if the request is heard as coming from unit actively engaged in research, it's heard more favorably.

The short example above reveals the interactions between the scene of writing-program research and the acts, purposes, and audience available there. I next examine them individually.

Purposes: Integrity, Advocacy, Instrumentality, Identity

Among many purposes for writing-program research, four are most significant. The first I call *integrity,* by which I mean studies that examine some feature to see if it's doing what the program claims or aspires for it. Research to the ends of integrity creates pictures of goals, practices, and outcomes for the purpose of interpretation, reflection, or change. A key focus of accreditation, integrity judges fit and consistency, but it also goes beyond. After all, a college could state a goal to "break our students' spirit and will," but we would question (I hope!) that goal's legitimacy.

Assessment research is the most obvious manifestation of the purpose of integrity. Assessment focus on questions of "how well" or "what happens when?" How well do our students write after/as a result of this particular course? What is the effect this pedagogy or technology? Assessment tends to address practical, immediate, and local concerns, from whether to change a curriculum to whether to change a budget, teacher, or administrator.

How one does it depends largely on who or what is being assessed (the students, the course goals/pedagogy/content, the teachers, the program?), the artifacts chosen (surveys, papers, tests?), and the audience. Let's take "the student." If the aim is to say, for each student in a program, how well he or she can do a certain kind of writing, then one needs writing from each individual.[1] One generally sees this kind of assessment in institutions that have some kind of writing-competency requirement. Students at Carleton College, for example, must have a writing portfolio passed by a faculty committee before they can graduate.

On the other hand, one can ask how well students "as a whole" are doing or, related to that, a course is fulfilling its goals. In this case, researchers don't need to examine work from every single student. Instead, they can rely on a random sample of the population, which cuts down time and energy tremendously. How big a random sample? Statistical formulae can tell the confidence level for various sample sizes; the formulae are a function of the size of the population being studied, though the sample size needed quickly flattens out, which is why political campaigns can get by making national claims after polling fewer than two thousand citizens.

random.
sampling

An example helps. In the writing program at the University of Denver, we wanted to know how well our students did certain kinds of writing at the end of their first-year courses. We asked them to turn in a portfolio that demonstrated that kind of writing. Evaluating all 900 portfolios would have required lots of resources, but we calculated that analyzing a random sample of about 260 of them would give us a confidence level of 95 percent and a confidence interval of +/- 5 percent in our findings, a terrific savings of time. That's what we did, then. With these comments on sampling and statistical principles, I'm just making the point that most assessment research ultimately uses measures expressed quantitatively.

Assessment can also serve the purpose of *advocacy,* seeking to garner resources, change practices, and create beliefs through research. Obviously tied to integrity, advocacy can have an internal orientation, for example, as one group of faculty conducts a study to persuade colleagues to revise course goals. More common, however, advocacy serves an external, sometimes adversarial purpose: to justify the program's existence, gain a new faculty line, approve a new course. In terms of assessment, I think of Ed White's often-cited dictum, "Assess or be assessed," with its implied tussle for definitional and methodological high ground. Now, advocacy needn't entail research; appeals to theory, authority, or common sense may win the day. But as writing programs operate in data-driven environments of accountability, they generally need empirical evidence for their claims. A common example is the argument replicated on numerous campuses to cap writing-class enrollments at a prescribed size. Brandishing CCCC and NCTE statements on best practices is often met with, "So what? Show me that smaller classes lead to better student outcomes." In this environment, advocacy occurs through research that generates measurements subject to statistical reasoning.

A third research purpose is *instrumental.* By this I mean studies undertaken less to achieve a direct goal than to accomplish a more oblique rhetorical purpose. In some cases, this may happen less through a specific finding than through the activity itself. Two local studies will illustrate.

When I came to the University of Denver in 2006, I met dozens of colleagues who were eager to improve student writing on campus. During that first year, attending countless meetings, I eventually grew weary of the assertion, "Most of my students can't even write a single correct sentence," which was generally deployed to show that, however good their intentions, professors' desires to teach writing were, alas, hamstrung until students met certain prior conditions. I recognized the claim as wrong. I knew my colleagues lacked the concepts and vocabulary to characterize the real shortcomings of student writing (and I granted the existence of shortcomings, just not in their terms), but after awhile I got impatient explaining the nature of writing and writing problems only to hear, "Yeah, but they still can't write a single correct sentence." I settled on an empirical intervention. The method and results of the study are clearest in my introduction to the final report's summative table:

> In the fall of 2007, we analyzed errors in a random sample of 215 papers selected from a corpus of 700 papers written by first-year students at the University of Denver in Fall 2006, using a taxonomy mainly based on work by Andrea Lunsford and Robert Connors. Papers came from a wide range of courses across the discipline at DU; none came from writing or composition courses. These 215 papers contained 330,803 words, in 17,606 sentences, an average of 18.79 words per sentence, an average paper length of 1538.6 words. Ten trained raters, all lecturers in the DU writing program, analyzed and reported errors in 25 different categories. The table below summarizes the results. One finding is that students made an average of 1.5 errors per 100 words. At least 82% of the sentences were error free; we say "at least" because many of the sentences that contained errors contained more than one, so we know the percentage of "clean" sentences is higher. How much so, we cannot say without a different kind of analysis. These findings counter conventional lore that ✓ student writing is rife with error.

The motivation for this study was instrumental. I had no particular desire to know the number and pattern of errors among Denver students, but I was interested in shifting campus conversations about writing to more productive terms. However interesting the study's findings were, had I lacked the larger reason to generate them, I would have focused program resources differently. Perhaps this is reflected in the rhetoric of the paragraph above, which I'm chagrined now to recognize as passive aggressive in the way it deploys numbers more to silence readers than to engage them.

More recently, I wanted to initiate more ambitious writing in the discipline projects on campus. A challenge was finding the right strategy. One approach, obviously, is to persuade individual departments that they have both the teaching opportunity and professional responsibility to be more intentional about how they assign and teach writing. However, to convince busy professors who feel avalanched by administrative initiatives is to climb a steep rhetorical hill. Incentives in the form of stipends to attend workshops can lessen the incline, and a mandate from a dean or provost can flatten it altogether, albeit at the cost of faculty buy-in. Weighing these options, I figured that while faculty might be cool to altruism and resentful of mandates, they do value research—or at least the research they produce and control. So I developed a project that invited departments to submit proposals for researching writing in their own majors. As WPA, I would pay modest stipends to two professors and two undergraduates from each participating department; they would join two writing professors to constitute a research team. The charge? Describe and analyze the amount, kinds, and quality of writing that X majors complete, the pedagogies employed, and the beliefs and attitudes about writing, both by students and by professors. The outcomes? A ten-to-fifteen-page report that the department "owns," a report primarily descriptive but with a section of implications; while the writing program gets a copy, any further distribution is at the department's discretion. (Many departments on their own volition have sent them to deans and other administrators, recognizing the benefits of a cogent assessment report.) In the first eighteen months of this strategy, we completed studies with nine departments.

The result was an effective form of curriculum and faculty development. Rather than paying stipends to attend workshops of a limited duration, we involved faculty and students over several weeks, not only the team members collecting and interpreting data but also those providing it, through interviews, surveys, assignments, and analyses of syllabi/assignment. Certainly, the research findings were useful as departments determined what they wanted to do with writing (about half the departments actually made curricular changes). But I'm convinced that the act of finding was more important than the findings themselves. If my writing program colleagues and I, as outsiders, had collected and analyzed data for each department, the effort would have lacked impact.

Finally, the purpose of program research can be to build identity, whether for the program, the researcher, or both. As I noted earlier, a reputation as a researcher can carry a strong ethos, even in the humdrum of program administration. Such is the academic capital of research. This ethos is almost independent of the research's particular nature. A WPA who studies workplace writing that has little connection to his or her program may, nonetheless, accrue useful prestige because of that work. Of course, some types of study more closely align with identity building.

Among them are local archival and historical projects. While knowing the history of a given program may provide levers for change, such research is often more basic than applied (in ways I explain below). I learned recently that the University of Denver, in the late forties and fifties, enjoyed some national prominence in the teaching of writing. The campus held an institute each summer, bringing together teachers and notables from around the country, among them Porter Perrin, then president of NCTE (Sherman). Doing the archival and textual scholarship to flesh out that history (Who were the central faculty? What did they teach and publish? Are there syllabi in the archives, even student papers?) would create a nice story for the alumni magazine—and also a longer legacy to which the current program could hitch itself.

Audiences: Local and Professional

Implicit in purpose is audience. When Rose and Weiser characterize program research's goal as "leading a sound, yet dynamic, writing program," they imply success as measured by the quality of the writing program that pursued it. Purely (and excessively) applied, research toward those ends would aim solely at internal audiences. And yet the very existence of Rose and Weiser's book, not to mention the call for publication in the WPA bylaws, betrays such limited readerships. One way to keep the narrow focus would be to regard published WPA research simply as providing models of how to, important less for any particular findings than as an exemplars for conducting one's own studies. But it's more reasonable to recognize at least two audiences: local readers of research done to improve the neighborhood and the writing program's lot in it, and profession-al readers, by which too-cute hyphen I'm emphasizing scholars in the larger disciplinary landscape.

The narrowest local audience, of course, is the program itself, producing work to foster reflection, perhaps for internal advocacy ("I'll convince my colleagues that . . .") but just as likely for reflection. For such audiences, context and method are clear and compelling, so these studies convince us with less fuss than would be needed to reassure our chemist colleagues.

A wider sphere, still local, is the campus, in whole or constituent parts. Given a school's diverse nature, its many readers necessarily can't share a writing program's knowledge base, orientations, or research dispositions. (For example, in three separate WAC workshops, I had faculty from across campus read Michael Carter's award-winning and, to my mind, perspicuous, article on four academic writing traditions; nearly to a colleague, they found it difficult and badly written, even wrong.)

I'm as critical of logical positivism as any current compositionist, but the fact is that many colleagues and administrators across campus—not to mention beyond in boards and legislatures—are most persuaded by the apparent rigor of statistical measures. One hard truth for folks grounded in hermeneutic or humanistic inquiry is that when the purpose is to show efficacy or need, then we need to use the rhetorical strategies that work for our audience, not us. I recently had ten minutes and five PowerPoint slides in which to show our board of trustees that our new first-year writing program was working. I used scores and percentages, tables and t-tests. Quotations from professors, explanations of assignments, or case studies of students wouldn't have done it. This situation, like many local ones, arose quickly and needed a quick response. Fortunately, certain pieces of data are common to many such situations, and having that information close at hand frees time to work on the more pressing issues. I've included as an appendix a list of information that writing-program administrators and researchers should find useful to compile in advance of a specific need.

A key dividing line between local and professional audiences has to do with the kinds of authorization one needs to conduct the research. Research involving people differs from that involving plants or protons by requiring permission from a campus institutional review board (IRB), whose job is to assess risks and rewards to subjects of given projects, then grant or withhold permission to proceed. Most IRBs exempt local assessment research, invoking those provisions of the federal code for protection of human subjects that address educational research, most pointedly:

> 46.101 (b) Unless otherwise required by Department or Agency heads, research activities in which the only involvement of human subjects will be in one or more of the following categories are exempt from this policy:
> 1. Research conducted in established or commonly accepted educational settings, involving normal educational practices, such as (i) research on regular and special education instructional strategies, or (ii) research on the effectiveness of or the comparison among instructional techniques, curricula, or classroom management methods. (U.S. Department of Health and Human Services)

"Exempt" does not mean "not subject to review"; IRBs generally reserve the right to name a study exempt. Purely internal studies ("Let's score fifty portfolios and discuss the results at a faculty meeting") often fly beneath the IRB radar, exempted from exemption. Presentation or publication in external professional settings always requires IRB action.

Writing for a professional audience has larger challenges, of course. Not least is climbing the threshold of significance and general application. Right or wrong, most scholars in composition studies dismiss "show and tell" research: Here's what I learned from this study on my campus. The extent to which findings connected to theories or broad trends is the extent to which program research ultimately finds publication. Exacerbating the situation is that, unlike, say, science disciplines that have a tradition of publishing "notes" and similarly short studies, composition trades on the substantial article. Much research, then, never leaves the local server. The crunch occurs when a WPA somewhere needs empirical evidence—any empirical evidence, even if from a single campus somewhat like hers—to answer a skeptical provost. Reed Way Dasenbrock once observed that there are no poststructuralists in administrative foxholes. That would certainly include WPAs under duress.

Certainly, its topic largely determines whether a study finds professional readers. But an additional factor is how it sets a context. Each year, my writing program surveys all first-year students about their high school writing experiences. The information is locally useful, helping us plan courses by understanding the concepts, attitudes, and genre knowledges that our students bring to campus. Now, the broad subject of writing transfer is nationally vital these days. Teachers, scholars, and WPAs have a stake in understanding what students carry from one writing situation to another, including high school to college. If we carefully characterize the demographics of our students (type of school, geographic region, test scores, gender, and so on), our modest study moves from internal assessment to national research on this issue.

That's the kind of work that Gerald Nelms and Ronda Leathers Dively did in their study of writing transfer between first-year composition and writing-intensive major courses at Southern Illinois University Carbondale. Their project included two phases: a detailed survey completed by thirty-five GTAs teaching in the first-year program and a focus-group discussion involving five instructors teaching in departments throughout the university. In many respects, this is a modest sampling for a modest project that clearly has local values for the campus but that might seem, from my stark depiction, unpromising for national publication. And yet, with a forty-item, works-cited page, Nelms and Dively clearly connect this research to larger conversations.

In doing so, they write for the "inner layer" of professional audiences: writing-program directors looking for ideas or research bearing on their own programs. They read it in journals like *WPA: Writing Program Administration, Assessing Writing,* or the *WAC Journal,* in books on programmatic perspectives, and on listservs (most centrally WPA-L), or they hear it in programmatically oriented conference panels.

Broader professional readerships are those of composition studies writ large, in journals from *CCC* to *Written Communication*, and research in these venues often contributes to broader knowledge about writing. Consider, for example, a report on two years of Stanford's longitudinal study of writing, written by Jenn Fishman, Andrea Lunsford, Beth McGregor, and Mark Otuteye. On the one hand, this is programmatic research, carried out under the auspices—and with the finances—of the Stanford Writing Program, that identified the 189 student participants. And yet, at least in terms of this article, the study doesn't focus on the program but, rather, on the broader conceptual issue of how students engage writing done in guise of performance versus in the name of academic ritual. The point is not to assess the Stanford program, and while this study's findings have implication for "improving" teaching there, the implications are cast more broadly, as meaningful to the teaching of writing generally. In terms of the last axis I'll introduce, the research act is more basic than applied.

Acts: Applied and Basic

By nature, and even by early definition, much writing-program research is applied, undertaken to answer questions, or make arguments in well-defined situations. The knowledge generated is going to get used—perhaps to change goals, perhaps to train teachers, perhaps to shape pedagogies—and the researcher knows that going in. Most assessment projects and advocacy projects fit under this rubric, especially those pursued in the context of ongoing teaching improvement, where findings are expected to reshape methods and goals, producing a new set of artifacts subject to new assessment, and so on.

For example, at Denver we developed a new course that had five goals, two of which were:

1. Students will develop a reasonably sophisticated awareness of academic research traditions (for example, text-based/interpretive; measurement-based/empirical; and observational/qualitative) and develop some facility in writing using at least two of them.

2. Students will develop a reasonably sophisticated awareness of rhetorical/conventional differences among various academic discourses and develop some facility in writing with at least two of them.

We analyzed portfolios of student writing gathered after the first quarter of teaching the course. They were disappointing. Considering these findings in the context of our teaching practices in this lightning-fast ten-week quarter, we finally concluded that the real problem was in the nature of the goals themselves. We revised them:

1. Demonstrate practical knowledge of academic research traditions (for example, text-based/interpretive; measurement-based/empirical; and observational/qualitative) through effectively writing in at least two of those traditions.

2. Demonstrate an understanding of rhetorical/conventional differences among various academic disciplines or groups of disciplines.

Among other things, we modified the expectation that students would demonstrate facility in writing at least two academic discourses; even our very best students did not. Now, we would likely have recognized the original goals as too ambitious without the study, but the evidence of student writing got us there more quickly and concretely and provided a comparative basis for the second year's study.

As central as it is, applied writing-program research is not the only kind. The particular scene, agent, and agency of writing programs also make them fertile sites for basic research. Researchers in this mode seek not (or not directly) to generate knowledge useful for decision making; rather, they use the program as a source of data or analytic labor, a means to an ends more broad or basic than answering a question like, "How can we improve teaching methods in our program?" An example can clarify.

Several years ago, I became interested in differences in how men and women wrote personal essays. Specifically, I wondered about two dimensions. First, was there a difference between the types of stories told by men versus women in terms of a scale we ended up calling "triumph to tragedy"? Essays toward the former end would dramatize a celebratory moment (scoring the winning touchdown, making a friend, learning a positive truth), while essays toward the latter would dramatize a defeat or bitter moment (fumbling on the goal line, the death of a relative, meeting disappointment). Second, was there a difference between men and women in how they represented their agency in the essay? Did they portray themselves as differently responsible for the narrated events ("I did or caused that"), as recipients of them ("Someone or something did that to me"), or as more "neutral" observers?

For one year, the writing program I was directing at Illinois State University had a common syllabus for our first-semester course. One assignment, in a nutshell, was to build a personal essay through narrating a lived experience.[2] This meant we had a corpus of three thousand essays easily at hand, especially because students turned in portfolios at the course's end. In these pre-IRB days, it was unproblematic to choose a sizeable random sample of a few hundred essays for analysis. Furthermore, because I was teaching a graduate course in research methods at the time, I thought the project would be a good hands-on experience for students (in framing questions, sampling, scoring, statistical analysis, and so on), especially since everyone enrolled in the graduate course had been a TA in the course from which we drew the sample. The writing program offered a convenient means for exploring research questions that, ultimately, had relatively little significance for the program itself.

Of course, any "means to ends" project has ethical dimensions. In the case just cited, we drew the sample essays from writings done in response to "naturally" existing assignments designed to achieve course goals to develop certain aspects of student writing. It would have been quite a different matter to ignore course goals or student needs simply to make an assignment convenient to a researcher in an advantaged position. That's the kind of situation that begs for IRB review.

Putting It Together: Three Axes Cubed

Figure 11.1 represents the interactions and permutations of the axes I've just explained. Given the sixteen different cells in the cube, I'll spare naming and discussing each. Instead, I'll suggest that this graphic representation shows the many forms that writing-program research takes today. In each case, the work is effective to the extent it is rhetorical, matching purposes and audiences. This is a hard lesson to learn for writing scholars who are steeped in historical, theoretical, and interpretive traditions and who are used to making arguments to professional colleagues who share those backgrounds and orientations. That's the case with much writing-program research, but it's not the case for all of it, especially for studies aimed to inform or persuade people who are not us, whether campus administrators, readers of the *Chronicle of Higher Education*, or congressional higher-education staffers.

Many types of program research do directly enact Rose and Weiser's definitional ends of "developing, sustaining, and leading a sound, yet dynamic, writing program." Among them are applied studies for the purposes of integrity, advocacy, and instrumentality, primarily aimed at local audiences within and beyond the program. But there just as many studies aimed at professional audiences for purposes both applied and basic, studies accurately labeled as "writing program research" because they're carried out under aegis and with the resources of the program. They exist less to improve "my program" than to shape wider understandings of writing, in ways sometimes large but more often incremental.

In both cases, if the work is done well, research helps develop, sustain, and lead writing programs in two powerfully indirect ways. First,

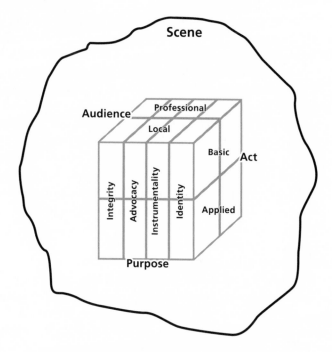

Fig. 11.1. Types of writing program research.

because programmatic research is almost inevitably collaborative, given the complexity of programs and the implications of any findings, the very doing of it serves as program development. It makes a faculty reflective by giving it something on which to reflect. More important, it embodies our ethical obligation to audit and analyze what we know and practice in the name of writing and teaching. However much research has evolved from the founding days of WPA, that ethical imperative has not. Second, program research is ultimately identity building, in terms of both ethos and ethics. Most crassly, doing it creates ethical intellectual capital, marking programs as substantial entities serious about professional matters and not just sweeping bodies through classrooms.

Obviously, this kind of intellectual capital can also serve individual researchers' interests as well as their programs'. This includes graduate students or junior faculty members as they seek jobs or advancement, for the implication of someone having done program research is that "here's a scholar willing and able to think broadly about larger efforts and institutional interests." However, there are at least two limitations or risks that graduate students and junior faculty face. One is the challenge of access. One is potentially asking numbers of faculty to allow class visits or observations, participate in interviews or provide other data, or provide or allow access to student artifacts. All this potentially happens in pursuit of questions that at least complicate faculty's teaching lives, maybe even at the risk of negative findings or portrayals. Someone in the role of WPA, especially someone senior, can invoke a status that a beginning researcher usually cannot. To the extent that the latter can align his or her research questions with the programs mission or goals, the researcher will have an easier time getting access to the program's faculty, students, or artifacts. In terms of the three axes described above, such researchers will tend to garner easier access for projects that are local and applied, with the purpose of integrity or advocacy. Those most clearly serve the program's interests.

After all, there is an opportunity cost for any research project, especially programmatic ones. Attention to one set of questions means lack of attention to another; if I interview my colleagues about one set of practices, it's harder for me also to interview them about a second or a third. The people who control access to writing-program resources continually have to judge competing research or assessment possibilities, not only on their individual merits but also in terms of the opportunities given by choosing one over the other. Recently, a doctoral candidate at another institution e-mailed me a very compelling request to have a number of my faculty and their students complete an extensive questionnaire about the technologies and writing. I'm sympathetic to the research question and supportive of graduate students; however, I'm also quite sensitive to how many times I can go to my colleagues and ask them to participate in a study.

That brings me to my second cautionary note for graduate students and faculty pursuing writing-program research: the opportunity costs they themselves face. Choosing, for the sake of access, to address the program's interests comes at a cost of other types of research that might better advance the individual's interest. The profession currently has a bias for research acts that are more basic than applied and for research scenes that are more professional than local, to cite two of the axes discussed. For a beginning scholar, then, his or her interests and the program's may be at odds, at least in terms of how projects get conceived. I do believe this is changing, as the growing culture of evidence in higher education increases the demand for more applied and local research in our published scholarship. In this volume, Richard H. Haswell nicely articulates that need. Still, beginning scholars need to understand tensions between projects they might elect and projects a program might elect for them.

For more senior scholars, especially those having administrative responsibilities, writing-program research bears somewhat fewer risks. Because their local identities are more closely bound with their programs and because professional advancement as an administrator prizes accomplishments beyond publication, they can "afford" to take on projects that foreground instrumentality and identity, with a lower level of concern about whether those projects are basic or applied, local or professional. In that sense, they have more in common with the type of WPA as researcher posited over thirty years ago in the WPA bylaws.

It may seem that I have struck a somber chord here at the end, but my purpose isn't to conclude in a pessimistic minor key. After all, I do believe that realms of writing program research are varied, and by exploring three axes and the options available in each, my goal is to reflect existing realities and rich possibilities. We need to think beyond programmatic research as narrow variations of assessment. However, it may be that certain types of projects better fit scholars at different points in their careers. Fortunately, careers are long and what we need to learn about and through writing programs is endlessly vital.

Appendix: The WPA's Digital Cupboard

Most general cookbooks have a section listing staple items that every kitchen should have on hand: flour, pepper, canned tomatoes, and so on. You want to have these around so that when it comes to a particular recipe, you can focus on getting the specialty ingredients and on the cooking itself. In a real pinch, you can make something without going to the store, even if it's tuna noodle casserole or egg salad.

In similar fashion, WPA's benefit from a handy basic set of documents and data; when the need comes to generate a report, proposal, or self-study, you can focus on the ingredients specific to the task rather than on gathering staples. Following are items I suggest for the writing program's digital cupboard, stored not in Tupperware but in Word documents, ready to deploy even on quick notice, as when the provost metaphorically invites herself to lunch tomorrow or needs a report.

• Program mission, vision, and goals statements

• Course numbers and titles, catalog descriptions, detailed goals and requirements, section caps; a standard syllabus or a representative pair of syllabi

- Number of sections and seats offered in each of past four terms plus total actual enrollments

- Overall GPA and grade distributions for each course in the program

- Complete list of teaching faculty for each of past four terms, including courses/sections taught, faculty status (TT, GTA, part-time, and so on), and degrees and expertise. (You will find it convenient to collect CVs or brief CVs electronically from everyone each year.)

- Description of placement or credit processes (AP, for example) along with number of students affected by these in the past four terms

- List and status (sophomores, TAs, part-timers, and so on) of writing-center consultant staff; number of consultations and different people using the center

- Employment conditions for each category of faculty (TT, lecturer/instructor, GTA, part-time): salary range, load, benefits, offices and equipment, support, and the like

- Operating budget, broken into main categories

- Position descriptions for everyone with administrative responsibilities

- Paragraph(s) explaining reporting lines, budget-development process, and program review

- List and descriptions of all programmatic committees, with their membership and charges, as well as any committees external to the program that have a significant bearing on the program

Notes

1. Here it's worth noting the differences between a direct measure (for example, judging a sample of the kind of writing one is assessing) and an indirect measure. Indirect measures are usually chosen for convenience; for example, if the goal is to assess students' abilities to produce arguments, a multiple-choice test about logical fallacies is more efficiently administered and scored than is having students write an argument. However, as the previous example illustrates, indirect measures are only as good (or, to use a more technical term, as valid) as they are strongly correlated with the phenomenon being studied. Mainly because of problems with validity, composition studies prefers direct measures.

2. Instituted at the request of busy TAs, it was dropped by consensus after one year's run, as all of us perceived that teachers were being less reflective and creative than when they designed their own courses.

Works Cited

Carter, Michael. "Ways of Knowing, Doing, and Writing in the Disciplines." *College Composition and Communication* 58.3 (2007): 385–418. Print.

Council of Writing Program Administrators. "Bylaws." *WPA: Writing Program Administration* 1.3 (1978): 13–15. Print.

Dasenbrock, Reed Way. "Why There Are No Poststructuralists in Administrative Foxholes." *ADE Bulletin* (Fall 2000): 22–25. Print.

Fishman, Jenn, Andrea Lunsford, Beth McGregor, and Mark Otuteye. "Performing Writing, Performing Literacy." *College Composition and Communication* 57.2 (2005): 224–52. Print.

Hesse, Douglas. "Error in DU Student Writings." *Microsoft Word* file.

Nelms, Gerald, and Ronda Leathers Dively. "Perceived Roadblocks to Transferring Knowledge from First-Year Composition to Writing Intensive Major Courses: A Pilot Study." *WPA* 31.1–2 (2007): 214–40. Print.

Rose, Shirley, and Irwin Weiser. *The Writing Program Administrator as Researcher: Inquiry in Action and Reflection.* Portsmouth: Boynton/Cook, 1999. Print.

Sherman, Thelma R., ed. *Publications of the Fifth Workshop in Basic Communication.* Denver: U of Denver P, 1947. Print.

U.S. Department of Health and Human Services. "Title 45, Public Welfare, Part 46: Protection of Human Subjects." *Code of Federal Regulations.* 15 Jan. 2009. Web. 28 Dec. 2011.

12.

Institutional Critique in Composition
Studies: Methodological and Ethical
Considerations for Researchers

Steve Lamos

Institutional critique in composition studies attempts to analyze and to
reform the complex and often problematic institutional spaces, both academic and nonacademic, in which writing, language, and literacy instruction occurs. This scholarship focuses on the discursive and the material
dynamics of institutional activity—what James E. Porter, Patricia Sullivan,
Stuart Blythe, Jeffrey T. Grabill, and Libby Miles characterize in their
Braddock Award–winning 2000 *College Composition and Communication* article as the "bureaucratic structures," "organizational roles and responsibilities," "work models," "lines of authority and communication,"
and "alignment of and interaction between personnel" utilized within
institutions as well as the "physical structures—economies, architectures,
bureaucracies, interorganizational relations, and physical locations" central to institutional operation (626–27). It also uses knowledge of discursive
and material dynamics to advocate for institutional change and reform:
As Porter et al. stress, institutional critique is "not interested in simply
reporting how evil institutions are . . . critique needs an action plan" (613).

Contemporary institutional critique takes a number of forms. One
form employs spatial-analysis techniques designed to illuminate how
and why contemporary institutional spaces have been configured in ways
that privilege certain groups at the expense of others. Common spatial-
analysis techniques include "postmodern mapping," which is designed
to illuminate "how space is both constructed and inhabited, designed to
achieve certain purposes (and not others)" (Porter et al. 623); "boundary
interrogation," which allows researchers to analyze "power moves used to
maintain or even extend control over boundaries" (Porter et al. 624); and

"third-space" analysis, which seeks to articulate "what kinds of real and imagined spaces are 'out there,' beyond academia, what kinds of spaces constitute being 'in here' (within the ontological regions of academia), and what kinds of spaces are created at the intersection" (Mauk 380).[1] Another form of institutional critique employs rhetorical analysis designed to promote "story-changing"—that is, to "change the dominant story about the work of writing instruction" (Adler-Kassner 2) by identifying

> where we have the most influence and the loudest voices—at our local levels. We can think about who we can reach out to, learn from, and enlist as allies. And with them, we can develop a communication plan that helps all of us shape and communicate messages about writers and writing to audiences who might just attend to those messages—and change the stories that they tell. (Adler-Kassner 163)[2]

A third form of institutional critique adopts a critical historical approach to analysis that is designed to illuminate how and why particular localized institutional configurations have emerged over time. This type of approach is designed to help scholars and activists "discern the roles [we] have played and might still play in relation to institutional forces that curtail or facilitate access" to higher education (Tassoni 118).[3]

Each of these forms of institutional critique requires researchers to be familiar with what Paul V. Anderson characterizes as "text-based" and "person-based" methods for conducting research (63)—that is, methods for analyzing published documentary materials regarding institutions (e.g., published scholarship or archival material) and methods for analyzing data obtained through interactions with institutional actors (e.g., interview and observational data). Each of these forms further requires researchers to balance a desire to produce site-specific analysis of identifiable institutional contexts with an ethical obligation to protect "the rights, privacy, dignity, and well-being" (CCCC, par. 1) of the individual institutional actors (e.g., administrators, bureaucrats, teachers, staff, and the like) working within these contexts. In light of these important requirements, I argue that researchers interested in institutional critique must be prepared to grapple with at least three specific methodological/ethical issues at some length:

1. How best to gain access to and gain permission to use data relevant to the institutional contexts being studied
2. How best to reference both the institutions and individuals being analyzed within the context of a specific account—that is, by real name? by pseudonym? by some combination?

3. How best to deal with the perception that institutional critique necessarily represents a kind of "bad news" (e.g., Newkirk)

I explore each of these issues with the aid of insights drawn from the composition/English studies literature as well as from my own attempts to generate institutional critique of the Educational Opportunity Program (EOP) rhetoric program at the University of Illinois at Urbana-Champaign, one version of a "basic writing" program for minority students that operated from the late-1960s through the early 1990s.[4]

Researching Institutions: Access and Permission Issues

Researchers planning on conducting institutional critique can use a number of avenues to obtain information about the institutional contexts of specific interest to them. These individuals can, for instance, visit official institutional or programmatic archives presided over by one or more professional archivists, utilizing the material contained therein according to the stated rules of the archive.[5] They can also arrange for a series of interviews with key institutional actors past and present and/or a series of site observations, utilizing the data gathered in these ways in accord with prearranged human-subjects protocols.[6] More than likely, however, researchers will also need to obtain other institutional information not available in either official archives or otherwise available through interviews and observations. As Barbara L'Eplattenier and Lisa Mastrangelo note, this need often arises because material related to institutional function is "often destroyed or hidden in a multitude of files" (xx), a problem exacerbated by the fact that "administrative decision-making often occurs in ways that are never [officially] recorded; informal decision-making, trade-offs, and unexplained accommodations are common" (xx). As a result, researchers will likely find themselves needing to work extensively within the "hidden archive," the

> old file boxes in the attic; the yellowed, hand-written essays in the bottom drawers; the textbooks thankfully overlooked during the last office cleanings; the records of forgotten meetings; and the indispensable memories of departmental personalities upon which . . . history could be built. (Henze, Selzer, and Sharer vi)

The hidden archive may contain a range of key documents ranging from "[o]fficial documents such as departmental reports, program memos, syllabi and catalogues" (Henze, Selzer, and Sharer ix) to "uncatalogued, undigested, uninterpreted . . . personal copies of books, notes, and papers that mattered to those who read and wrote in that place, at particular moments, on unique rhetorical occasions" (Moon 2).

Questions about how best to access and use the hidden archive are various: Where might such hidden archival materials be most likely to exist? Who will be able to provide researchers with access to these materials and under what conditions? Who will be able to provide researchers with explicit permission to use these materials and under what circumstances? And, although I cannot necessarily offer definitive answers to these sorts of questions, I can suggest that researchers try out a number of strategies to help them locate, access, and obtain permission to use material from this hidden archive.

To begin, researchers should plan to spend time early during the course of the their projects browsing through actual old file cabinets, bookshelves, closets, drawers, and other (public) physical locations within the particular institutional contexts that interests them. They should also plan to spend some time asking knowledgeable institutional actors (e.g., administrators and/or administrative staff) about other places and locations in which such materials might exist. As Gesa Kirsch and Liz Rohan remind us, "exploring a place and re-seeing a place as an archive" (5) can offer crucial insights into the context under study. Furthermore, throughout these searches, researchers should keep in mind the importance and value of what Kirsch and Rohan describe as "serendipity," that is, the ways in which "a hunch, a chance encounter, or a newly discovered . . . artifact" (4) can lead to new information. In other words, although researchers will not likely be able to predict ahead of time where they may encounter a hidden archive, they certainly can be prepared to seize upon those encounters that do ultimately present themselves.

Researchers should also plan to seek explicit permission—ideally, written permission—to use the materials that they encounter within the hidden archive, and they should do so as early in the research process as possible. In order to obtain such permission, researchers might present documents that they have obtained from a hidden archive to the individual or group responsible for it—for example, a head administrator within the division or unit housing the archive; a professional archivist from elsewhere in the institution; the actual individual or group author(s) of the documents themselves—while asking for explicit permission to analyze and quote from these documents directly.[7] Researchers should also be prepared to make specific arguments about why this sort of information deserves to be made public: for example, by drawing explicit connections between information that they wish to use from the hidden

[margin handwritten note: re-seeing a place as an archive]

archive and any information that is already publicly available from more "official" sources such as published scholarship; by articulating specific reasons that the hidden information in question ought to be disseminated to the larger public; and/or by discussing specific or disciplinary institutional insights that might be gained from the dissemination of information from this archive.

Such issues of access and permission have certainly shaped my own work with the EOP rhetoric program. When I first began my work with this program back in 2002, I spent a great deal of time perusing the official University of Illinois archives for specific information about the EOP program and its EOP rhetoric component. I also spent significant time conducting IRB-approved interviews with individuals who had been directly or indirectly involved with these programs. These kinds of data-gathering activities proved immensely useful to my research, affording me crucial insight into key issues within the history of the program. Nonetheless, I realized rather quickly that I could not find nearly as much documentary information about the actual day-to-day workings of the EOP rhetoric program as I would have liked: as a marginalized "basic writing" program within a marginalized institutional program for high-risk minority students, official documentary information about the program was fairly scarce.[8]

Fortunately, after talking to a number of individuals, including the department head at the time and several staff members who had been at Illinois for decades, I was directed to a wall of file cabinets in a locked basement room, given a set of keys, and granted verbal permission to analyze and quote from them for the purposes of my research. These archives, all kept in something of an ad hoc fashion by English Department administrators throughout the years, contained a host of EOP rhetoric documents that had not been given over to the official archives.[9] These documents ultimately proved invaluable to my work, offering countless insights into the evolution of EOP rhetoric that would have remained invisible had I simply restricted myself to more "official" materials.

Several years later, however, I ran into a permissions problem of sorts involving these hidden materials. While attempting to publish my first account of one episode within the history of EOP rhetoric, the editor and reviewers of the journal with which I was working wanted written permission (not simply oral permission) for me to cite from these English Department archives. I therefore immediately contacted the current department head in order to request such permission, making sure to present him with two things: first, a copy of the actual article that I had written (including a list of all materials that I had taken from this hidden archive); second, a list of published scholarly articles and books that had already referenced the EOP program and its administrative actors publicly. In so doing, I aimed to demonstrate how my work in the hidden archive was designed to offer institutional analysis and critique rather than institutional "dirt" on specific administrators; I also tried to suggest that I was referencing events and people that were already part of public scholarly discourse concerning this program at Illinois. Fortunately, the head was gracious enough to grant me retrospective written permission to quote directly from this material, and I was able to publish this piece in due time.

Describing Institutions: The Ethics of Naming Places and People

As noted above, institutional-critique scholarship routinely requires researchers to strike a careful balance between institutional specificity and accountability on the one hand and the individual rights and privacy of people within a specific institutional setting on the other. The need for such balance manifests itself explicitly within the choices that researchers can make with respect to naming institutional contexts and the institutional actors within them.

Researchers performing institutional critique have several choices regarding naming issues. They might, for instance, choose to reference both institutional contexts and institutional actors by real names, an approach that I have characterized elsewhere as "overt-historical" along the lines of what one might see in traditional historical scholarship. Conversely, they might choose to reference contexts and actors by pseudonym, an approach that I have described as "covert-qualitative" along the lines of what one might see in traditional ethnographic scholarship. In still other cases, researchers might choose to reference places by real name while referencing individuals by institutional title or pseudonym only, an approach that I have termed "hybrid-institutional."[10] As a quick example of this hybrid-institutional approach to naming, consider John Paul Tassoni's article "(Re)membering Basic Writing at a Public Ivy: History for Institutional Redesign." Within this institutional critique of basic writing at Miami University in Ohio since the mid-1970s, Tassoni is quite specific in terms of his discussion of specific institutional events and contexts. He discusses at great length, for instance, the specific details of the English Department's caustic reaction to the 1974 "Students' Right to Their Own Language" document (109–14). However, even as he discusses this specific history, he references administrators by their institutional title alone as his default approach to issues of naming—for example, discussing a

"Miami University English Professor" (101) or describing a "respondent" within this controversy (109)—in ways affording an amount of privacy for these individuals. Or, to put things another way, Tassoni's hybrid-institutional approach to naming allows him to be as specific as possible about the institutional context of Miami while allowing him to be somewhat general about the actual people involved.

In my view, this hybrid-institutional approach to naming offers the best chance of striking a needed balance between institutional specificity and individual privacy within institutional critique. One analogy that I have used to explain this is that of a basketball coach using *X*'s and *O*'s on a whiteboard while diagramming specific plays: This coach can explain the dynamics of a particular play in a particular game context perfectly well without calling (unnecessary) attention to the individual identities or personalities of particular players. A hybrid-institutional approach to naming operates in a similar way by focusing readers' attention squarely upon institutional dynamics rather than upon the thoughts, beliefs, and actions of identifiable individuals.

Issues of naming have proven quite central within my work with EOP rhetoric. When I first began analyzing the program, I tried to reference both places and people throughout my account by real names in keeping with a sort of overt-historical approach. However, the same journal editor and reviewers mentioned above expressed concern that my using real names might seem threatening to some of the administrators discussed within my institutional critique, especially given my direct focus upon issues of race and racism. At the same time, the head who granted me retroactive permission to cite from the English Department archive also asked me to try "anonymizing" my account wherever possible in order to minimize any such possible threat.

These concerns led me to perform a concerted search of the literature aimed at seeing how other people doing institutional critique work chose to reference or not to reference places and people. In turn, this search led me to identify and adopt explicitly this hybrid-institutional approach to naming within all of my work with the EOP rhetoric program, one that I explain as follows in a footnote from my "Language, Literacy, and the Institutional Dynamics of Racism" piece:

> I deliberately refer to all Illinois administrators throughout this piece by institutional title alone rather than by title and personal name. I do so in order to place analytical emphasis upon the institutional discourses and practices that these individuals enacted rather than upon their personal beliefs or values. I realize, of course, that this

choice may strike some as unusual given the trend in contemporary historical work to refer to the real names of institutional actors.... I realize, too, that this decision may strike others as problematic (or even cowardly) given my explicit desire to understand and critique the operation of racism within the history and evolution of composition studies, a racism that was, in fact, promulgated in part through the choices and decisions of real administrators with real identities. ... It is my strong belief, however, that this decision allows me to perform detailed critical analysis while at the same time minimizing the possibility that I might do unnecessary harm to the professional or personal reputations of individual people for decisions and actions with which they were involved nearly four decades ago and about which they may well feel differently today. (73n5)

It is through this sort of approach that I personally try to strike a workable balance between institutional specificity and individual privacy.

Reporting on Institutions: Mitigating Concerns about "Bad News"

A final issue that seems particularly important for researchers to consider stems from the fact that attempts to perform and write up institutional critique might frequently be perceived as conveying "bad news" (Newkirk 3). Given that the explicit goal of institutional critique is to identify, map, and reform problematic institutional power relationships, it seems likely that some individuals within the institution may equate such critique with bad news, perhaps even restricting current or future access to institutional information as a consequence. For these reasons, institutional critique demands careful attention to Jennie Dautermann's warning that "writing studies that address social issues can appear threatening to the institutions under study and thus threaten researcher access as well. We have not yet found adequate ways to critique the assumptions of institutions and cultures while depending on their good graces for the continuation of our work" (242).

Researchers can, nonetheless, employ several strategies in order to minimize the risk of their work being perceived merely as bad news. They might, for instance, discuss overtly the goals of institutional critique with the administrators and/or other individuals most likely to be concerned about bad news, perhaps even stressing Porter et al.'s admonition that the goal of this sort of work is not "simply reporting how evil institutions are" but rather to formulate some sort of "action plan" designed to foment positive change (613). Researchers might also mitigate such concerns by making explicit some of the access/permission and naming choices that they adopt. In other words, by being transparent and deliberate concerning such choices (e.g., by obtaining permission to use information as early as possible and by using names that stress institutional dynamics rather than individual identities), researchers may be less likely to make institutional gatekeepers feel as though their goal has been merely to disseminate bad news.

These strategies have also proven crucial for me in my own work. For instance, when I have tried to explain the nature of my work to administrators and others, I have stressed repeatedly that my goal is to generate critique aimed at understanding institutional dynamics, not at generating "he-said/she-said" accounts of the thoughts, beliefs, and actions of identifiable individuals. (In fact, I actually derived the footnote that I quote above from a series of e-mails that I wrote to the department head and the journal editor mentioned previously. In this e-mail, I tried to describe explicitly what I thought the purposes of institutional critique were and why I thought that specific naming choices were most appropriate given these purposes.) Furthermore, I have tried to solicit feedback about my work throughout the drafting and publication process from several administrators intimately familiar with the past and present program, asking them directly whether or not the account seems balanced.[11] And, so far, responses have been generally favorable: One of the early deans of EOP remarked that my account of the earliest years of the program was "remarkably" similar to his own recollections in the ways that it emphasized both the significant strengths and significant weaknesses of the program; another current administrator suggested that, in his view, my account offered useful critique of the program without dwelling unnecessarily upon the purported individual beliefs and values of identifiable people. Of course, I cannot claim that no one has perceived or will perceive my critique of EOP rhetoric to be "bad news." I can claim, however, that I have tried to emphasize throughout my work that my analytical goal is reform-minded institutional critique, not the generation and delivery of bad news per se.

Conclusion

I have spent a fair amount of time recently at conferences and elsewhere talking with other individuals who are also performing various kinds of institutional-critique projects. And, in almost every single one of these discussions, questions regarding access and permission, of reference and naming, and of mitigating "bad news" have come up during the course of conversation, for example, "Where did you find that incredible letter?"

"Did you have any trouble convincing so-and-so to let you analyze this interaction?" "How and why did you choose to describe the people whom you reference in this piece in the ways that you did?" "How has the current administration responded to your work?" Throughout this brief chapter, I have tried to offer readers some preliminary answers to such questions in ways that I hope prove useful to the important project of understanding and reforming problematic institutional power dynamics across a variety of settings.

Notes

1. See, for instance, both Grabill and Flower for analyses of specific community literacy organizations, Mauk for analysis of the dynamics of writing instruction at his home community college, Taylor for analysis of writing instruction within his home historically black institution, McGee for analysis of writing program structure and function at her home institution, and Grego and Thompson for analysis of their Studio approach to basic writing instruction as implemented within two different institutions in the southern United States.

2. See, for instance, Adler-Kassner and Herrington for analysis of story-changing work pertinent to issues of institutional "accountability." See also Rhodes for discussion of story-changing work related to the "branding" of writing instruction by the Council of Writing Program Administrators.

3. See, for instance, Parks; Smitherman; and Kynard for historical critiques of the CCCC organization and its "Students' Right to Their Own Language" statement; DeGenaro and Tassoni for historical work on basic writing at their home "public ivy" institution; and Hoogeveen for historical discussion of writing instruction at his home historically black institution.

4. EOP rhetoric at Illinois constituted one of the largest efforts on the part of a predominantly white university in the post–Civil Rights era in the United States to meet the perceived language and literacy needs of "high-risk" minority students. For more detailed background about this program, see my article "Language, Literacy and the Institutional Dynamics of Racism."

5. For discussions of methodological and ethical choices relevant to work with "official" archival data, see Connors; L'Eplattenier and Mastrangelo; Moon and Donahue; Kirsch and Rohan; and Ramsey, Sharer, L'Eplattenier, and Mastrangelo.

6. For discussions of methodological and ethical choices related to work with interview and observation data, see Kirsch and Mortensen; Anderson; CCCC "Guidelines"; Dautermann.

7. The question of who can ethically and legally decide questions of access to materials within archival collections remains thorny even for professional archivists. The Society of American Archivists (SAA) notes, for instance, that professional archivists face a quandary with respect to issues of permission as they attempt to balance the need to "promote open and equitable access to . . . the records in their care without discrimination or preferential treatment" (par. 10) with the need to "protect the privacy rights of donors and individuals or groups who are the subjects of records" (par. 12). One particularly important set of permissions involves the idea

of authorship: Are institutional documents "authored" by identifiable individuals, or are they "authored" by the institution more generally? How does a given answer to this authorship question influence the ways in which a researcher seeks permission to analyze and quote from these documents? I grapple with aspects of these important authorship questions within my "'What's in a Name?'" piece.

8. Tassoni has made much this same point when suggesting that programs like basic writing tend to be "absent from [official institutional memory] . . . at least as that memory is represented in the archives and in the minds of those whom the archives represent" (107).

9. I was also told by someone that many more documents were literally set on fire by one disgruntled director in the late 1970s as a means to protest the institution's treatment of the program—a story that I have never been able either to confirm or deny.

10. For a detailed discussion of these terms, see my article "'What's in a Name?'"

11. I must note that I did not ask each living person referenced in this account to read and respond to my drafts before publication in the ways that ethnographers are sometimes encouraged to do (e.g., Bogdan and Biklin), largely because I see my work as primarily "text-based" and focusing on public documents rather than "person-based" and focusing upon individual beliefs, values, and ideals.

Works Cited

Adler-Kassner, Linda. *The Activist WPA: Changing Stories about Writing and Writers.* Logan: Utah State UP, 2008. Print.

Adler-Kassner, Linda, and Susanmarie Herrington. "Responsibility and Composition's Future in the Twenty-First Century: Reframing Accountability." *College Composition and Communication* 62.1 (2010): 73–99. Print.

Andersen, Paul V. "Simple Gifts: Ethical Issues in the Conduct of Person-Based Research." *College Composition and Communication* 49.1 (1998): 63–89. Print.

Bogdan, Robert C., and Sari Knapp Biklin. *Qualitative Research in Education.* 5th ed. Boston: Pearson, 2007. Print.

Conference on College Composition and Communication. "Guidelines for the Ethical Conduct of Research in Composition Studies." *National Council of Teachers of English.* 2003. Web. 7 Apr. 2009.

Connors, Robert. "Dreams and Play: Historical Method and Methodology." Kirsch and Sullivan, *Methods and Methodology* 15–36.

Dautermann, Jennie. "Social and Institutional Power Relationships in Studies of Workplace Writing." Kirsch and Mortensen, *Ethics and Representation* 241–59.

DeGenaro, William. "Why Basic Writing Professionals on Regional Campuses Need to Know Their Histories." *Open Words: Access and English Studies* 1.1 (2006): 54–68. Print.

Flower, Linda. *Community Literacy and the Rhetoric of Public Engagement.* Carbondale: Southern Illinois UP, 2008. Print.

Grabill, Jeffrey T. *Community Literacy Programs and the Politics of Change.* Albany: State U of New York P, 2001. Print.

Grego, Rhonda, and Nancy Thompson. *Teaching/Writing in Thirdspaces: The Studio Approach.* Carbondale: Southern Illinois UP, 2008. Print.

Henze, Brent, Jack Selzer, and Wendy Sharer. *1977: A Cultural Moment in Composition*. West Lafayette: Parlor, 2008. Print.

Hoogeveen, Jeffrey L. "The Progressive Faculty/Student Discourse of 1969–1970 and the Emergence of Lincoln University's Writing Program." *Local Histories: Reading the Archives of Composition*. Ed. Gretchen Flescher Moon and Patricia Donahue. Pittsburgh: Pittsburgh UP, 2007. 199–219. Print.

Kirsch, Gesa E., and Liz Rohan, eds. *Beyond the Archives: Research as a Lived Process*. Carbondale: Southern Illinois UP, 2008. Print.

———. "Introduction: The Role of Serendipity, Family Connections, and Cultural Memory in Historical Research." Kirsch and Rohan, *Beyond the Archives* 1–9.

Kirsch, Gesa E., and Patricia A. Sullivan, eds. *Methods and Methodology in Composition Research*. Carbondale: Southern Illinois UP, 1992. Print.

Kirsch, Gesa E., and Peter Mortensen, eds. *Ethics and Representation in Qualitative Studies of Literacy*. Urbana: NCTE, 1996. Print.

Kynard, Carmen. "'I Want to Be African': In Search of a Black Radical Tradition/ African-American-Vernacularized Paradigm for 'Students' Rights to Their Own Language,' Critical Literacy, and 'Class Politics.'" *College English* 69.4 (2007): 356–86. Print.

L'Eplattenier, Barbara, and Lisa Mastrangelo, eds. *Historical Studies of Writing Program Administration: Individuals, Communities, and the Formation of a Discipline*. West Lafayette: Parlor, 2004. Print.

Lamos, Steve. "Language, Literacy, and the Institutional Dynamics of Racism: Late-1960s Writing Instruction for 'High-Risk' African American Students at One Predominantly White University." *College Composition and Communication* 60.1 (2008): 46–81. Print.

———. "'What's in a Name?' Institutional Critique, Writing Program Archives, and the Problem of Administrator Identity." *College English* 71.4 (2009): 389–414. Print.

Mauk, Johnathon. "Location, Location, Location: The 'Real' (E)states of Being, Writing, and Thinking in Composition." *College English* 65.4 (2003): 368–88. Print.

McGee, Sharon. "Overcoming Disappointment: Constructing Writing Program Identity through Postmodern Mapping." *Discord and Direction: The Postmodern Writing Program Administrator*. Ed. Sharon James McGee and Carolyn Handa. Logan: Utah State UP, 2005. 59–71. Print.

Moon, Gretchen Flesher, and Patricia Donahue. *Local Histories: Reading the Archives of Composition*. Pittsburgh: Pittsburgh UP, 2007. Print.

Newkirk, Thomas. "Seduction and Betrayal in Qualitative Research." Kirsch and Mortensen, *Ethics and Representation* 3–16.

Parks, Stephen. *Class Politics: The Movement for the Students' Right to Their Own Language*. Urbana: NCTE, 1999. Print.

Porter, James E., Patricia Sullivan, Stuart Blythe, Jeffrey T. Grabill, and Libby Miles. "Institutional Critique: A Rhetorical Methodology for Change." *College Composition and Communication* 51.4 (2000): 610–42. Print.

Ramsey, Alexis, Wendy Sharer, Barbara L'Eplattenier, and Lisa Mastrangelo, eds. *Working in the Archives: Practical Research Methods for Rhetoric and Composition*. Carbondale: Southern Illinois UP, 2010. Print.

Rhodes, Keith. "You Are What You Sell: Branding the Way to Composition's Better Future." *Writing Program Administration* 33.3 (2010): 58–77. Print.

Smitherman, Geneva. "CCCC's Role in the Struggle for Language Rights." *College Composition and Communication* 50.3 (1999): 349–76. Print.

Society of American Archivists. "Code of Ethics." *Society of American Archivists.* 2003. Web. 27 Feb. 2008.

Soliday, Mary. *The Politics of Remediation: Institutional and Student Needs in Higher Education.* Pittsburgh: U of Pittsburgh P, 2002. Print.

Tassoni, John Paul. "(Re)membering Basic Writing at a Public Ivy: History for Institutional Redesign." *Journal of Basic Writing* 25.1 (2006): 96–124. Print.

Taylor, Hill. "Black Spaces: Examining the Writing Major at an Urban HBCU." *Composition Studies* 35.1 (2007): 99–112. Print.

13.

Longitudinal Writing Research in (and for) the Twenty-First Century

Jenn Fishman

Echoing the primary question of this anthology, "What does it mean to study writing in the early twenty-first century?" this chapter asks what it means to study writing longitudinally in the new millennium. It is a difficult question to address. Already, a little more than ten years into the century, there are as many answers as there are longitudinal projects. Diverse in subjects, methods, and materials, longitudinal writing research includes panel, case, and multiyear cohort studies, and it examines an ever-expanding range of writers, types of writing, and sites of writing activity. That is not to say longitudinal research lacks common cause or common ground, however. Studies conducted over the past forty-odd years reflect researchers' shared interest in writing development, and together extant books, articles, conference presentations, and institutional reports confirm researchers' collective commitment to improving what is known about writing and enhancing available resources for writers as their praxes change over time.

My own perspective on longitudinal research is shaped by nearly a decade of experience. I became a researcher with the Stanford Study of Writing in 2001 at the same time 189 undergraduates agreed to participate. Working with this group alongside principal investigator Andrea A. Lunsford and coresearchers Marvin Diogenes, Erin Krampetz, Paul Rogers, and Laurie Stapleton, I learned about everything from study design to designing study SWAG (or "stuff we all get"). I also learned how writing—as an act, an assignment, a job, a chore, a challenge, a desire, an agency—fit into Stanford students' busy lives. Perhaps the most unexpected lesson I learned was about research itself. My long-term relationship to the study participants combined with the ongoing process of data analysis taught me that conducting longitudinal research means becoming a historian of the present. That is to say, when we undertake longitudinal research, we methodically document contemporary writing, creating records of the immediate past (i.e., yesterday, last week, last year). Although much of our attention is focused on the present, and we work always with the future in mind, when we interpret our data, we also construct histories of writing or systematic accounts of the past. While procedurally this has always been the case, twenty-first-century writing changes quickly, and the speed with which recent examples become anachronistic heightens our need for historical orientation. As a result, to study writing longitudinally means designing projects, collecting data, and disseminating findings that can illuminate the past productively.

Critical history making

In this respect, longitudinal research is part of a long tradition of critical history making. In 1918 when literary critic and historian Van Wyck Brooks coined the phrase "a usable past," he described history as a rhetorical project with genuine cultural and material significance (339). In 1999, Joseph Harris dedicated the fiftieth anniversary issues of *College Composition and Communication* to this idea, gathering essays that offered "ways not simply of reconceiving our past as a field but of reshaping our actions as writers, teachers, intellectuals, activists, and administrators" (343). Taking up this gauntlet as longitudinal writing researchers involves more than reexamining past studies and current projects; it also entails reconceptualizing the work that lies ahead. To that end, this chapter asks:

- What can—and should—we learn from past longitudinal research?

- What can—and should—we learn from recent and ongoing studies?

- What histories can—and should—be told through future longitudinal projects?

Certainly, experienced researchers will have preliminary answers to these questions, but it is important for prospective researchers also to reply. In addition, these are questions for administrators, educators both within and outside the schools, policy makers, commentators, and writers themselves: everyone whose actions and decisions have short- and long-term consequences for contemporary writing and its histories.

Longitudinal Writing Research, 1963–2000

In 1963, Richard A. Braddock, Richard Lloyd-Jones, and Lowell Schoer identified longitudinal research as a "promising type of investigation," and subsequent scholars have agreed (32). In "Basic Writing," Mina

Shaughnessy argues, "Writing is a slow-developing skill that should be measured over longer periods of time than a semester" (146), and David Bartholomae and Linda Flower cite longitudinal research as the best way to capture writers' "'natural' learning sequence" along with the "effects" and "durability of learning" over time (Bartholomae 268; Flower 256). Although there is no comprehensive bibliography of the studies that put these assertions to the test, Robert J. Tierney and Margaret Sheehy usefully examine longitudinal studies of literacy development from early childhood through the college years, and Paul Rogers provides a richly detailed survey of college-level longitudinal case studies. In addition, several scholars incorporate longitudinal research overviews into larger projects, most notably Marilyn S. Sternglass, Patrick Dias and Anthony Paré, Richard H. Haswell, Lee Ann Carroll, and Erin McClure Krampetz. Covering everything from basic writing to workplace writing to ESL writers' development, these resources provide researcher/historians with not only a strong starting place for examining past work but also an initial basis for judging whether and how longitudinal research has met its promise.

Longitudinal reviews often begin with Walter Loban's thirteen-year study of California schoolchildren, James Britton's eight-year study of school-aged writers in England, and Janet Emig's watershed work on the composing process of twelfth graders. In the 1980s, researchers paid increasing attention to college writing, and 1990s researchers increased their efforts to study a greater diversity of writers. While study designs have varied across the decades, cohort studies and individual case studies have come to the fore. As Scott W. Menard explains, nothing else "allows the measurement and analysis of intraindividual changes in cognition and behavior" over time (6). Mirroring larger trends in writing research, experimental or quasi-experimental examples are in the minority, while hybrid studies that draw heavily on different ethnomethodologies are more common. Many of the best-known longitudinal studies fit this description, including a cadre of college writing research conducted during the 1990s and discussed in well-known academic monographs: *Academic Literacies* by Elizabeth Chiseri-Strater (researched 1987–88; published 1991), *Writing like an Engineer* by Dorothy Winsor (1996), *Time to Know Them* by Marilyn Sternglass (1989–95; 1997), *Writing in the Real World: Making the Transition from School to Work* by Anne Beaufort (1992–93; 1999), *Persons in Process* by Anne Herrington and Marcia Curtis (1989–93; 2000), and *Rehearsing New Roles* by Lee Ann Carroll (1994–98; 2002).

Although these books represent a range of academic (and workplace) perspectives, they share a pedagogical stance. Most writing researchers are also teachers, and they approach development not as change or growth but as learning or the situated acquisition of knowledge and skills, the contextualized refinement of concepts and practices, and the self-reflective accumulation of experiences that shape individuals' behavior as well as their sense of self. This attitude transfers from the first-year writing classroom, where many studies begin, to advanced writing classes and coursework across the curriculum. The same attitude also informs researchers' analysis of instructional settings, testing situations (Sternglass), self-directed academic writing (Carroll), and early workplace endeavors (Winsor; Beaufort). These examples remind us that all writers are students in the sense that all writers are "persons in process" or individuals learning "to construct coherent selves through writing" and "to make themselves understood through their writing" as they move through curricula, professional training, and time (Herrington and Curtis 354). Despite the extremely linear, chronological momentum of these studies, the patterns of development they reveal are seldom straight lines. Instead, longitudinal research generally confirms that writing development is as recursive as writing processes. As Sternglass reports, "[The] development of complex reasoning strategies over time does not produce consistent improvement" even when improvement does occur (59), and Carroll similarly observes that students struggle with different tasks at different times as they ride the "roller coaster" of college writing (49).

In the studies cited above, as in longitudinal studies more generally, researchers' pedagogical stance combines advocacy with inquiry and underscores the idea that research can—and should—support writing education. In this sense, longitudinal research has a strong politics, which is student centered. In fact, given the prominence of writers' own experiences and voices, we might think of *A Time to Know Them* as not only Sternglass's research but also stories that belong to Linda, Joan, Ricardo, Chandra, Delores, Audrey, Donald, Carl, and Jacob. By the same token, we can connect *Academic Literacy* with Anna and Nick; *Writing like an Engineer* with Jason, Al, Chris, and Ted; *Persons in Process* with François, Lawrence, Nam, and Rachel; and so on. Delving into these writers' lives, researchers' stance aligns with critical pedagogy, social constructivism, and social epistemic rhetoric. As Sternglass writes, the "worldviews of all students impinge on their attempts to make sense of the academic perspective," and "the effects of gender, race, ethnicity, class, and ideology" cannot be ignored (295). Studies undertaken in the 1990s in particular reflect a general consensus, as researchers amplified their efforts to understand how writers develop not only as proficient communicators but also as individuals who are African American, Latina or Latino, Korean, Vietnamese, Chinese, white, lesbian, gay, male, female, working class, middle class, disabled, first-generation American, and so on.

This body of work is representative of the larger contribution past longitudinal research made to twentieth-century writing studies, extending from Shirley Brice Heath's *Ways with Words* and other longitudinal research of childhood literacy to Deborah Brandt's study of life-long writing development in *Literacy in American Lives*. Nonetheless, it is important to ask whether longitudinal research has met its promise. In "Documenting Improvement in College Writing," Richard H. Haswell answers, "No." As he correctly notes, past longitudinal studies suffer from design limitations, flawed or failed approaches to data analysis, and a dearth of convincing and shared measurements of change, and additional problems lie just beyond the scope of his assessment. Although some studies may be weakened by participant attrition (5), studies with large cohorts can become "treadmills of data collecting" if they take in more information than researchers can handle effectively (Filer with Pollard 59). Longitudinal researchers also frequently lack funding and other kinds of resources. There is not enough discussion about ethical issues that arise during long-range studies, nor has there been enough attention paid to the unique types of collaboration that longitudinal studies can require, both among researchers and between researchers and study participants.

All of us involved in longitudinal projects during the first years of the twenty-first century worked with an acute awareness of these issues, and collectively we wish we could brag about finding a solution to at least one of the above problems. Instead, it is more accurate to say we have been using longitudinal research as a tool that can, through ongoing use and refinement, help us illuminate different aspects of writing and its study.

Longitudinal Writing Research, 2000–Present

As part of the writing-research resurgence over the last decade, longitudinal studies have proliferated. Read as histories of the present, they document writing development against the backdrop of new writing practices, technologies, and sites. Recent studies also reflect researchers' heightened awareness of writing as not only product and process but also performance or activity mediated by a complex of interrelated material and rhetorical circumstances. One constant across recent work is the evolution of researchers' pedagogical stance, which is perhaps now best understood as a commitment to *paideia* or writing education that supports not only standard academic and professional goals but also active community participation. This attitude informs researchers' latest inquiries into the experiences of both individual writers and groups of writers from different social and cultural backgrounds; it also frames recent efforts to make longitudinal research an agency for education change.

Not surprising, schools have remained a prominent site of longitudinal inquiry, even as researchers set formal education into broader contexts, and college-based projects continue to be at the fore led by Nancy Sommers's study at Harvard (1997–2001), the Stanford Study of Writing led by Andrea A. Lunsford (2001–6), and the study of undergraduates Doug Hesse and his colleagues conducted at the University of Denver (2006–10). Both the Harvard and Denver studies concentrated on the college years, while at Stanford we followed our cohort for an additional postgraduate year. At Harvard, Sommers focused on academic writing and collected five hundred pounds of examples, while Stanford students uploaded more than fourteen thousand academic and nonacademic texts into an electronic database. Sharing a broad approach, the Stanford and Denver studies redefined college writing to include personal, extracurricular, workplace, and professional compositions, and they brought new attention to new media. The Stanford database includes a cache of e-mail, PowerPoint presentations, and web texts, while Denver students were encouraged to submit "poems, fiction, or other self-sponsored writings; emails; writings for websites, blogs, wikis or other digital media; posters, brochures, journals, sketchbooks, and so on" (Hesse, "Overview"). Representing more than ten years of continuous data collection, these three studies have amassed an overwhelming amount of writing, which places enormous demands on all of us as researcher/historians. At the same time, by creating an unprecedented archive of college writing, these studies have also created equally rich opportunities for research innovation.

Although longitudinal research is not synonymous with assessment, a growing number of long-term projects capitalize on the data-rich, site-specific nature of longitudinal research by including an assessment component. By making this choice, researchers take on unique responsibilities, collaborators, and audiences, and the stakes can be high, especially if program funding or accreditation is in involved. For these reasons, not all longitudinal researchers wish to engage in assessment, and not all studies are designed to do so successfully. However, long-range assessment can be a powerful resource for the writing community in the present era of evaluation fixation, which the twenty-first century inherited from the "psychometric climate" of the 1980s and the "decade of assessment/ accountability" that followed (Park 1; McLeod). Against this backdrop, longitudinal research offers educators a proactive role in evaluation, and it engages their expertise as teachers, scholars, and administrators. Just as Lee Ann Carroll's Pepperdine study began in conjunction with a general education review (32), a team of researchers at New Hampshire University started a multiyear project while reevaluating their first-year writing requirement (Edwards), and Hesse has promised to "use rich direct measures to assess the quality of student writing and writing instruction" through his study ("Assessing"). Likewise, longitudinal assessment can directly benefit students, who gain opportunities for analysis and self-reflection that testing rarely affords. Especially if writing teachers and administrators can integrate multiyear projects into their programs and curricula, longitudinal research stands to become a cornerstone of twenty-first-century writing education.

Recent scholarship confirms this idea, suggesting additional contributions by longitudinal studies. As Hesse observes, large cohort studies add to "the sparse professional literature comprising longitudinal studies of writing," and they contribute uniquely robust, data-driven findings to a variety of topics ("Overview"). As Sommers and Deborah Saltz demonstrate, longitudinal research can illuminate college students' "common struggles and abilities" (127), and, they argue, based on Harvard Study data, effective college writing development may depend on students' willingness to play the role of "novice-as-expert" in the early college years (145–46). Similarly, Stanford Study of Writing findings both enhance ongoing scholarly conversations and initiate new lines of discussion. As we continue to analyze the study participants' paths from first-year composition and the general education curriculum into different majors and postgraduate activities, our data illuminate the developmental role of student-teacher interactions, students' experiences with different languages and cultures, their ideas about intellectual property, and their deliberate uses of performance to address the challenges of inventing not only the university but also themselves (Fishman, Lunsford, McGregor, and Otuteye).

A potentially inexhaustible resource, recent longitudinal studies also address numerous other subjects. As Gerald Nelms and Rhonda Leathers Dively comment, longitudinal research indicates that teaching to transfer is possible (215–16), and studies by Anne Beaufort, Elizabeth Wardle, and Linda S. Bergman and Janet Zapernick substantiate this claim. Outside the four-year college or university, Smokey Wilson and (together) G. Genevieve Patthey-Chavez, Paul H. Dillon, and Joan Thomas-Spiegel offer longitudinal perspectives on community-college writers' development;

Katherine Schultz focuses on adolescents' in- and out-of-class writing; and Lauren Rosenberg examines how older adults use writing to rewrite their life stories. Elsewhere, Sally Barr Ebest turns longitudinal attention to graduate teaching assistants, while Janet Alsup studies preservice secondary teachers, and Diane Stephens and her colleagues examine the pedagogical practices of four working elementary-school teachers. Responding to William Hart-Davidson's call for "more expansive and longitudinal accounts of individual or group writing strategies" in digital domains (169), James Hartley offers two case studies, Gloria Mark examines the "conventions in distributed electronic work" that evolve among a single group of professional writers over the course of five years (267), and Patrick W. Berry, Gail E. Hawisher, and Cynthia L. Selfe offer global perspective in *Transnational Literate Lives*.

Future Longitudinal Writing Research

As we take up the mantle of history and look ahead to future projects, it is imperative we ask new questions. Rather than wondering if longitudinal research has met its promise or can, we should ask what longitudinal researchers can—and should—promise to address through new studies. In "Documenting Improvement," Haswell offers one answer, arguing by his own example for the virtues of focusing on methodology. Specifically, he makes a case for what we might call FRM projects, or research that is "feasible, replicable, and meaningful" (308). Although FRM is neither as catchy nor as polemical as what Haswell has identified as replicable, aggregable, data-driven, or RAD research, the idea may be as important. Feasible and meaningful are terms that can—and should—invite fieldwide deliberation about how and why we conduct longitudinal studies, while "replicable" can and should be interpreted broadly to mean not only rigorous scientific replication but also deliberate and appropriate use of shared research designs, protocols, and evaluative procedures across various kinds of studies. As a combined mantra and heuristic, FRM can also prompt us to ask: What is feasible for me to collect, organize, and analyze? What meaningful conclusions can I draw from the data I gather? How many study participants can I handle? How many coresearchers can I work with? How will this be a meaningful experience for graduate and undergraduate researchers? How will my study test previous researchers' findings? And how will others be able to replicate and test my work?

I think about these questions in relation to the project I would most like to do next: a six-year study of writing at my undergraduate alma mater, Kenyon College. My reasons for picking Kenyon are several. In general, we need to expand the range of sites where longitudinal research takes place, and small liberal arts colleges are one of many underrepresented locations. As a discipline, rhetoric and composition is more aware of its large university roots than its small college heritage, and though Kenyon has no formal rhet-comp tradition, it is an institution with a long-standing and well-earned reputation for writing excellence. I am as interested in what we can learn from its history, which extends back to the 1820s, as from its contemporary students. Since the campus is relatively remote, even with the ever-encroaching suburban sprawl of nearby Columbus, Ohio, Kenyon also presents a unique opportunity for studying the sociability of writing, which will occasion a shift in focus. While many longitudinal researchers, myself included, have asked how writing creates and is created by individual writers, with the Kenyon Study, I hope to learn more about how writing creates and is created by a community over both short (i.e., six years) and extended (i.e., nearly two hundred years) periods of time.

The Kenyon project I have envisioned also promises to make explicit the historical and historiographical aspects of longitudinal writing research. If conducting this kind of research in and for the twenty-first century means conducting histories of writing, we need to do more to fulfill our promise. If we are going to conduct FRM research and create a usable past for writing educators, we need historical methods in our research courses, and we need to identify shared exigences for our work. The latter means making better use of the opportunities conferences provide and supporting the development of resources like REx, the Research Exchange Index.[1] We might also benefit from an event like the 2003 Alliance of Rhetoric Societies conference, a three-day cross-disciplinary think tank for rhetoric scholars, and we will most certainly benefit from new projects and publications as they appear.

Note

1. REx is the most recent iteration of the Research Exchange. More information can be found at http://researchexchange.colostate.edu/.

Works Cited

Alsup, Janet. "Speaking from the Borderlands: Exploring Narratives of Teacher Identity." *Identity Papers: Literacy and Power in Higher Education.* Ed. Bronwyn T. Williams. Logan: Utah State UP, 2006. Print.

Bartholomae, David. "The Study of Error." *College Composition and Communication* 31.3 (1980): 253–69. Print.

Beaufort, Anne. *College Writing and Beyond: A New Framework for University Writing Instruction.* Logan: Utah State UP, 2007. Print.

———. "Developmental Gains of a History Major: A Case for Building a Theory of Disciplinary Writing Expertise." *Research in the Teaching of English* 39.2 (2004): 136–85. Print.

———. *Writing in the Real World: Making the Transition from School to Work.* New York: Teachers College P, 1999. Print.

Bergman, Linda S., and Janet Zapernick. "Disciplinarity and Transfer: Students' Perceptions of Learning to Write." *Writing Program Administration* 31.1–2 (2007): 124–49. Print.

Berry, Patrick W., Gail E. Hawisher, and Cynthia L. Selfe. *Transnational Literate Lives in Digital Times.* Logan: Computers and Composition Digital/Utah State UP, 2012. Web.

Braddock, Richard A., Richard Lloyd-Jones, and Lowell Schoer. *Research in Written Composition.* Champaign: NCTE, 1963. Print.

Brandt, Deborah. *Literacy in American Lives.* New York: Cambridge, 2001. Print.

Britton, James, Tony Burgess, Nancy Martin, Alex McLeod, and Harold Rosen. *The Development of Writing Abilities (11–18).* London: Macmillan, 1975. Print.

Brooks, Van Wyck. "On Creating a Usable Past." *Dial* 764 (April 1918): 337–41. Print.

Carroll, Lee Ann. *Rehearsing New Roles: How College Students Develop as Writers.* Carbondale: Southern Illinois UP, 2002. Print.

Chiseri-Strater, Elizabeth. *Academic Literacies: The Public and Private Discourse of University Students.* Portsmouth: Heinemann, 1991. Print.

Dias, Patrick, and Anthony Paré. *Transitions: Writing in Academic and Workplace Settings.* Cresskill: Hampton, 2000. Print.

Ebest, Sally Barr. *Changing the Way We Teach.* Carbondale: Southern Illinois UP, 2005. Print.

Edwards, Mike. "UNH07 A3: The UNH Longitudinal Study." *Vitia.* 16 Oct. 2007. Web. 8 Dec. 2008 <http://www.vitia.org/wordpress/2007/10/16/unh07-a3-the -unh-longitudinal-study/>.

Emig, Janet. *The Composing Processes of Twelfth Graders.* Urbana: NCTE, 1971. Print.

Filer, Ann, with Andrew Pollard. "Developing the *Identity and Learning Programme*: Principles and Pragmatism in a Longitudinal Ethnography of Pupil Careers." *Doing Research about Education.* Ed. Geoffrey Walford. London: Falmer, 1998. 57–76. Print.

Fishman, Jenn, Andrea A. Lunsford, Beth McGregor, and Mark Otuteye. "Performing Writing, Performing Literacy." *College on Conference Composition and Communication* 57.2 (2005): 224–52. Print.

Flower, Linda. *The Construction of Negotiated Meaning: A Social Cognitive Theory of Writing.* Carbondale: Southern Illinois UP, 1994. Print.

Harris, Joseph. "From the Editor: A Usable Past: CCC at 50." *College Composition and Communication* 50.3 (1999): 343–47. Print.

Hart-Davidson, William. "Studying the Mediated Action of Composing with Time-Use Diaries." *Digital Writing Research: Technologies, Methodologies, and Ethical Issues.* Ed. Heidi McKee and Dànielle DeVoss. Cresskill: Hampton, 2007. 153–70. Print.

Hartley, James. "Longitudinal Studies of the Effects of New Technologies on Writing: Two Case Studies." *Writing and Cognition: Research and Applications.* Ed. Mark Torrance, Luuk van Waes, and David Galbraith. Amsterdam: Elsevier, 2007. 293–306. Print.

Haswell, Richard H. "Documenting Improvement in College Writing: A Longitudinal Approach." *Written Communication* 17.3 (2000): 307–52. Print.

———. *Gaining Ground in College Writing: Tales of Development and Interpretation.* Dallas: Southern Methodist UP, 1991. Print.

———. "NCTE/CCCC's Recent War on Scholarship." *Written Communication* 22.2 (2005): 198–223. Print.

Heath, Shirley Brice. *Ways with Words: Language, Life, and Work in Communities and Classrooms.* Cambridge: Cambridge, 1983. Print.

Herrington, Anne, and Marcia Curtis. *Persons in Process: Four Stories of Writing and Personal Development in College.* Urbana: NCTE, 2000. Print.

Hesse, Doug. "Assessing Student Writing and Writing Instruction at the University of Denver." *University of Denver Writing Program.* Web. 8 Dec. 2008. <http://www.du.edu/writing/documents/Writing_Assessment_The_University_of_Denver.pdf>.

———. "Quick Overview: A Longitudinal Study of Undergraduate Writing at the University of Denver." *University of Denver Writing Program.* Web. 8 Dec. 2008. <http://www.du.edu/writing/documents/Longitudinal_Study_of_Writing_at_University_of_Denver.pdf>.

Kitzhaber, Alfred. *Themes, Theories, and Therapy.* New York: McGraw-Hill, 1963. Print.

Krampetz, Erin McClure. *Writing across Cultures and Contexts: International Students in the Stanford Study of Writing.* MA thesis. Stanford U, 2005. Web. 10 Dec. 2008.

Loban, Walter. *The Language of Elementary School Children: A Study of the Use and Control of Language and the Relations among Speaking, Reading, Writing, and Listening.* Champaign: NCTE, 1963. Print.

Mark, Gloria. "Conventions and Commitments in Distributed CSCW Groups." *Computer Supported Cooperative Work* 11 (2002): 349–87. Print.

McLeod, Susan, Heather Horn, and Richard H. Haswell. "Accelerated Classes and the Writers at the Bottom: A Local Assessment Story." *College Composition and Communication* 56.4 (2005): 556–80. Print.

Menard, Scott W. *Handbook of Longitudinal Research: Design, Measurement, and Analysis.* Amsterdam: Elsevier, 2008. Print.

Nelms, Gerald, and Rhonda Leathers Dively. "Perceived Roadblocks to Transferring Knowledge from First-Year Composition to Writing-Intensive Major Courses: A Pilot Study." *WPA Journal* 31.1–2 (2007): 124–49. Print.

Park, Taejoon. "An Overview of Portfolio-Based Writing Assessment." *Working Papers in TESOL and Applied Linguistics* 4.2 (2004): 1–3. Web. 2 Dec. 2010. <www.tc.columbia.edu/academic/tesol/.../pdf/TaejoonParkForum.pdf>.

Patthey-Chavez, G. Genevieve, Paul H. Dillon, and Joan Thomas-Spiegel. "How Far Do They Get? Tracking Students with Different Academic Literacies through Community College Remediation." *Teaching English in the Two-Year College* 32.3 (2005): 261–76. Print.

Rogers, Paul. "North American Longitudinal Studies of Writing." *Traditions of Writing Research.* Ed. Charles Bazerman, Robert Krut, Karen Lunsford, Susan McLeod, Suzie Null, Paul Rogers, and Amanda Stansell. Oxford: Routledge, 2009. 365–77. Print.

Rosenberg, Lauren. "'You Have to Knock at the Door for the Door Get Open': Alternative Literacy Narratives and the Development of Textual Agency in Writing by Newly Literate Adults." *Community Literacy Journal* 2.2 (2007). Web. 10 Dec. 2008.

Schultz, Katherine. "Looking across Space and Time: Reconceptualizing Literacy Learning in and out of School." *Research in the Teaching of English* 36.3 (2002): 356–90. Print.

Shaughnessy, Mina. "Basic Writing." *Teaching Composition: Ten Bibliographical Essays*. Ed. Gary Tate. Fort Worth: Texas Christian UP, 1976. 137–68. Print.

Sommers, Nancy. "The Call of Research: A Longitudinal View of Writing Development." *College Composition and Communication* 60.1 (2008): 152–64. Print.

Sommers, Nancy, and Deborah Saltz. "The Novice as Expert: Writing the Freshman Year." *College Composition and Communication* 56.1 (2004): 124–49. Print.

Stephens, Diane, Gail Boldt, Candace Clark, Janet S. Gaffney, Judith Shelton, Jennifer Story, Janelle Weinzirl. "Learning (about Learning) from Four Teachers." *Research in the Teaching of English* 34.4 (2000): 532–65. Print.

Sternglass, Marilyn S. *Time to Know Them: A Longitudinal Study of Writing and Learning at the College Level*. Mahwah: Erlbaum, 1997. Print.

Tierney, Robert J., and Margaret Sheehy. "What Longitudinal Studies Say about Literacy Development/What Literacy Development Says about Longitudinal Studies." *Handbook of Research on Teaching the English Language Arts*. 2nd ed. Ed. James Flood, Diane Lapp, James R. Squire, and Julie Jensen. Mahwah: Erlbaum, 2003. 171–91. Print.

Wardle, Elizabeth. "Understanding 'Transfer' from FYC: Preliminary Results of a Longitudinal Study." *Writing Program Administration* 31.1–2 (2007): 65–85. Print.

Wilson, Smokey. *"What about Rose?": Using Teacher Research to Reverse School Failure*. New York: Teachers College P, 2007. Print.

Winsor, Dorothy. *Writing like an Engineer: A Rhetorical Education*. Hillsdale: Erlbaum, 1996. Print.

PART THREE

Reconceptualizing Methodologies and Sites of Inquiry

14.

Quantitative Methods in Composition Studies: An Introduction to Their Functionality

Richard H. Haswell

A canny, skeptical lot, writing program administrators handle problems on a weekly basis, all the way from students wanting to avoid trouble down to politicians wanting to cause it. Not surprising, then, that a certain amount of the traffic on the WPA listserve (WPA-L) consists of requests for "solid evidence" or "verifiable information." Especially during hard times, hard data are a godsend. This is why quantitative inquiry can be a friend to WPA work, indeed to all branches of composition studies. What kind of friend is the main issue this chapter ponders.

Crisis: Calling for Data

During September, October, and November of 2008, twenty-nine different pleas for quantified information were posted on the WPA-L. Here are five.

- What are the wages paid to adjuncts and peer tutors around the nation?

- Have writing studios recorded measurable outcomes?

- What is the academic fate of students bringing dual credit in composition with them to college?

- Do we have data showing that exemption from first-year writing should not be awarded on the basis of a score of 4 on the Advanced Placement essay?

- Are there data showing that first-year writing improves student retention in college?

It is not difficult to understand that these requests for hard data arise from palpable crises. WPAs need to make certain administrative decisions for which specific information is crucial or need to deal politically with certain stakeholders who are swayed by numbers—deans, legislators, cross-campus colleagues, the public (see the chapter by Hesse in this volume).

What is difficult to understand, however, is the paucity of replies to such pleas on the WPA-L. As it turns out, currently there are no surveys of tutor and adjunct wages, no efforts to measure writing studio outcomes, and few studies connecting dual-credit in composition and retention in college. These and most of the other data hoped for are nonexistent or scanty at best. No doubt, lack of hard data is part of the reason the WPAs were posting their queries in the first place. It seems the need for quantitative research in the composition field is a crisis in itself.

Apophasis: Tabling Some Issues

On the WPA-L, concurrent with voices hoping for the availability of quantified data are voices doubting the validity of quantified data. One respondent mentioned Steve Street, who declared that teachers should be "leery of diagnosing the ills of higher education with the tools of statistical analysis." The teacher-student "interface" is neither experienced nor communicated via numbers, says Street. When you step in poop, "you reach for a stick, not a calculator."

Well, when I step in an aporia, I reach for an apophasis, and Street's activity of "diagnosing" is as classic an aporia as you can find, as hermeneuticists have long noted. In this chapter on quantitative methods, I am not going to wrestle with the philosophical controversies associated with quantification, such as the distinction between "data" and "facts."[1] Nor will I restate the logical rebuttal of Street's charge against numbers.[1] Nor will I support quantitative research by laying out the rich variety of methods at its disposal, such as survey, text analysis, ethnography, prediction, quasi-experiment, meta-analysis.[2] Nor will I advocate combining the qualitative and the quantitative since that is a point well made by Bob Broad in this volume (see also Johanek).

Instead, I will start with the cheerful, pragmatic assumption, held by most quantitative researchers, that numbering obeys ordinary human impulses, as natural as totting your change before you start putting it into the vending machine. My argument is simply that quantitative data gathering and data analysis are an everyday way that humans perceive and act; that in research procedures, they involve straightforward and useful functions; and that in outcome, they have benefits that uniquely serve practitioners and researchers. My main approach will be simply to look at some quantitative studies in the field of composition to see how they work and what they offer.

Taxis: Delimiting Some Terms, Setting Some Assumptions

But first we need to accept some terms.

Datum is a once-occurring historical act that the researcher cannot change. A student's comment in class is a datum. Anne Haas Dyson observed a six-year-old student sticking to her forehead a scrap of paper on which she had written "I hate math" and then deliberately facing her teacher (119–20)—an act Street would label an "interface" but still a datum. Datum assumes that humans apprehend life in circumscribable pieces. How then does a research systematize them?

Dimensionalizing is one systematic thing that can be done with a datum. A dimension is constructed by a researcher as a frame to hold a datum. Note that the quantitative method assumes that dimensions can be created by humans, not only "found" in nature. Dyson could have constructed a dimension called "creative" to hold her student's behavior with the scrap of paper. Instead, she chose to dimensionalize it as "unofficial practice." Dyson finds other data falling into that category, so dimensionalizing is a way to move from datum to data (Farkas and Haas). There is nothing that humans cannot dimensionalize. Dimension is called *trait* in psychology, *feature* in text analysis, *behavior* in ethnography, *variable* in statistics.

Counting is another systematic thing a researcher can do with a datum, naturally following from the assumptions that data can be circumscribed and dimensionalized. Once Dyson created the dimension of "unofficial practice," her data can be quantified, although in her published piece she declines to do so. At a minimum, simply the number of instances that fall into the frame can be counted ("categorical" data). If there is nothing that cannot be dimensionalized, then there is nothing that cannot be counted or turned into a "measure."

Comparing is another systematic thing a researcher can do with dimensionalized and counted data, allowing data to be set alongside other data and both judged. Quantitative researchers sometimes assume comparability and sometimes contest it. Can the findings from the data used in one investigation be tested in another—are they *replicable*? Can one researcher's data be extended by another's—are they *aggregable*? Can data in one research context apply to another context—are they *generalizable*? Can dimensionalized data from one discipline be meaningful in another—are they *commensurable*?

Quantitative research is any in which the researcher takes data crucial to the study and systematically dimensionalizes, counts, and compares them.

Although simple, this notion of number research helps dismantle some false dichotomies between "quantitative" and "qualitative" research. It is easy to see why quantitative methods have been used not only in empirical studies but, often, in research called ethnographic, grounded, participant-observer, action, contextual, inductive, field-based, and humanities-based.

Hypothesis: Positing Four Functions of Quantitative Methods

What then do quantitative methods and assumptions, reaching across so much scholarly ground, distinctively offer composition researchers, from experimenters to exegetes? I posit four functions and illustrate each with an example of recent research.

Insight. Quantification can "see" phenomena that unaided human perception cannot, especially in situations that swamp observers with complex washes of data.

Transgression. Quantification can change the way teachers and administrators conceive of their field, sometimes debunking myths that have prevailed for decades.

Challengeability. Quantification employs methods deliberately designed to make possible the support or falsification of its findings.

Persuasion. Quantification offers a kind of conviction that may move many stakeholders in the fields of discourse, rhetoric, and literacy, serving as agent of social, political, disciplinary, and instructional change.

Exegesis: Interpreting Some Pieces of Quantitative Research

A look at some studies will clarify these functions and some of the distinctive assumptions, motives, and moves of the quantitative method. The four functions and studies are *insight* with Luuk Van Waes and Peter Jan Schellens, "Writing Profiles: The Effect of the Writing Mode on Pausing and Revision Patterns of Experienced Writers"; *transgression* with John R. Hayes, Jill A. Hatch, and Christine Murphy Silk, "How Consistent Is Student Writing Performance?"; *challengeability* with Ellen Lavelle, "The Quality of University Writing: A Preliminary Analysis of Undergraduate Portfolios"; and *persuasion* with Richard H. Haswell, "Class Sizes for Regular, Basic, and Honors Writing Courses."

Insight in Waes and Schellens, "Writing Profiles"

One of the great unknowns in language studies is exactly how people go about composing extended pieces of discourse. For researchers, part of the challenge is the unthinking nature of the act of writing, where, because cognitively it is so highly complex, the writer automatizes and intuits much of it. There are major limits to what authors can tell researchers, even in think-aloud procedures, or to what observers can see, even with video cameras. Into this internal, swirly weather of the composing act, quantitative methods of inquiry allow insight that other methods do not enjoy.

Van Waes and Schellens had twenty experienced writers each draft two reports, one report using a computer and the other using pen and paper. The word-processed drafting was analyzed with software that recorded all revisions as well as the time lapse between keystrokes (in $\frac{1}{16}$ of a second). The videotaped pen-and-paper drafting was transferred to the computer, letter by letter in real time, so that equivalent information (e. g., acts of revision and length of pauses between words) was available for both modes of writing. The result was a massive digital log of minute bits of information.

What can be seen in it? Not much by the human eye, which tends to be dazzled by even small clusters of unsystematized datum points. Van Waes and Schellens assume that the problem can be tackled by creating a number of machine-countable dimensions, for instance, the average length of pauses that were followed by creation of new text compared to average length of pauses followed by revision of text already written. These and other countable dimensions located for Van Waes and Schellens what they call "writing profiles." Here are three of their five profiles.

Profile 1: "Initial planners," who spent above-average time before writing, whose pauses were relatively long during writing, and who made relatively few revisions.

Profile 3: "Fragmentary Stage I writers," who spent little time before starting to write, who made only brief pauses during writing, and who made almost all of their revisions in their first draft, few in their final draft.

Profile 4: "Stage II writers," who took their time before writing, paused infrequently during writing, and made many revisions but most of them in the final draft.

How were these and two other profiles seen and extracted from this grain bin of data? The researchers relied on statistical counting procedures, using cluster analysis and discriminate analysis to locate mutually exclusive combinations of measures. Unaided, no human could have seen these combinations. Call it statistical insight, if you wish. It becomes human insight, we can assume, if it makes sense to humans.

One human sense is the way these profiles line up with the two writing modes, computer and pen-and-paper. No writer adopted profile 3 while composing on paper, but nine out of the twenty did so while word processing, and none adopted profile 4 on the computer, while nine did so with pen and paper. As the twenty writers switched from one writing mode to the other, eighteen of them changed profile. Van Waes and Schellens must have been surprised and delighted to find such strong evidence to add to the debate among literacy specialists over whether a writing tool, the computer, will change our composing habits. The researchers would have been able to see little of the evidence without the help of quantitative methods of analysis.

Transgression in Hayes, Hatch, and Silk, "How Consistent Is Student Writing Performance?"

If, with quantitative methods, numbers can force their own insight, then quantitative researchers have a strong motivation to use them if they want to counter untested assumptions held by teachers, administrators, and themselves (Haswell, "Textual"). One widely held belief involves consistency in student writing performance. Administrators seem to trust that a student who writes at a certain level of performance on one task will, uninstructed, continue to do so on subsequent tasks—hence, students are placed into basic-writing courses on evidence of one placement essay. For their part, composition teachers seem to believe that students will, instructed, either remain at the level of their first essay or show steady improvement from assignment to assignment.

Now if there is one pattern of data sets that quantitative researchers are most alert to, it is variability, the way data points on a dimension are inconsistent.[3] So when Hayes, Hatch, and Silk follow the assumption common with quantitative researchers everywhere that teacher beliefs need to be tested, they do so in the simplest quantitative way, by recording the variability in the quality of essays a student produced, in sequence, over a semester. Their findings transgress much teacher lore.

Hayes, Hatch, and Silk had qualified judges, not the teachers, rank essays students submitted for the four most substantial assignments in a number of composition courses. Here is a snippet of the outcomes, just the rankings from one judge on eight students from one course. Nineteen students total were in the course, so 1 is best, 19 is worst.

Student	Assignment 1	Assignment 2	Assignment 3	Assignment 4
A	1	3	5	1
B	2	15	19	4
C	3	11	14	14
D	4	1	12	2
E	5	4	4	15
F	6	8	1	6
G	7	13	11	11
H	8	18	2	9

SOURCE: Hayes, Hatch, and Silk, "How Consistent Is Student Writing Performance?," 35.

The way one paper poorly predicts the next paper here continues for the other eight students in the class, and it is the same picture with the other judges and other classes. The average correlation between one essay and the next, for all the students rated, is 0.2. That is close to random.

I do not know if Hayes, Hatch, and Silk set out with iconoclastic assumptions and intentions, but for over a century in composition studies, quantitative investigations have found no lack of idols to topple. They have shown precollege testing unable to predict college writing performance, professional writers using fewer explicit transitions than do students, students not always benefiting from peer critique, workers on the job often composing pieces straight through with no revision, with scores of other findings that run contrary to disciplinary dogma. Do you hanker to *épater la bourgeoisie*? Take up numbered inquiry. What quantitative researchers know and relish is how little quantification it sometimes takes to produce shock.[4]

Challengeability in Lavelle, "The Quality of University Writing"

Quantitative methodology has its critics, among them quantitative researchers, who as a lot are as skeptical as WPAs. Researchers will be the first, for instance, to assume that the uneven progress shown by Hayes, Hatch, and Silk's scores might change were the rating done by the teachers of the students. Quantified researchers, in fact, cannot avoid that assumption because it emerges from one inherent quality of the quantitative method, falsifiability (Popper 83–190). Since the analysis used, the data reported, and the findings derived are countable, they are accountable. Counterfindings can be produced, for instance, by recomputing the math or replicating the research design. One of the most powerful motives of quantitative researchers is the desire to publish representations of the real world that can be challenged.

Falsifiability is by no means an assumption of all discourse produced by composition scholars. Great swatches of it look like this: "Instead of showing students how to write readable essays, I follow the spirit of Dewey and just show them efficient ways to produce the required words in a serviceable time." This assertion cannot be contradicted by any amount of counterevidence. What this teacher-scholar has done in the classroom cannot be replicated because it is undocumented personal history. Furthermore, key words in the assertion—"readable," "spirit," "efficient," and "serviceable"—are Plastic Man terms, pliable enough to escape any dispute. The sentence reflects a Teflon-coated mode of discourse that creates, in Dasenbrock's phrase, "a cozy solipsism" (560).

By contrast, Lavelle's quantitative inquiry is challengeable. It asks if students improve their writing during the undergraduate years, one of the most fractious questions in writing research. For instance, long ago Alfred Kitzhaber documented decline, recording senior writing as worse than first-year writing on a spectrum of writing traits. Four decades later, on a different spectrum of measures, I recorded improvement ("Documenting"). Lavelle's findings seem to support Kitzhaber's. She compared an essay that each of thirty students had written in their first year for their composition class with an essay written three or four years later for a course in their major. On a number of dimensions, including holistic rating, the students' later writing tended to fare worse than their earlier.

Now I, for one, have reservations about Lavelle's study. The mean differences between early and later writing are miniscule for such a small sample, and the calculation of significant differences that found statistical confidence in them is a one-sample t-test, which seems inappropriate. The point, however, is not these or other reservations, but the way she chose a research method, quantification, that allows them to be made. Every step of her inquiry is clearly enough specified to be challenged—sample, measurement, evaluation, statistical analysis. The one-sample t-test is an unambiguous calculation with well-established parameters of use, and by choosing it, Lavelle asked for an audit. What motivates this kind of research? Among other things, to pledge honesty in public and to throw down the gauntlet. To publish quantitative research takes, among other things, courage.

Persuasion in Haswell, "Class Sizes"

Quantitative researchers assume, largely from experience, that raw data can be agent to change. They know that in our culture, numbering holds a compulsive draw, seen everywhere from the "Index" in *Harper's Magazine* to the dollar-cost figure put on hurricanes twenty-four hours after landfall. They infer that academicians are not immune from the attraction. A way to put this, perhaps unflattering, is that researchers choose quantitative tactics because they wish power—or, perhaps more accurate, because they feel other methods may have fewer teeth. Consider my motives to create an online list of composition-class caps on enrollment.

WPAs have long fought to keep class sizes down, administrators to keep them rising. So in 1998, I put on line a list of enrollment caps in first-year, advanced, and honors writing courses at institutions across the nation. I update the compilation every so often. Currently, it has data from over 230 colleges. Technically, this repository of information is the most dubious of samples. The information is self-reported. I've never tried to stratify it, for instance to add more data from private or two-year institutions, which are poorly represented. Yet, this sleaziest of data dumps has had some sway. To date, I know of eleven institutions where information from my list has entered into reports to higher administration, and several where the list helped in lowering class caps.

Where lies the persuasive force? Even when quantity is crudely dimensionalized and systematized, new and powerful dimensions can be inferred. Some trends can be seen at a glance in my data, for instance, that the more prestigious the school, the lower the class sizes. Viewers can find personal trends, noting the way their institution has higher caps than do their peer institutions. Here an array of datum points, simply arranged (institution, type of course, size of enrollment cap), is helping foster educational change. Did I assume this from the start? Of course. Why else would I take the trouble?

Praxis: Diving In Once More

I am not saying that quantitative research is or should be a lax or unlettered enterprise. Conducted well, that is, conducted as it only should be, it is as rigorous as any other kind of scholarly research. And as technical. In just the four pieces I have discussed, researchers worked with standard deviation, interrater reliability, degrees of freedom, p-values, t-tests, Latin square design, Wilcoxon matched-pair signed-rank tests, profile typology, cluster analysis, discriminant analysis, outlier exclusion, and Z-value recalculation. How does a young scholar in composition studies learn stuff like this? Worse, how does an old one?

In 1976, Mina P. Shaughnessy suggested that many basic-writing teachers needed "catching up" as much as did their students. She outlined a "developmental scale" that charts degrees of professionalization. Today, most compositionists have traversed her first three stages: protecting the academy from criticism, acculturating students to the ways of the academy, and trying to understand students and self. The rub is her fourth stage ("diving in"), which she says begins with awareness of our ignorance of students and teaching subject and continues with our willingness to uncover "more accurate data" by "rigorously" applying research methods, some of them quantitative (238). Let me carry on with Shaughnessy's vision of professional growth and list some steps a scholar might take who is attracted to quantitative research and willing to dive in. The steps are not sequential.

Take courses in statistics and research methods. You cannot ride backseat with quantity. Begin with the basic courses so you get a firm grasp of underlying notions such as measurement scales, variable dependence and independence, sampling error, frequency distribution, variance, correlation, predictability, and regression.

Read quantitative studies with an eye on method. Instead of skipping the tables, study them. If you cannot smoke out a statistical maneuver, e-mail the authors. According to the rules of the quantitative game, they are obligated and should be happy to explain.

Hook up with a savvy researcher. Learning to quantify is like learning to tango. A roomful of beginners will never teach one another. Introductory books on empirical or quantitative methodology, such as Mary Sue MacNealy or Janice M. Lauer and J. William Asher, are trustworthy surveys of advice, caution, theory, and research design. But they cannot impart the feel of the actual quantitative dance.

Start your own investigation with what you want to know. The only sane impetus for doing quantitative research is pursuit of the not known or poorly known. It is possible for researchers to launch studies in order to gain tenure, placate a dean, use up money, or for other reasons that sooner than later, if they are the only reasons, will suck the soul dry. A piece of quantitative research usually takes time. The researcher needs to outlast it, and what drive lasts longer than intellectual curiosity?

Start small. Exploratory or pilot studies can try out a gamut of dimensions with few participants or few texts, in order to trim hypotheses and variables for a full-bodied study later. Reviews of research are also good starters. Replications, much needed in composition studies, make another workable place to begin, since design and statistical procedures are already established.

Embrace rigor. As it has been used to qualify quantitative research, "rigor" is a vintage Plastic Man word. But there is an inner frame to the word worth saving. Let's give it a name of even more vintage: honesty. Once systematized and dimensionalized, a research direction must be followed without deviation. Fudging is a cardinal sin, reporting false data the unpardonable sin. Whatever else the motives, the quantitative researcher must be happy in documenting disappointment.

Synchoresis: Conceding a Final Point

For their 2007 book, *Becoming a Writing Researcher*, Ann Blakeslee and Cathy Fleischer asked their students why they have a fear of research: "Many conjured up images of men in white lab coats (and it usually was men). . . . Many also thought initially of more experimental and quantitative types of research." The authors allay their students' fear by declaring, "Writing research tends to be more qualitative" (9) and by omitting quantitative research methods from their book.[5] Of course, in some fields where writing research is conducted—psychology, for example—their quantitative assertion of "tends" could be proven inaccurate and so proven by quantitative means. But if they are talking about composition studies only in U.S. English and rhetoric departments, their assertion of "tends" is correct. Stateside, the majority of compositionists do not do quantitative research.

A fact, as the WPA-L continues to show us, that has no bearing on the need of composition studies for quantitative research.

Notes

1. See Charney, "Empiricism Is Not a Four-Letter Word"; Haswell, "Textual Research and Coherence."

2. See Lauer and Asher, *Composition Research*; MacNealy, *Strategies for Empirical Research*; and in the current volume, Sheridan, "Making Ethnography Our Own"; Haas, Takayoshi, and Carr, "Analytic Strategies, Competent Inquiries."

3. Many quantitative researchers assume, from experience, that the most insightful statistical computation is not the mean (as the uninitiated sometimes think) but variance, which calculates the degree to which data points deviate from the mean.

4. See Hayes, Hatch, and Silk, "Does Holistic Assessment Predict Writing Performance?" for more data.

5. Blakeslee and Fleischer's implication that women in composition studies do not conduct quantitative research will puzzle Jocelyne Bisaillon, Darsie Bowden, Annie Brown, Davida Charney, Ann Chenoweth, Gail Corso, Jill Cummings, Tiane Donahue, Olga Dysthe, Patricia Ericsson, Sarah Freedman, Lynn Goldstein, Christina Haas, Sarah Hudelson, Cindy James, Carmen Lee, Ilona Leki, Eva Lindgren, Jianda Liu, Andrea Lunsford, Karen Lunsford, Susan MacDonald, Susan McLeod, Peggy O'Neill, Kelly Ritter, Carol Rutz, Elizabeth Wardle, Katherine Wills, and a crowd more who do.

Works Cited

Blakeslee, Ann, and Cathy Fleischer. *Becoming a Writing Researcher.* Mahway: Erlbaum, 2007. Print.

Charney, Davida. "Empiricism Is Not a Four-Letter Word." *College Composition and Communication* 47.4 (1996): 567–93. Print.

Dasenbrock, Reed Way. "Truth and Methods." *College English* 57.5 (1995): 546–61. Print.

Dyson, Anne Haas. "Staying in the (Curricular) Lines: Practicing Constraints and Possibilities in Childhood Writing." *Written Communication* 25.1 (2008): 119–59. Print.

Farkas, Kerrie, and Christina Haas. "A Grounded Theory Approach for Studying Writing and Literacy." *Socially Responsible Research Methods for Writing and Literacy.* Ed. Katrina M. Powell and Pamela Takayoshi. New York: Hampton, forthcoming.

Haswell, Richard H. "Class Sizes for Regular, Basic, and Honors Writing Courses." *Archives and Professional Resources.* CompPile. Sept. 2008. Web. 18 Apr. 2009.

———. "Documenting Improvement in College Writing: A Longitudinal Approach." *Written Communication* 17.3 (2000): 307–52. Print.

———. "Textual Research and Coherence: Findings, Intuition, Application." *College English* 51.3 (1989): 305–19. Print.

Hayes, John R., Jill A. Hatch, and Christine Murphy Silk. "Does Holistic Assessment Predict Writing Performance? Estimating the Consistency of Student Performance on Holistically Scored Writing Assignments." *Written Communication* 17.1 (2000): 3–26. Print.

———. "How Consistent Is Student Writing Performance?" *Quarterly of the National Writing Project* 17.4 (1995): 34–36. Print.

Johanek, Cindy. *Composing Research: A Contextualist Paradigm for Rhetoric and Composition.* Logan: Utah State UP, 2000. Print.

Kitzhaber, Alfred. *Themes, Theories, and Therapy: Teaching of Writing in College.* New York: McGraw-Hill, 1963. Print.

Lauer, Janice M., and J. William Asher. *Composition Research: Empirical Designs.* New York: Oxford UP, 1988. Print.

Lavelle, Ellen. "The Quality of University Writing: A Preliminary Analysis of Undergraduate Portfolios." *Quality in Higher Education* 9.1 (2003): 87–93. Print.

MacNealy, Mary Sue. *Strategies for Empirical Research in Writing.* New York: Longman, 1998. Print.

Popper, Karl R. *The Logic of Scientific Discovery.* New York: Basic Books, 1959. Print.

Shaughnessy, Mina P. "Diving In: An Introduction to Basic Writing." *College Composition and Communication* 27.3 (1976): 234–39. Print.

Street, Steve. "Mad about Numbers." *Chronicle of Higher Education.* 11 Dec. 2008. Web. 18 Apr. 2009.

Van Waes, Luuk, and Peter Jan Schellens. "Writing Profiles: The Effect of the Writing Mode on Pausing and Revision Patterns of Experienced Writers." *Journal of Pragmatics* 35.6 (2003): 829–53. Print.

WPA-L List. *Archives: Arizona State University.* Sept.–Dec. 2008. Web. 18 Apr. 2009.

15.

Strategies and Passions in Empirical Qualitative Research

Bob Broad

In day-to-day professional conversations, I comfortably and proudly refer to myself as a "qualitative researcher." When contributing to a book on research methods, however, I have to exchange that easy comfort for critical reflection and ask myself what I am even talking about when I so gladly self-identify and what forces shape my methodological choices. So I begin this chapter with a brief taxonomic investigation that marks—and then blurs—boundaries between qualitative and quantitative analyses and between empirical and textual data. After clarifying what sort of research I do and don't typically pursue, I move on to the more vexing—and more interesting—question of *why*, generally, some researchers favor empirical-qualitative methods over textual and quantitative methods. I trust that both the taxonomic demarcations and the exploration of murky methodological motives offered here will help readers better understand how choices among research methods enter into, and play out in, researchers' lives and the field(s) of English studies, including rhetoric and composition.

Choosing among Methods: Words and Numbers

Matthew B. Miles and A. M. Huberman distinguish qualitative from quantitative methods in the simplest possible way, stating that qualitative methods take as their main type of data "words rather than numbers" (15). This is a fair and useful enough border to draw as a taxonomic starting point, yet it demands further exploration because the interests of qualitative researchers are both broader and narrower than the distinction suggests.

I see Miles and Huberman's numbers versus words distinction as too narrow and exclusive. As Cindy Johanek in *Composing Research*, Kristie S. Fleckenstein, Clay Spinuzzi, Rebecca J. Rickly, and Carole Clark Papper in "The Importance of Harmony," and Richard H. Haswell in the current volume point out, quantitative and qualitative researchers should and do often borrow from each other's domains of data. In my work, I have regularly made use of quantitative data to provide overviews of findings and to explain choices in narrowing data that lead up to the close, qualitative analysis that is typically my research focus. For example, in my studies of writing-assessment dynamics at "City University," I used tables with numbers to show that the themes I selected for close discursive analysis (e.g., significance, liveliness, mechanics, expectations) were those about which my participants spoke most frequently and at the most length.[1] These quantitative data demonstrated for my readers that the topics emphasized in my research possessed "emic" legitimacy: they were the same topics that most concerned the people I was studying.

Granted, my treatments of numbers were both rudimentary in their level of sophistication and secondary in theoretical significance when compared to my analyses of qualitative (discursive) data. Nevertheless, I am happy to recognize and agree with Johanek, Fleckenstein, Spinuzzi, Rickly, and Papper, and Haswell (among others) that we qualitative researchers should and do make meaningful and effective use of numbers, just as our quantitatively oriented colleagues often frame their in-depth experimental and statistical analyses with prefatory offerings of discursive data (e.g., anecdotes). In the midst of all this methodologically liberal congeniality, however, it is important to remember that qualitative and quantitative researchers most often use "the other kind of data" in ways that are noticeably more basic than, and secondary to, their primary methodological commitments and goals. In other words, our strategically and rhetorically necessary crossing of the words-numbers boundary should not distract us from the deeper paradigmatic differences between those who choose to conduct and those who are most persuaded by qualitative vs. quantitative research.

Choosing among Methods: People and Texts

Paradoxically, I also find Miles and Huberman's numbers-versus-words distinction too broad and inclusive. As a qualitative researcher in rhetoric and composition, working in an English studies program that emphasizes and encourages connections among various aspects of our field(s), I am conscious that identifying words as the main data for qualitative research tags *all* colleagues in my department (and across the field English studies) as qualitative researchers. Now, if that's okay with my colleagues, it's okay with me; I love my colleagues, and I admire their work. But I also want to be able to distinguish my methods from theirs. So I call myself an empirical researcher to differentiate my work from the chiefly textual research that predominates in our field (and in my department). Most of our English studies colleagues take published written texts as their main pool of data (see any issue of *College English*, *JAC*, or *PMLA*) for analysis, and this is what distinguishes them as *textual*-qualitative researchers. By contrast, the data that most keenly interest *empirical*-qualitative researchers are drawn from things people do, say, and write in day-to-day life, in what Norman K. Denzin and Yvonna S. Lincoln call "the world of lived experience" (introduction 8). The primary focus of the empirical-qualitative researcher is relationships and interactions among people, not published texts.

Having established this textual/empirical distinction among those of us who use mainly words as our research data, I must now blur it, just as above I needed to blur the distinction between those investigators who use mainly verbal versus mainly numerical data. Textual researchers often provide anecdotes from empirical, lived experience (e.g., personal stories, classroom scenarios) as introductions to and frames for their textual analyses. And empirical researchers in English studies nearly always frame their research questions and data analyses with literature reviews that ground their empirical projects in a textual history and a textually established line of inquiry and argument. So, just as qualitative and quantitative researchers draw from each other's domains, so do empirical and textual researchers. We cannot usefully distinguish among ourselves according to which kinds of data we use, since we all use both kinds. We can and should, however, be distinguished by the kinds of data and kinds of analyses that lie *at the heart* of our research projects. Looking into the heart of things, we usefully and meaningfully separate out the context-freeing (objectivist, experimentalist, quantitative) from the context-preserving (interpretive, naturalistic, qualitative) methods of analysis, and among those using words as our chief kind of data, we distinguish the textual researchers from the empirical. So, to be informative and precise about my methodological dispositions, I need to identify myself as an *empirical* (main kind of data: people's lived experiences, not published texts) *qualitative* (main kind of analysis: interpretive, not objectivist) researcher.

* uses empirical to mean — people's lived experiences

Blinded to Our Passions: The Inescapability
of Interestedness and Stance

> It is good for researchers to make their preferences clear.
> —Miles and Huberman, *Qualitative Data Analysis*

In her book *Composing Research*, Johanek recommends a "contextualist paradigm" for developing and choosing research methods. She emphasizes that research questions should dictate methods rather than vice versa. This simple, yet powerful formulation helped overcome much of the partisan rancor that had characterized quantitative/qualitative debates for decades, and we should award Johanek partial credit for the spirit of methodological pragmatism with which it seems to me English studies is currently blessed. Several of the contributors to this volume (including Haswell, Hesse, Fleckenstein, and I) enthusiastically share the strategic/ pragmatic view that rhetorical contexts should drive methods and that the most effective research methods in any given rhetorical situation (e.g., particular audiences and purposes) will depend on the specifics of that situation.

I welcome and participate in this strategic-rhetorical-pragmatic spirit in composition and rhetoric research, yet I also want to problematize it to a degree because in the process of writing this chapter on empirical qualitative research, I have concluded that choices among research methods are not as purely rationalistic and strategic as we might wish, believe, or pretend. Deep-seated intellectual desires and predilections are also in play. It is this intriguing interaction between methodological choices that are strategic and those that stem from personal preference, between methods as context-driven and methods as profoundly and personally prejudged that the remainder of this chapter explores.

I regularly teach my department's graduate seminar "Research Methods in Composition." Each time I've taught the course since Johanek's book was published in 2000, that text has been the first and perhaps most important thing I assign my students to read. Enacting all the qualities mentioned above—context-responsiveness, rhetorical awareness, methodologically strategic thinking—Johanek's text helps my students learn the most important lesson I have to offer them: to be cosmopolitan and strategic in crafting research questions and methods.

Yet, I always scratch my head over these sentences from Johanek's introduction: "I have *no personal preference* for any one kind of research method. . . . I am merely curious about everything—as I imagine you to be, too. Narrowed, *personal attachment to methodological choices cloud* [*sic*] *our vision* of what those choices are in the first place" (4, emphasis added). Commenting on this passage, I respectfully point out to my students that if Johanek had no "personal preference for" quantitative methods, if she were free of "personal attachments to methodological choices," then her book would not exist because she would not have felt enough urgency to write it. To the contrary, she perceived the quantitative methods she clearly loves being marginalized and devalued in the field of composition (particularly in the journal *Research in the Teaching of English*), so she joined the struggle to save them from oblivion. Like Haswell's chapter in this volume and Davida Charney's 1996 article "Empiricism Is Not a Four-Letter Word," Johanek's *Composing Research* serves the clear and valuable purpose of correcting the uninformed and mistaken assumption held by some of our colleagues that quantitative methods are just not useful and may even be, well, uncool. Only authors with a personal predilection for quantitative methods are likely to notice this problem, and they are also the ones most likely to persuade readers to include quantitative methods in their research toolkits. Notice how strategic thinking about methods therefore sometimes relies upon awareness—and even celebration—of one's "personal attachments to methodological choices." This is the paradox I am trying to unravel.

When considering the pros and cons of "personal preference" and "personal attachment" in scholarly inquiry, some awareness of the field of phenomenology comes in handy. Phenomenology helps us understand how empirical data—what we observe, notice, and care about in the world—are revealed, obscured, filtered, and shaped by our values and beliefs. We have all seen how, in the broader discourse of the sciences (as in the passage from Johanek quoted above), such *interested* values and beliefs are often criticized as "narrow biases" and "blind prejudices" in contrast to a purer, value-free rationalism.[2] Pamela Moss elegantly formulates the phenomenologists' rebuttal to the objectivist critique of *interestedness*: "'[H]ermeneutic philosophy,' which is reflected in the writings of Heidegger and Gadamer, recognizes that the reader's preconceptions, 'enabling' prejudices, or foreknowledge are inevitable and valuable in interpreting a text. In fact, *they make understanding possible*" (7, emphasis added). Following Moss, I argue that it was precisely Johanek's preconceptions, enabling prejudices, and foreknowledge passionately favoring quantitative methods that inspired her to write her important book. I assign Johanek's text in my research-methods course and begin with it precisely because it is an intelligent, articulate, impassioned argument from a scholar who has as resoundingly clear a "personal preference" for and "personal attachment" to quantitative inquiry as I (the professor of the methods course) have a personal preference for and personal attachment to qualitative inquiry. Acknowledging such predispositions does not mean we devalue, misunderstand, or shun each other's favored methodologies; it simply helps us understand and be more aware that we may have a strong personal preference for one paradigm over another, and we probably also have special gifts for conceiving and executing research projects within our favored research paradigms. Furthermore, the dispositional self-awareness on behalf of which I am arguing helps us stay alert to our need to be strategic and rhetorical and not to slide unaware into our favored or familiar methodological groove when the context calls for a different approach.

Before us, then, lies a delicate and complex puzzle: a book (Johanek's *Composing Research*) clearly written out of a pure and abiding passion for quantitative methods that also argues against allowing such passions to "cloud" our strategic, pragmatic methodological choices. The current chapter is an attempt to illuminate and understand this seemingly contradictory relationship between our deeply felt methodological proclivities and our rationalist, contextualist, rhetorical, and methodological strategizing. I believe the most powerful determinant of one's methodological choices may be a deep-seated epistemological *orientation*. In other words, we may approach certain research questions with a strong preemptive impulse to frame our inquiries quantitatively or qualitatively, textually or empirically. I have become convinced that methodological preferences run exceptionally deep and are quite difficult to explain—or are even immune from explanation. If this is true, then methodological decisions may sometimes be less straightforwardly strategic and more predetermined or prejudged according to our epistemological inclinations than a purely pragmatic, contextualist view of research methods supposes.

The Making of an Empirical-Qualitative Researcher

> [Q]ualitative researchers study things in their natural settings,
> attempting to make sense of, or to interpret, phenomena in
> terms of the meanings people bring to them.
> —Denzin and Lincoln, introduction

In what ways and contexts do we choose our methods, and in what ways and contexts do our methods choose us? Writing this chapter, I've come to understand just how difficult these questions are to answer. The most promising method I can devise to serve as a start on this line of inquiry is to offer a reflective, personal-methodological narrative. I turn to a personal narrative not because I believe my methodological story to be exceptional or exemplary but rather because when tracing the interplay of intellectual desire and rhetorical effectiveness, my story is the only set of data to which I have access. I believe it would be helpful to our field if more researchers reflected and wrote openly about their personal methodological passions and stories.

I expect most of us choose a career in English studies driven and guided by two deeply felt emotions: (1) the eager *joy* we feel when reading and writing texts critically and creatively, and (2) our firm *faith* that doing this textual work is a noble, worthy, and socially valuable activity. I still remember the car ride to my first day of preschool in 1964 and the struggle and excitement of verbally spelling out my name ("B-O-B-B-Y") in a halting response to my mother's challenge. That euphoric buzz of literacy—both reading and writing—continued through grade school (where I savored the exotic aquamarine and magenta labels of the SRA Reading Laboratory Kit) and high school (where my Panglossian optimism and idealism were shaken by Orwell's *1984*, Goulding's *Lord of the Flies*, and Huxley's *Brave New World*) and ran on through undergraduate and graduate work. So it is not surprising that I began my journey as a publishing English studies scholar firmly rooted in the realm of literary textual research: reading published literary texts, asking questions about those texts, and composing answers to those questions. This is what I did through the earlier part of my graduate studies, and one of my earliest publications, an essay on Toni Morrison's *Beloved* ("Giving Blood"), enacts this classic textual-qualitative approach to literary inquiry.

Even while working on that exclusively textual project, however, I was already beginning to integrate interviews and observations into other inquiries, and full-blown empirical-qualitative methods (observations, interviews, study of unpublished documents, recordings of discussions and interviews, transcripts, and so on) quickly followed. My essay in the journal *Works and Days* combined textual study of various social and literary theories and their relationship to pedagogical and political practice with interviews of three different "kinds" of scholars: feminist, socialist, and liberal. What drove me to add empirical-qualitative data to the textual materials out of which I was crafting scholarship? I felt a powerful attraction to integrate "live" conversations into what would otherwise be traditional textual research because I believed that distinctive and valuable kinds of knowledge were created in the *interplay* between the empirical and the textual spheres (e.g., getting scholars talking about how their readings compared to and influenced their classroom teaching practices) that could not be achieved within the realm of the strictly textual, and I fervently desired those additional dimensions of knowledge.

This is the right moment to observe that the hunger for empirical, in-the-world (versus on-the-page or on-the-screen) data is shared by quantitative and qualitative researchers, even though our quantitatively oriented colleagues sometimes conflate "hard facts" (empirical data) with numbers. The empirical-qualitative researcher wants to work mainly with hard facts that are discursive.

My first publication in the field of writing assessment was a theoretical, text-based inquiry into the troubled relationship between the positivist-quantitative tradition of "scoring" students' writing and constructivist-interpretive assessment methods like portfolios. "'Portfolio Scoring': A Contradiction in Terms" was textual-qualitative research that employed one empirical anecdote—the story of "Martha"—to illustrate some of the problems I wanted to address. Just as a quantitative researcher may import appealing anecdotes to illustrate findings arrived at through statistical methods, as a textual-qualitative researcher I was dabbling in the empirical realm without a system or method to guide me. Incidentally, this is exactly the sort of treatment of data for which qualitative researchers are sometimes criticized: "cherry-picking" anecdotes to support conclusions arrived at without a clear system of data analysis.[3] Recognizing the valid critique of such dilettantish treatments of empirical data, with the support of—and rigorous challenges from—my dissertation advisers I educated myself further and learned the qualitative research method called grounded theory.

<u>Grounded theory</u> is a system for developing and validating findings based on analysis of empirical, discursive data.[4] The key qualities that won grounded theory my methodological loyalty were its systematic and comprehensive approach to data analysis. Grounded theory is the qualitative method that does the best job, in my view, of meeting qualitative researchers' most urgent responsibility: to actively seek out interpretations contrary to what they might have hoped or expected to find, and to ensure that interpretations and findings are "emic," that is, that they are deeply rooted in the interpretive framework(s) of research participants. Most of my scholarship over the past fifteen years has employed grounded theory methods because they offer the critical and creative leeway favored by humanistic and textual researchers while also providing the analytical transparency and the rigorous validation processes characteristic of traditional, quantitatively oriented, experimentalist methods.[5] To put it another way, grounded theory enables qualitative research to be taken

seriously as a source of insight and truth by people who are neither humanists nor English studies majors but rather administrators and colleagues steeped in the discourses of the physical sciences.

Getting *Heart* Back into the Conversation

The current chapter is a call for our field to add researchers' enthusiasm and curiosity to the array of contexts that comprises our ecological understanding of methodological options and choices. This last chapter section looks at three recent discussions of research methods in writing studies that I believe could have been even more helpful and productive if they had directly addressed the topic of researchers' methodological passions.

In *The Function of Theory in Composition Studies*, Raul Sanchez develops his theory of "the writtenness of theory." One of the results he hopes for from his efforts at theoretical transformation sounds a lot like a call for a shift in the focus of writing research from the textual to the empirical: "[C]omposition theory can move closer toward explaining what writing is and how writing works in the world. Writing happens, and composition researchers can watch it happen and make claims about it, or they can look at the artifacts it leaves behind and make claims about writing as a result" (9). I am persuaded and excited by Sanchez's theoretical work, and I believe he is likely to have some of the effect on shaping research in rhetoric and composition for which he hopes: to move the field toward incorporating more empirical data and methods into composition research. In the context of this chapter, however, I find myself also asking: Why do some rhetoricians need a marked theoretical shift to move them toward what Sanchez calls "humanistic inquiry" (10), while others already pursue just such empirical inquiry without need of a new theoretical framework for the discipline? Here again, I believe that our varied histories, cultures, and values may predispose some of us toward such methods, while others may require persuasion, such as the arguments Sanchez posits.

Along similar lines, in "The Importance of Harmony: An Ecological Metaphor for Writing Research," Fleckenstein, Spinuzzi, Rickly, and Papper offer an intensive and stylish argument for letting the metaphors of *harmony* and *ecology* guide our efforts as researchers. These coauthors explore how communities, individuals, purposes, questions, and audiences (among other elements) interact to shape research questions and research methods. I find myself impressed by the breadth with which they take in the interconnected universe of research methods. However, I was surprised to find no explicit place in their methodological ecosystem for the researcher's intellectual background, wishes, desires, and goals. As should be obvious by now, I strongly advocate adding this missing element to our conversations about research methods.

Of all the commentators I have read on passions and methods, Haswell (this volume) comes closest to addressing directly the issue of researchers' proclivities and yearnings when he describes some scholars (including himself, I presume) as "attracted or compelled to quantitative research." Haswell offers this additional valuable advice: "A piece of quantitative research usually takes time. The researcher needs to outlast it, and what drive lasts longer than intellectual curiosity?" Frankly acknowledging the role of methodological "attraction" and "drive," Haswell frames the issue mainly in terms of finding a desirable research *question*. I fully agree with Haswell's advice here, but I want us to add the researcher's heart to the constellation—or, in the terms of Fleckenstein, Spinuzzi, Rickly, and Papper, to the ecosystem—we examine when we try to understand researchers and the forces that shape their *methods*.

Attraction, compulsion, drive, desire, enthusiasm, passion—these words, all used by Haswell, are the key terms driving my reflective inquiry into researchers and their methodological choices. How and why did I, for example, move from the comfortable, familiar, and relatively tidy world of textual humanities research into the (at that time, to me) alien and (still) complicated, messy world of empirical qualitative research? I believe it was to resist what I perceived to be the potentially paralyzing insularity of exclusively textual research. Offering advice to young writers of creative nonfiction, Annie Dillard warns, "Never, ever, get yourself into a situation where you have nothing to do but write and read. You'll go into a depression. You have to be doing something good for the world, something undeniably useful; you need exercise, too, and people" (xiv). The text-bound depression against which Dillard warns matched too well with some of what I saw going on around me in the academy, and empirical methods seemed to me a potent cure. "The province of qualitative research," write Denzin and Lincoln, "is the world of lived experience" (introduction 8). If I was going to make my career in the academy, I wanted to interject into its often rarified discourse what Robert W. Connell memorably calls "a good dose of awkward facts" (3). It wasn't just others' ideas that seemed to me to cry out for raw material from the outside world, it was also my own. Already firmly committed to qualitative theories and methods, I saw empirical data as a powerful lever by which I could get myself, in Peter Elbow's words, "to end up thinking something you couldn't have started out thinking" (15). Including the empirical world in my research also seemed to boost the utility and transformative power for which I yearned. In Marge Piercy's words, "The pitcher cries for water to carry / and a person for work that is real" (2–3).

The taxonomy with which I began this chapter connects to the thesis with which I conclude. I believe that many of us pursue qualitative scholarly research because it is our proclivity as humanists and lovers of textuality. My movement as a researcher from primarily textual to primarily empirical was more strategic and political, though still rooted in deeply felt commitments and desires (e.g., "to be of use"). I believed that my scholarship would interest and persuade a broader audience—including university administrators, public officials, and other public audiences—if it included a hefty dose of empirical data, analyzed comprehensively and systematically, as grounded theory requires. I want my work in writing assessment to make a discernible difference in the workings of the world, including classroom assessments, large-scale assessments, and assessment policy. I believed—and still believe—that we have a stronger chance of transforming more of the world with empirical-qualitative research than we do with exclusively textual research because empirical data register with more readers as relevant, accessible, and in-the-world than does solely text-based theorizing.

My strong preference for working with empirical data using qualitative methods is simultaneously one of personal predilection and one of strategy. My choices do not imply criticism of others' alternative choices because I favor those methods toward which I feel the strongest "attraction" and "drive" (to use Haswell's terms), and other researchers inevitably do the same. When those with divergent proclivities (prominently Charney, Haswell, and Johanek) make their cases for other methodological choices, they not only make me more self-aware and remind me to be more strategic but also strengthen the field of writing studies by writing from—and about—their own passionate preferences and thereby diversifying our methodological thinking.

Ironically, our willingness to acknowledge and work with our personal preferences (whether qualitative or quantitative, textual or empirical) turns out to be highly strategic and rhetorical. Such self-awareness allows us to make methodological choices that enhance our ethos and our audience effectiveness depending on the rhetorical situation. As Haswell recommends, we gain ethos when we select research projects about which we care deeply and that can sustain our interest. Research projects we can love are also those on behalf of which we can be the most eloquent and persuasive with our audiences. We are strongest as researchers when we combine our methodological passions and strategies.

Notes

1. For examples of tables with numbers, see my "Pulling Your Hair Out" and *What We Really Value.*

2. See Guba and Lincoln, chapter 1, for a robust discussion of this history.

3. See Flower, "Cognition, Context, and Theory Building."

4. See Glaser and Strauss, *Discovery of Grounded Theory*; Strauss and Corbin, *Basics of Qualitative Research*; and Charmaz, "Grounded Theory."

5. See Broad, "Reciprocal Authorities in Communal Writing Assessment," "Pulling Your Hair Out," and *What We Really Value*, and Broad and Theune, "What We Value in Contemporary Poetry."

Works Cited

Broad, Bob. "Pulling Your Hair Out: Crises of Standardization in Communal Writing Assessment." *Research in the Teaching of English* 35.2 (2000): 213–60. Print.

———. "Reciprocal Authorities in Communal Writing Assessment: Constructing Textual Value within a 'New Politics of Inquiry.'" *Assessing Writing* 4.2 (1997): 133–67. Print.

———. *What We Really Value: Beyond Rubrics in Teaching and Assessing Writing.* Logan: Utah State UP, 2003. Print.

Broad, Bob, and Michael Theune. "How We Evaluate Contemporary Poetry: An Empirical Inquiry." *College English* 73.2 (2010): 113–37. Print.

Broad, Robert (Bob) L. "Giving Blood to the Scraps: Haints, History, and Hosea in Morrison's *Beloved.*" *African American Review* 28 (1994): 189–96. Print.

———. "'Portfolio Scoring': A Contradiction in Terms." *New Directions in Portfolio Assessment.* Ed. Laurel Black, Donald A. Daiker, Jeffrey Sommers, and Gail Stygall. Portsmouth: Boynton/Cook, 1994. 263–76. Print.

———. "Power in the Classroom: Theory, Pedagogy, and Politics." *Works and Days* 16 8.2 (1990): 75–86.

Charmaz, Kathy. "Grounded Theory: Objectivist and Constructivist Methods." Denzin and Lincoln, *Handbook* 509–35.

Charney, Davida. "Empiricism Is Not a Four-Letter Word." *College Composition and Communication* 47.4 (1996): 567–93. Print.

Connell, Robert W. *Making the Difference: Schools, Families, and Social Division.* Sydney: Allen, 1982. Print.

Denzin, Norman K., and Yvonna S. Lincoln, eds. *Handbook of Qualitative Research.* 2nd ed. Thousand Oaks: Sage, 2000. Print.

———. "Introduction: The Discipline and Practice of Qualitative Research." Denzin and Lincoln, *Handbook* 1–28.

Dillard, Annie. "Introduction: Notes for Young Writers." *In Fact: The Best of Creative Nonfiction.* Ed. Lee Gutkind. New York: Norton, 2005. xi–xviii. Print.

Elbow, Peter. *Writing without Teachers.* New York: Oxford UP, 1973. Print.

Fleckenstein, Kristie S., Clay Spinuzzi, Rebecca J. Rickly, and Carole Clark Papper. "The Importance of Harmony: An Ecological Metaphor for Writing Research." *College Composition and Communication* 60.2 (2009): 388–419. Print.

Flower, Linda. "Cognition, Context, and Theory Building." *College Composition and Communication* 40.3 (1989): 282–311. Print.

Glaser, Barney G., and Anselm L. Strauss. *The Discovery of Grounded Theory: Strategies for Qualitative Research*. Chicago: Aldine, 1967. Print.

Guba, Egon, and Yvonna S. Lincoln. *Fourth Generation Evaluation*. Newbury Park: Sage, 1989. Print.

Johanek, Cindy. *Composing Research: A Contextualist Paradigm for Rhetoric and Composition*. Logan: Utah State UP, 2000. Print.

Miles, Matthew B., and A. M. Huberman. *Qualitative Data Analysis: A Sourcebook of New Methods*. Beverly Hills: Sage, 1984. Print.

Moss, Pamela A. "Can There Be Validity without Reliability?" *Educational Researcher* 23.2 (1994): 5–12. Print.

Piercy, Marge. "To Be of Use." *To Be of Use*. Garden City: Doubleday, 1973. 2–3. Print.

Sanchez, Raul. *The Function of Theory in Composition Studies*. Albany: State U of New York P, 2005. Print.

Strauss, Anselm, and Juliet Corbin. *Basics of Qualitative Research*. Thousand Oaks: Sage, 1998. Print.

16.

Community-Based Research and the Importance of a Research Stance

Jeffrey T. Grabill

I have always been interested in how people use writing to get work done in the world. That one sentence is how I understand my research, and that sentence goes some way toward explaining why I choose projects (when I get a choice). Because of this interest, rhetoric and composition has sometimes been a difficult fit. I tend to understand "the world" as "not school," and so I tend to focus on writing in community or workplace domains. Because of the critical importance of "work" as a category of activity, I consider technical and professional writing a home. However, because of my interest in things community-based (and public, civic), that field can also be a challenging fit for my work. Rhetorical studies does concern itself with how writing works in public domains, but its history and strong historiographic traditions make situated studies of mundane literacies, technologies, and work difficult to value.

I start with this bit of personal history because it identifies *community* as a particular domain that poses a set of research problems, beginning with disciplinary and field issues. Those disciplinary and field issues have methodological implications. This chapter offers community-based research as a particular approach to research in communities, and I am doing so in order to offer tools for making methodology. Research methodologies, which I understand as a theoretical articulation of ideologies, methods, and practices (see Sullivan and Porter) and developed with respect to particular people, places, and things (like a school). Methodologies developed within particular disciplinary or field contexts may not travel well when moved to new places, people, and their things (like a community). As Patricia and James Porter argue, we must make methodologies in order to research, and that suggests the need for methodological revisions when confronted with community-based research.

Community-based research needs to be understood as naming a set of methodological approaches.[1] The first part of the chapter is about that approach to research and situate that discussion in my own efforts to understand writing in communities. The second part unpacks two implications of community-based research for how we research writing in communities. First, community-based approaches ask us to study how people use writing to do work in the world on their own terms and in their own interests, and some approaches demand that researchers support and facilitate that work. Second, as a methodology, community-based work asks us to reconsider key methodological terms and concepts like method and practice. However, the key difference between community-based research and related methodologies resides in what I call a *research stance*. A stance should be understood as a position or a set of beliefs and obligations that shape how one acts as a researcher. Therefore, I focus this chapter on the concept of "stance." My argument is that stance is the single most important issue to consider when researching in or with communities and needs to be better understood in any conversation about research methodology.

Community-Based Research and Methodological Difference

I have adopted a particular way of talking about research methodology that is based on the methodological arguments of Sullivan and Porter and tracks closely with their concepts and vocabulary. These authors make some careful and powerful arguments that are worth discussing again, as they are necessary for understanding how I have engaged community-based research and why I understand stance as such an important idea. Perhaps the most significant move they make in this framework is to distinguish between *method* and *methodology*. For Sullivan and Porter, *methodology* is the proper "larger" term for thinking about research. A methodology is a theory of research, and any given methodology articulates concepts like stances, methods, and practices.[2] The distinction between method and methodology is important. In Sullivan and Porter's model, something like "ethnography" is not a method. It is a methodology, which means that a particular approach to ethnography has an ideological component (a theory of human relations), a practice component (how people actually constitute their relations with each other) and a method component (tools). This is why I wrote earlier of the existence of various *approaches* to research that share enough theoretical consistency to be understood as alike (methodological) yet are distinct in their deployment.[3] This is also why I will insist later that simply calling oneself an ethnographer or community-based researcher is not sufficient for understanding one's own research practice or communicating that to others (the concept of "stance" helps us with precisely this problem). A model such as the one articulated by Sullivan and Porter allows us to discuss methodologies yet account for their differences. Indeed, methodology is a concept that contains a host of issues: disciplinary histories, values, and training; personal commitments and ideologies; the pressures of the research situation.

This grounding with respect to a concept like methodology is necessary to understand any discussion of community-based research methodology. *Community-based research* (CBR) is usefully understood as a variant of action research or participatory action research and is often discussed in this way.[4] From action researchers, community-based researchers draw on the practice of working with people to answer questions and solve problems—as opposed to researching "on" people and their problems. By foregrounding action, research projects tend to move between capacity building, problem solving, and theorizing. As Schafft and Greenwood comment, "[Action research] projects include capacity building, theory and hypothesis development, conventional research activities, action design and ongoing evaluation of outcomes in which the local knowledge of the relevant stakeholders makes as much a contribution to the process and the professional knowledge of the outside social researchers" (25). Like larger discussions of action or participatory action research, discussions of CBR often focus on power and ethics or questions of why research is conducted, by whom, in whose interests, and to what ends.[5] Many researchers are concerned with representation and identity and also with positionality and self-reflection in terms of understanding what motivates and sponsors research.

The key difference between action research and community-based research concerns the role of "community" in the structure and conduct of an inquiry. This difference plays out in a number of ways. Most obviously, community-based research takes place with a community (though sometimes just *in* a community). Community-based research is generally thought of as research that involves citizens working with professionally trained researchers in a community-driven process to answer local questions or solve local problems. Many varieties of inquiry travel under the CBR name. At my institution, for instance, I would characterize a great deal of work as research *in* communities or *on* communities, but within my institution, all such work is understood as community based. The ethical question of "in" or "with" is a real question, but it plays out quite differently in various disciplines, and so it is wise to listen carefully to how community-based researchers describe their work and to be generous and careful in responding to this work and when thinking about research design.[6] In general, then, CBR researchers value and focus on developing the relationships necessary to engage community members in the practices of research, analysis, and writing.[7] Because CBR is action driven, activities like education, political and social change, and policy making are often explicit project goals. Stoecker writes, "[I]n the best CBR projects, people are also planning strategy, recruiting participants, changing organizations, and producing policy" (8). Conducting CBR is extremely difficult because communities must be well organized, and researchers must be open and flexible in order for projects to be successful.

With that brief overview of CBR, it should be possible to see any number of correspondences with research conversations within rhetoric and composition, particularly the critical methodological tradition that is perhaps best represented by the work of Sullivan and Porter. But what makes CBR different from these larger research conversations? What is important about *community*-based research? I highlight two issues. One is perhaps distinctly related to CBR—the place of community in an inquiry. The other, the importance of relationships to research, is not unique to CBR but manifests itself quite differently in communities.

The first issue is the place of community in any inquiry. I have written previously about the role of community in research design, and I will not repeat those arguments in detail here.[8] But a short version of that argument is that the idea of community is not sufficiently interrogated in rhetoric and composition, leaving it largely to mean "context" or "background." Sometimes it is used to attach significant, positive meaning to a project—that is, community work is de facto ethically good work. Instead, I argue that the concept and possibility of community itself must become a primary object of inquiry for any community-based study. Identifying and understanding—indeed, constructing—community are community-based researcher's primary obligations and, therefore, become issues of *stance* for one interested in conducting community-based inquiries. A researcher is under some obligation to construct the community as part of the project. As a pragmatic issue, for instance, a researcher has to figure out who and what constitute "the community" in a given case in order to work with communities. This pragmatic issue dovetails with a more conceptual argument that communities don't exist ready-formed and discoverable. We construct them as we work. This is just as true for a community organizer as it is for a community-based researcher.

A good example of how these issues play out is work in a community called "Harbor" (Blythe, Grabill, and Riley). In this project, constructing community was a primary task, and the resulting constructions of "community" were key project deliverables that had both procedural and epistemological value. In that project, my colleagues and I worked as part of an organization called Technical Outreach Services for Communities (TOSC). To help TOSC do its work, we looked for ways that people drew boundaries (e.g., us versus them) and otherwise characterized the nature of the community. Characterizations of this community depended first on who was doing the characterization, with the most obvious distinction being between those who were clearly outsiders and those who at least lived in or near Harbor. Distinctions such as this (and there were many others) had enormous practical, political, *and* epistemological power. In missing these multiple characterizations of community, it would have been very easy for us to make serious errors in research practice. In starting from the *stance* that "communities don't exist," we collected and mapped a number of accounts of community. Based on those accounts, we worked with individuals and groups who were quite diverse inside that community but looked the same from the outside. One of the methodological imperatives of CBR is to construct community as part of that work. This imperative (discussed below) is part of a CBR stance.

The second issue important for CBR is the importance of relationships to research. Although not unique to CBR, researching in communities without paying attention to relationships may make projects literally impossible to initiate or complete. I write about the importance of building relationships in more detail as a research practice in other places,[9] and it is an exceedingly difficult issue to explain. Yet, all research, especially all community-based research, is a function of good relationships with the individuals and groups who facilitate and participate in a project. This is an obvious point. However, it is invisible in the research literature and is a serious problem for novice researchers in particular. A story might help to explain what I mean. In that project in Harbor, the key community participant refused to meet with me for a year. She would talk to me on the phone. She would talk to me face-to-face at public meetings. But she refused to meet with me one-on-one, and she refused to be a "research participant" for political reasons that I understood (and that we needed to understand more fully as part of constructing this community). By chance, I ran into her in a restaurant in Harbor, and that plus the fact that we discovered a shared interest in the "precautionary principle" changed her mind about participating in the project. Dumb luck, yes, but this change was also a function of a relationship constructed over time. What we learn from CBR, I believe, is the necessity of moving slowly and committing oneself to getting to know people, listening to people, and demonstrating one's usefulness before the more formal processes of research design can begin.[10] These issues are part of a CBR *stance*. Relationships take time and are fundamental to CBR. And so the stance of a community-based researcher is shaped by this obligation to foreground relationship building and maintenance. There are no shortcuts in good CBR.

On the Value of Stances

I have been alluding to the concept of stance because I think that studying writing in communities presents particular problems for researchers that the concept of a research stance can help solve. That is, the key differences with respect to researching writing in communities are not issues of ideology or method, and they are not precisely issues of practice (though practice is terribly important). Stance is critical, particularly early in a research process, because a stance is an identity statement that enables a researcher to process methods and make decisions. By "research stance," I mean something like a "position" relative to issues like purposes, goals, and methods for research. In other words, one's stance as a researcher is an answer to these questions:

- researcher identity. Who am I personally? as a researcher? in relation to my discipline?

- purposes as a researcher. Why research?

- questions of power and ethics. What are my commitments with respect to research?

A research methodology doesn't answer these questions. Neither does ideology. Or ethics. But in articulating a stance, a researcher draws on these ways of thinking about research to create a position that researchers must develop in order to make wise decisions throughout a research process. A stance can help researchers drop a plumb line through the mess of research itself, providing guidance for decision making and even for tracking when and how one's stance changes. It might be useful to think that a stance precedes choices regarding methods. This is true when researchers have a sense of who they are and why they are researching before forging ahead. The relationship between stance and method is interactive. recursive, and framed, ultimately, by the larger theory of research at

If we reflect on CBR as a set of methodological approaches for studying writing in communities, we have at our disposal some tools for creating stances as community-based researchers. As I have presented CBR, constructing community as a research outcome and the importance of relationships to research practice are key methodological issues. But there are other important aspects of CBR: the preference for action and change as an outcome, privileging local and participant knowledge, and the value of "usefulness." Taken together, these methodological tools can serve as a heuristic for researchers as they figure out who they are as community-based researchers—their stance.[11] Let me close with a scenario that might illustrate how a stance works as a tool and why it can be productive.

Two summers ago, the community in which I live was afflicted by a series of killings. Some were located in an engaging and dynamic area of town where I had worked in the past. In the newspaper, I saw a story about a "take back the neighborhood" march that took place in that area of town, and I suspected that the director of a community organization in that area was not happy about this march. This organization facilitates community activities across a number of neighborhoods. It is a highly functional organization, and its director is a force in the community. When I called the director later that week to ask her about the march, she was indeed unhappy and told me that taking back the neighborhood wasn't necessary. It was never lost.

We discussed the role of communication in this situation and the fragility of community identity. What takes years to assemble can be destroyed in one summer. We had worked together a number of times in the past and so began to discuss what to do about this situation. How could her organization get better at creating and communicating identities? How could they leverage advanced information technologies for both the creation and delivery of messages? These are genuine questions. However, they do not necessarily require research to answer them. This is an important point. As an expert on communication, I could simply share my answers to these questions based on best practices and conventional wisdom. The decision to research is based, significantly, on how my stance informs that decision: Who am I as a researcher, what are my commitments, why research, and given answers to these questions, how might I assemble a project with my partners?

A number of elements in place in this scene make CBR possible. The most obvious issue, perhaps, is the relationship between me (and my university) and the director of that organization. Past work together is why I could call her and have this conversation and why she could have called me as well. These past relationships are clearly important, but even more important is the value of *maintaining* that relationship through new, shared work (a key part of my stance). If maintaining the relationship is a priority, then many decisions during a research process will be informed by this principle. Indeed, good research relationships are productive. They generate data, enhance understanding, and increase the likelihood of useful solutions. My point is that even the decision to research is shaped by who we are as researchers, a researcher identity that is a function of a stance. Think of how differently this scenario plays out if we decide in advance of the inquiry that because we are a "qualitative researcher" or an "ethnographer" or something else, then we must enter the research scene by leading with our disciplines, our politics, or our methods. Instead, we lead with something much more subtle. Given the CBR stance that I have articulated here, we should *follow* with methods—with decisions about method choice and practice—because we cannot know, yet, which tools of collection and analysis are best for the given problems, people, and scenes at hand. And here we arrive at my argument: to research writing in communities, we must assemble our studies slowly, carefully, and based on an understanding of who we are as researchers and what it means to research, informed by issues that distinguish CBR from other methodologies. The key difference between CBR and other forms of research is that in this methodological approach, stance can make the difference between effective and ineffective inquiries. While I believe that stance is integral to all research practice, given a conscious CBR stance, it is possible to think about the best methods for constructing a community anew for each project, privileging action and change as outcomes, and valuing user (or local) knowledge—all important community-based research values.

The more that I struggle with research—and research seems to become more difficult the more that I do it—the more I realize that the truly difficult issues are rarely discussed. Our methodological literature is too well defined, too clean, too well lit. The stories we tell each other are difficult for me to square with experience. We can only learn how to do research by researching, and it is in those moments of learning that we come to understand, I believe, that issues like practice and stance are critical. With community-based research in particular, what distinguishes this approach to inquiry is not what we commonly discuss but rather what we rarely discuss: in this case, issues of stance. To be a community-based researcher means to adopt a particular identity as a researcher within this methodological approach. It means to construct a methodology around a set of obligations and commitments and to then practice that research with some thoughtfulness and care. It means, significantly, that community itself remains a central problem for our research.

Notes

1. I use the term *approach* deliberately in this chapter. *Approach* names a collection of associated methodologies. This allows a more limited use for "methods." As discussed in this chapter, we don't have a good shared methodological language, which means, for instance, that we write far too monolithically about methods as if methods (a) tell us how to research and (b) contain within them all the tools and issues that we need for research. I understand methods to be a much-smaller concept and as merely one of many concepts important to research methodology.

2. For more on practices, see Grabill, "Study."

3. Think here of research approaches that have strong ideological consistencies but have very different uses of methods or are practiced quite differently. These approaches might be said to have strong methodology commonalities, but in saying so, we are noting meaningful differences. See also note 1.

4. See, for instance, Stoecker. For more-detailed reviews of community-based research in other places, which might interest readers, see Grabill, "Community Computing"; Grabill, *Writing Community Change.*

5. My treatment here glosses over distinctions within and between action research and participatory action research, and for many, these distinctions are deep and meaningful. Stoecker, for instance, argues that action research is animated by a "functionalist" sociological tradition that values stability, cooperation, and a resistance to challenging existing structures and relationships. Participatory action research, in contrast, is animated by the tradition of "conflict theory" and therefore is interested in challenging existing systems and driving change.

6. This is another instance in which disciplines matter. Colleagues in other disciplines at Michigan State University do truly excellent community-based research that would not be understood as research "with" communities. But it is work that is of the highest quality with respect to their disciplinary traditions. It is also productive for their community partners.

7. In my experience, community partners rarely participate deeply and across the practices of a project. They are busy people with more work than they can do without participating in my work. We coordinate, we partner, and sometimes we collaborate. As a less-experienced researcher, I used to worry that my own practices did not measure up to the idealized practices articulated in methodological literatures. This is a useful worry. But I also think it is important to provide more-nuanced accounts of research practice so that we can become vigilant but not anxious researchers.

8. See Grabill, Writing Community Change.

9. See Grabill, "Study of Writing."

10. See Monberg on dwelling.

11. By "heuristic," I mean a thinking technology. This discussion is intended as a tool to help researchers think about what their stance might look like.

Works Cited

Blythe, Stuart, Jeffrey T. Grabill, and Kirk Riley. "Action Research and Wicked Environmental Problems: Exploring Appropriate Roles for Researchers in Professional Communication." *Journal of Business and Technical Communication* 22 (2008): 272–98. Print.

Grabill, Jeffrey T. "Community Computing and Citizen Productivity." *Computers and Composition* 20 (2003): 131–50. Print.

——. "The Study of Writing in the Social Factory: Methodology and Rhetorical Agency. *Cultural Studies Approaches to Technical Communication.* Ed. Blake Scott, Bernadette Longo, and Katherine V. Wills. Albany: State U of New York P, 2006. 151–69. Print.

——. *Writing Community Change: Designing Technologies for Citizen Action.* New York: Hampton, 2007. Print.

Monberg, Terese Guinsatao. "Writing Home or as the Community: Toward a Theory of Recursive Spatial Movement for Students of Color in Service-Learning Courses." *Reflections* 8.3 (2009): 21–51. Print.

Schafft, Kai A., and Davydd J. Greenwood. "Promises and Dilemmas of Participation: Action Research, Search Conference Methodology, and Community Development." *Journal of the Community Development Society* 34, no. 1 (2003):18–35. doi:10.1080/15575330309490101. Print.

Stoecker, Randy. "Creative Tensions in the New Community Based Research." *Researching with Communities: Grounded Perspectives on Communities in Research.* Ed. Andy Williamson and Ruth DeSouza. Auckland: Muddy Creek, 2007. 7–24. Print.

Sullivan, Patricia, and James Porter. *Opening Spaces: Writing Technologies and Critical Research Practices.* Westport, CT: Ablex, 1997. Print.

17.

Conducting Writing Research Internationally

Karen J. Lunsford

When I was attending graduate school in English/writing studies at the University of Illinois at Urbana-Champaign, I never imagined that I would become involved with research on writing in international venues. After all, I was not specializing in English as a second or foreign language (as the field was then called). And while I was intrigued by contrastive rhetoric—a field that compares writing traits and argumentative patterns across cultures—I was not focused on it. Instead, I was specializing in writing across the curriculum (WAC) and writing in the disciplines (WID). At the time, WAC and WID seemed to me to be defined primarily in relation to first-year composition, as campus writing initiatives that extend writing instruction beyond the first-year writing course. Although I had read theory and studies by scholars outside of the United States, I did not consider myself as belonging to an international scholarly community.

Since then, that sense has changed as I have pursued my career at the University of California Santa Barbara (UCSB). Thankfully, sponsors such as Chuck Bazerman and Susan McLeod introduced me to their writing contacts in Brazil, Mexico, Bhutan, China, England, Norway, and Australia. In the past eight years, too, UCSB has hosted three international conferences dedicated to writing research. The Writing Research Across Borders (WRAB) conference in 2008 welcomed 650 participants from 32 countries. Out of the conference grew an edited collection of writing research that documents a recent and significant worldwide uptick in research on writing and writing instruction (Bazerman et al.). It appears that the first decade of the twenty-first century has seen global shifts in the exigencies for writing research, including shifts in the student populations that now attend postsecondary institutions, in publication practices for academic journals, and in educational reforms. Moreover, both the conference and the collection suggest that writing scholars today are looking beyond their national and disciplinary borders to create extensive professional networks. In short, just as previous decades were characterized by the "rhetorical turn" and the "cultural turn" in academia, the opening of the twenty-first century appears to have ushered in an incipient "international turn" in writing studies.

This chapter reflects on my own initiation into two international writing research projects centered at the University of Bergen, Norway (Universitetet i Bergen, or UiB). I have asked myself, "What does it mean to conduct writing research internationally?" and I have come to two different answers. The first project, a team effort to launch WAC/WID initiatives at UiB, illustrates the challenges in conveying concepts to colleagues when conducting research across national and disciplinary boundaries. The second project, my own imported study on science writing, suggests how vital it is for twenty-first-century writing scholars in all subfields to design projects in dialogue with international audiences. Together, both projects illustrate that to conduct writing research internationally is to become aware of tacit assumptions embedded in one's own academic background and preferred research methods. They further illustrate that scholars must continually reenvision those assumptions in light of the world's diverse research traditions, political agendas, and local contexts that shape approaches to writing. Before discussing the projects' differences, therefore, let me suggest that twenty-first-century writing scholars must consciously practice a new researcher role: the information broker.

Laying the Groundwork: Writing Researchers as Information Brokers

As a writing researcher, I have employed a range of quantitative and qualitative methods. In these projects, I have adopted different roles. At times, I have been a novice statistician, an interviewer, a participant observer, and an interface designer. In taking up international writing research, I initially imagined that I would be an ethnographer—and an outdated version of an ethnographer at that, an objective outsider who studies "other" cultures. As the next sections show, I do employ qualitative techniques found in ethnographies, especially interviews. However, as I worked with international colleagues to cross cultural boundaries and to find connections among our varied experiences with writing studies, I soon realized that my researcher role was quite different. More often than not, an international writing researcher is an information broker.

A *broker* is a concept from social-network analysis, a methodology that is used to study how people interact with each other. Social-network analysts define a social network by tracking who communicates with whom, about what, how often, and for what motives (e.g., assisting each other, companionship (Haythornthwaite 160). Typically, a social network will have distinct pairs or clusters of people who often interact with each other. In a business, for example, these clusters might be different work teams or departments. An information broker is an individual who has contacts with more than one cluster; he or she controls the flow of information from one part of the network to another (Haythornthwaite 177). The broker's ties with other network members may be stronger or weaker, depending on the number and quality of interactions. One of the broker's functions may be to translate materials among the clusters— sometimes literally translating from one language to another but more often recasting or explaining materials according to a cluster's viewpoints. For example, in an engineering firm, an information broker might be the technical writer of an engineering design team who is also responsible for conveying the team's plans to the firm's advertising department. Similarly, Theresa Lillis and Mary Jane Curry have reported on the wide variety of "literacy brokers," both professional (e.g., academics in a specific field, copy editors) and nonprofessional (e.g., friends), who assist nonnative speakers with writing academic articles in formal English. The broker maintains contacts with the clusters and may enable (or, in some cases, deter) connections among other members.

Information brokers are needed as writing studies becomes an international movement because, inevitably, building professional research networks across national boundaries also means crossing disciplinary boundaries. Writing can, and has been, defined in diverse ways at different times and places: as an "artifact, an individual capacity to act, a situated activity, a technology, or a mode of social organization" (Prior and Lunsford 82). Given the range of definitions, it is not surprising that different academic communities have emphasized distinct aspects of writing for instruction and research. These distinctions among different academic communities have been further sharpened as they have been institutionalized as academic departments in different geographical regions. In the United States, writing research has been primarily identified with English departments or (now) independent rhetoric or writing programs. In Europe and Australia, the departmental homes for writing research typically have been applied linguistics or cognitive psychology. In mainland China, the discipline is called writingology (Chen). In Latin America, writing research is often carried out under the auspices of writing centers, which are akin to independent research centers in the United States funded by national grants (e.g., the National Science Foundation) and may or may not have anything to do with providing student assistance. Globally, too, researchers have variously configured the relationships between college writing and primary- or secondary-school writing, and so the influence of education departments on writing studies also varies. Not least, the advent of new media literacies has also brought about new clusters of writing research in diverse departments, especially communications and new media.

These institutionalized divisions among the disciplines have had profound effects, particularly on opportunities for writing researchers to have access to information about each other's work. The departmental bureaucracies for promotion and tenure tend to reward scholars for adhering to a relatively narrow range of assumptions about which research questions ought to be asked and what research methods should be employed (Klein). Those assumptions are further reinforced as researchers publish in approved venues and attend conferences that target like-minded academics. To attend a conference outside of one's field takes extra effort, even more so if that conference is in another geographical region. For example, researchers worldwide were drawn to our interdisciplinary WRAB conference; however, several experienced difficulties in obtaining visas, despite starting the process months in advance. Even listservs and other electronic networking services tend to attract researchers from relatively narrow communities.

Adding to these disciplinary divisions is the fact that writing research often engages with writing instruction. Because writing instruction depends on specific institutional contexts, local pedagogies, and political mores, it may be difficult to see why research in one setting is relevant for scholars in another. And, from an international perspective, there are profound differences inherent in the U.S. branch of writing studies—most of all, its deep interest in first-year composition. Simply put, the first-year, campuswide, general-education composition course does not exist in most college/university systems worldwide. As I found myself explaining to WRAB conference attendees, the U.S. system favors a core liberal arts curriculum, often two years' worth of compulsory courses. In contrast, many countries' systems, especially those in Asia and Europe, may require more time in secondary school, and they typically track their college/university students more directly into majors and professions. The compulsory, general writing course, moreover, is the legacy of a U.S. institution, the English A course initiated in 1885 at Harvard University (Connors). That legacy has been powerful: Currently, there are over four thousand institutions of higher learning in the United

US → deep interest in FYC

States, and most have followed Harvard's lead. Consequently, each year, thousands of students take at least one early course focused on writing. For our international colleagues, the sheer number of students in U.S. writing courses sufficiently justifies why much U.S. scholarship has been concerned with aligning students' writing needs, academic requirements, and the purposes of an entry-level course.

That said, my own shift towards actively participating in international research projects parallels recent, broader movements in the United States. These movements have sought to expand the foci of writing studies by considering writing as a lifelong activity and by fostering new methods for empirical studies that are replicable, aggregable, and data-supported (Haswell). To be sure, there have been exchanges among international communities in the past, as when expressivist pedagogies in the United States drew upon the work of British scholars. However, the 1990s in the United States saw a wave called the new abolitionism (Connors) that sought to redefine the field by arguing that the required first-year composition course ought to be replaced with self-selected courses, writing centers, and a much more extensive use of WAC/WID initiatives. This increased attention to WAC/WID has aligned well with educational systems in other countries, which have variously integrated writing instruction within their degree programs. The challenge has been to identify the worldwide initiatives, for *WAC* and *WID* are U.S. terms. In 2006, Christopher Thaiss, Tara Porter, and Erin Steinke undertook the task of mapping these initiatives across the globe and surveying scholars associated with them, a study that is still in progress.

Only now, then, is a global network formally being identified to enable writing researchers to compare their experiences and to begin to consolidate their expertise. To a large extent, current academic networks are still informal. In my own case, the connection was first made over portfolios. As governments worldwide pressure educational institutions to provide measures of accountability, writing researchers have been seeking alternatives to high-stakes timed testing and have been recommending portfolio systems. In the past five years, for instance, the Norwegian government was convinced to mandate portfolio assessments for all seven public, full universities, with implications for another forty or so institutions (professional schools and "university-colleges" that have more-limited degree offerings). As this mandate was initiated, Professor Olga Dysthe was a visiting Norwegian writing scholar at UCSB. She conducted library research and queried her U.S. colleagues intensely about what defines a portfolio. Until she began questioning me, for example,

I had not considered fully the role of the reflective cover letter in distinguishing a portfolio from a mere collection of student texts. Olga and her colleagues went on to document multiple types of portfolios, and she tracked what happened when Norwegian faculty across the disciplines began to require them (Dysthe, Engelsen, and Lima). I have since used her definitive work to justify my own proposals to UCSB administrators to implement digital portfolios. In these brief exchanges, we were both information brokers, shuttling knowledge from one locale to the other. It was Olga's visit and her subsequent invitation to me to work on a grant with her at UiB that led me to become involved more extensively with two research projects centered in Norway.

Implementing a WAC/WID Initiative: A Cooperative Project

Since 2007, I have spent part of my summers engaged in a multiyear initiative at Bergen. I have been asked to model writing workshops for faculty and advanced (primarily master's) students in the humanities and the biological sciences divisions. In addition, I am a research consultant and partner, advising faculty on how to assess the impact of increased writing instruction. As an information broker in this research network, I have relied upon two well-known qualitative strategies to respond to the challenges of relaying concepts across our different cultures and research traditions: discourse analysis and defamiliarization.

The initial discourse challenge found me somewhat prepared because I had lived earlier in Europe, and those experiences had reminded me that histories are implicated within vocabulary terms. In this first case, the term was *collaboration*, a common topic in my scholarship. I knew that although Europeans also discuss *collaboration*, I could anticipate that terms such as *cooperative* or *partnership* might be preferred. Norwegians, among others, remember being occupied by Germany in World War II, when a "collaborator" was an informant to the Nazi regime. Still, the next challenge, a request for a faculty workshop, took me aback: Would I please address the red thread of writing instruction?

Red thread? Some rapid Googling told me that "the red thread" can be found in Chinese fairytales implying that disparate people and events are linked by an invisible-to-humans red thread of fate. Norwegian friends also added that a red thread might mark the correct pathway through a labyrinth, or it might be the most important string to find running across a tapestry, or it might be an extra thread twined into rope to identify the coils officially approved for use by the navy. But what would the red thread of writing instruction be?

To analyze why the metaphor was being used in this context, I deliberately began including it in my conversations with faculty to test when I was using it appropriately, and I asked them directly to reflect on the term. Faculty members' responses began to piece together an answer, as they referred to a process seemingly far removed from the concerns of writing instructors. In 1999, some two dozen nations in Europe and Scandinavia had come together to sign a bureaucratic agreement called the Bologna Declaration (or the Bologna Accord). The nations agreed to align their university degree requirements and their grade transcripts so that students could transfer more easily from one institution to another; there are currently over forty signatory nations. This massive bureaucratic reorganization provided the exigency for introducing other educational reforms, particularly increased requirements for student writing. Norwegian faculty, concerned about student performance, were seeking a more coherent writing curriculum. For these faculty, then, tracing the red thread of writing instruction meant linking students' experiences with writing both horizontally (across the classes they were taking in a particular year) and vertically (across the bachelor's degree through the higher degrees).

Once I had conducted this discourse analysis, I found myself as an information broker between two cultures both adopting and resisting the metaphor. On one hand, the faculty and I could identify opportunities for coordinating a sequence of writing assignments that built upon one another, both within and across classes. On the other hand, the metaphor felt to me decidedly teleological, suggesting that if only we could find the correct curricular sequence, students would write flawlessly. In my workshops, then, I emphasized the often recursive, "tangled" nature of writing processes.

Given my personal history and academic training, terms such as *collaborator* and *red thread* were highly visible as needing such analysis. More difficult were the assumptions that were tacit, the terms that I assumed were familiar and shared. Several moments reminded me to defamiliarize them, to see the familiar as strange. For instance, in talking with students and faculty about written arguments, I suddenly realized that some did not recognize the term *topic sentence*, even when translated. Similar issues have been reported by Christopher Thaiss in translating his questionnaires into many languages for the worldwide survey of WAC/WID initiatives: The writing concepts do not necessarily convert. Likewise, researchers tend to assume that they are referring to the same thing when they talk about methods. For example, I suggested to writing researchers situated within a psychology/education department that we might initiate a longitudinal study to learn how students respond to writing feedback. It took some time before we realized we were assuming different definitions for a study. I had assumed that it would be naturalistic (that we would observe techniques already being performed by teachers), and they had assumed that a study must contain both a control group and a trial group. Such incidents are common for multidisciplinary research teams, as studies on organizations have shown (Haythornthwaite, Lunsford, Bowker, and Bruce). The person best situated to realize that team members are speaking from different cultural or disciplinary perspectives tends to be the information broker.

The practice of defamiliarization also applies to the material conditions under which research is conducted. Tacit assumptions are embedded within technologies; for example, they determine which team members will be allowed access to an institution's course-management systems. They are embedded in the rhythms of the academic year, with coordination issues arising when team members' term lengths and holidays differ. They are embedded within institutional regulations, such as those that govern research with human participants. When tacit assumptions such as these are not recognized but are included in the research plans, they can delay or even derail projects. To succeed in working on a cooperative project, then, writing researchers need to develop checklists for areas of potential trouble. Aside from checklists, a willingness to embrace ambiguity in international projects has been helpful to me—for along with the ambiguity brought about by differences in languages and disciplines comes opportunity.

Studying Distributed Scientific Publication Systems

In the WAC/WID project, conducting research internationally has meant coordinating a large project with writing-research colleagues in another nation, and my role as an information broker has been emphasized because I was recruited explicitly as a consultant. However, I am also beginning to play a broker role when I conduct my own research projects. As mentioned earlier, one issue highlighted by the WRAB conference is that writing researchers worldwide are situated within different disciplines and contexts, and thus they have tended to be ignorant of each other's work. Writing-research problems and the theories that frame them are informed by distinct contexts, and they often are not in dialogue with other disciplinary or regional findings. By expanding my research networks into a new (to me) environment at UiB, I have been reminded to take into account perspectives that make my research richer and more relevant to a wider audience.

While at Bergen, I have expanded a project begun at UCSB. I have been studying how scientists construct their arguments across multiple online venues, or what I call *distributed publication systems* (see "Remediating"). For instance, a scientist may be required to submit not only a journal article (published in both a print and an online version) but also data to the field's central database, such as a genome database. By interviewing scientists located at UiB, I have become aware of an aspect of my research that I had not anticipated from consulting previous scholarship.

According to much scholarship on science writing and "impact factors," English has become the lingua franca of science (e.g., Cronin). The impact factor of a journal is determined by its citation record from the past two years, a formula that divides the number of citations the journal has received by the number of articles in those volumes. The highest-impact journals are those available in electronic formats and published primarily in English. As a result, one issue to study is how scientific English is becoming standardized. For example, many scientific journals have adopted "structured abstracts," which provide sentence-by-sentence templates to instruct contributing authors on how to write their abstracts. These standardized templates assist professionals for whom English is a nonnative language, and they ensure that the finished abstracts conform to a format that allows computer search engines to locate information more efficiently. In my own work, I have been interested in thinking about how such standards affect how scientific information is distributed online.

What I (and others) have overlooked, though, is that despite the impact of English publications, scientific materials are still widely distributed across not only media but also languages. Research on scientific writing cannot focus on just English materials but must take into account the effects of multiple, simultaneous translations. The Norwegian scientists I interviewed particularly emphasized this issue because problems of translation are inherent to their language. The history of their writing systems is unique. For over four hundred years (1380–1814), Norway was united with Denmark, and the written language was Danish. When the countries separated, the question became what language to use. Since then two written languages have evolved, neither of which is entirely congruent with any of the several spoken Norwegian dialects. One written language reflects Danish orthography (Bokmål); the other was artificially constructed by a linguist who converted elements taken from the various spoken dialects into a written form, Nynorsk. Both written languages are currently official. Norwegian writers, especially academics, routinely translate their writing from one form to another, in addition to translating their texts into other languages. Norwegian scientists, then, might expect to distribute their materials in a spoken dialect, in two native written forms, as well as in English.

For me, the consequence of these interviews was to make me more conscious of my responsibility to all of the clusters in my international research network. On one hand, as I develop my current research project, I will draw upon the Norwegian research in translation/writing studies and the scientists' experiences to complicate the notion that English is science's lingua franca, an assumption that prevails within the U.S. research communities that I know. On the other hand, I also need to draw upon an extensive WAC/WID experience in the United States to develop pertinent materials for the UiB context. The most common question I have received in the WAC/WID workshops, especially from graduate and postdoctoral students in the sciences, is how to coordinate writing multiple drafts of texts in multiple languages. As an instructor and researcher, I am still developing answers to that question, just as I am still adjusting my theory of distributed publication systems to take into account issues of translation.

Conclusion

I am excited to be living in this moment of writing studies history. In the three decades before 2000, writing researchers witnessed the emergence of strong, independent writing-research communities within different academic departments around the globe. Now, as the twenty-first century moves through its second decade, we are seeing a concerted effort to link these distinct research communities into a more consolidated, international movement. Writing comprises such a range of activities and practices, all differently constituted within local contexts, that we need multiple perspectives and methods to understand them. Not only will conducting writing research internationally entail working flexibly across disciplines and departments but it will also involve delving deeply into the historical, social, and political contexts that have shaped writing instruction worldwide. I confess to feeling somewhat overwhelmed at times as I contemplate how many studies I may need to read from research communities I am still discovering. Yet, that feeling subsides when I remember to converse with colleagues in this larger network: researchers who point out relevant materials, who help coordinate cooperative studies across national boundaries, who engage in dialogues with multiple communities, who meet the challenges of encountering new discourses and tacit assumptions, and who share their own experiences freely. Such activities define an information broker, a role vital to the success of today's scholarship.

Works Cited

Bazerman, Charles, Robert Krut, Karen J. Lunsford, Susan H. McLeod, Suzie Null, Paul Rogers, and Amanda Stansell. Preface. Bazerman et al., *Traditions of Writing Research* ix–xi.

——, eds. *Traditions of Writing Research*. New York: Routledge, 2009. Print.

Chen, Huijun. "Modern 'Writingology' in China." Bazerman et al., *Traditions of Writing Research* 3–16.

Connors, Robert. "The Abolition Debate in Composition: A Short History." *Composition in the Twenty-First Century: Crisis and Change*. Ed. Lynn Z. Bloom, Donald A. Daiker, and Edward M. White. Carbondale: Southern Illinois UP, 1997. 47–63. Print.

Cronin, Blaise. *The Hand of Science: Academic Writing and Its Rewards*. Lanham: Scarecrow, 2005. Print.

Dysthe, Olga, Knut Steinar Engelsen, and Ivar Lima. "Variations in Portfolio Assessment in Higher Education: Discussion of Quality Issues Based on a Norwegian Survey across Institutions and Disciplines." *Assessing Writing* 12.2 (2007): 129–48. Print.

Haswell, Richard H. "NCTE/CCCC's Recent War on Scholarship." *Written Communication* 22.2 (2005): 198–223. Print.

Haythornthwaite, Caroline. "Building Social Networks Via Computer Networks: Creating and Sustaining Distributed Learning Communities." *Building Virtual Communities: Learning and Change in Cyberspace*. Ed. K. Ann Renninger and Wesley Shumar. Cambridge: Cambridge University Press, 2002. 159–90. Print.

Haythornthwaite, Caroline, Karen J. Lunsford, Geoffrey C. Bowker, and Bertram C. (Chip) Bruce. "Challenges for Research and Practice in Distributed, Interdisciplinary Collaboration." *New Infrastructures for Knowledge Production: Understanding E-Science*. Ed. Christine Hine. Hershey: Idea, 2006. 143–66. Print.

Klein, Julie Thompson. *Crossing Boundaries: Knowledge, Disciplinarities, and Interdisciplinarities*. Charlottesville: UP of Virginia, 1996. Print.

Lillis, Theresa, and Mary Jane Curry. "Professional Academic Writing by Multilingual Scholars: Interactions with Literacy Brokers in the Production of English-Medium Texts." *Written Communication* 23.1 (2006): 3-35. Print.

Lunsford, Karen J. "Remediating Science: A Case Study of Socialization." *Re-mediating and Re-situating the Canons: A Cultural-Historical Remapping of Rhetorical Activity*. Ed. Paul A. Prior, Janine Solberg, Patrick Berry, Hannah Bellwoar, Bill Chewning, Lunsford, Liz Rohan, Kevin Roozen, Mary P. Sheridan-Rabideau, Jody Shipka, Derek van Ittersum, and Joyce Walker. *Kairos* 11.3 (2007). Web. <http://kairos.technorhetoric.net/11.3/index.html>.

Prior, Paul A., and Karen J. Lunsford. "History of Reflection and Research on Writing." *Handbook of Research on Writing: History, Society, School, Individual, Text*. Ed. Charles Bazerman. Mahwah: Erlbaum, 2007. 81–96. Print.

Thaiss, Christopher. "The International WAC/WID Mapping Project: Objectives, Methods, Early Results." Bazerman et al., *Traditions of Writing Research* 251–64.

Thaiss, Christopher, Tara Porter, and Erin Steinke. "The International WAC/WID Mapping Project." *University of California*. 2008. Web. 1 July 2009. <http://mappingproject.ucdavis.edu>.

18.

The Role of Activity Analysis in Writing Research: Case Studies of Emerging Scholarly Communities

Mike Palmquist, Joan Mullin, and Glenn Blalock

In this chapter, we reflect on the use of activity analysis to support scholarly inquiry in composition studies. Characterized by Flower as an extension of activity theory (Leontiev, "Genesis of Activity"; Engeström, "Activity Theory"), activity analysis provides a set of tools for "studying the nature of learning and knowledge making" (241–42), areas of particular interest to scholars in composition studies.

To illustrate its utility as an interpretive framework, we use activity analysis to study efforts to develop and maintain three websites that support scholarly work in composition studies: the WAC Clearinghouse, CompPile, and REx (the Research Exchange Index).[1] Our analysis shows how activity analysis can be used to understand how these sites—individually and as an emergent collective—serve as foci for and extensions of efforts to form communities of writing scholars. In our analysis, we address the impetus for the development of the sites, the challenges—or problematics—faced by the initial developers, and the challenges faced and strategies employed to expand the respective communities of scholars involved in their development and their use. The chapter concludes with our reflections on both the use of activity analysis as an interpretive framework within composition studies and the potential role community-developed, web-based digital tools might play in supporting scholarly practices.

Activity, Community, and Tools

Activity analysis provides a framework within which we can understand the development of sites such as the WAC Clearinghouse, CompPile, and REx as "a coherent, stable, relatively long-term endeavor directed to an articulated or identifiable goal" (Barab, Evans, and Baek 204).[2] Our analysis of these sites, like other work in this area over the past decade, follows Yrjö Engeström's elaboration of Aleksei Nikolaevich Leontiev's theories of activity.[3] Unlike Lev Vygotsky, whose work in activity theory focuses largely on the individual (or subject) engaged in activity, Engeström presents a more complex model of interaction among subjects, tools, and community, involving objects, outcomes, rules, contradictions, and division of labor (see fig. 18.1). A key feature of Engeström's treatment of activity theory is its ability to accommodate the activities and motives of participants whose relationships to each other are not immediately obvious.

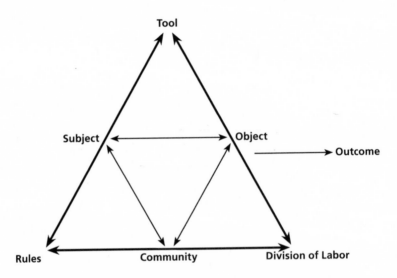

Fig. 18.1. Engeström's model of activity theory.

The development of the websites we consider within the interpretive framework of activity theory can be seen as a form of tool development (Leontiev, "Genesis of Activity"). The work of establishing and maintaining the sites, both individually and as a set of tools within a larger activity system (e.g., scholarly work within composition studies), can be understood as a sustained effort to adapt the sites to the needs of researchers and teachers in composition studies as well as teachers from outside the field who use writing in their courses. Development of the sites can also be understood as activity in relation to other systems (e.g., universities and professional organizations), which pursue related (and sometimes nested) goals: educating students, ensuring safe access to web-based instructional materials, or publishing scholarly work.

Within composition studies, the World Wide Web serves not only as a means of disseminating and archiving scholarly work but also as a focus for—and even an inducement to—community formation. Interrogating the role of the web in our scholarly work allows us to explore its impact on the field's communities of knowledge and practice. In particular, it allows us to consider the role of technology in shaping participation and roles within communities of knowledge and practice, its impact on our choices about how to share our work (both in progress and as finished products), and its effects on the roles we adopt regarding the formation and maintenance of scholarly communities. Interrogating our uses of the web also allows us to consider the design of the tools we create and use for these purposes and to reflect on how those tools affect access to and understanding of our scholarly work.

Sites of Research
WAC Clearinghouse

The WAC Clearinghouse can be understood as an activity system embedded within other, nested activity systems, including the larger Writing@ CSU website,[4] which supports writing instruction at Colorado State University and other institutions, the writing-across-the-curriculum (WAC) movement, and scholarly work within composition studies. Initially envisioned as a set of resources to support the WAC program at Colorado State University, the growing capabilities of the web made it clear that the planned site could also address the needs of teachers of writing at other institutions. Development of the site, which began in spring 1997, involved Bill Condon, Christine Hult, Linn Bekins, Nick Carbone, Gail E. Hawisher, Kate Kiefer, Donna LeCourt, Martin Rosenberg, Richard Selfe, and Mike Palmquist, among others. The site grew over more than a decade to the point where it has become a publisher of open-access academic journals and scholarly books as well as a home for an extensive collection of resources for the WAC community. It has also supported the development of related sites, such as REx, a site that is jointly supported by CompPile.[5]

As an activity system, the WAC Clearinghouse evolved from decisions made and actions taken by members of editorial boards of journals affiliated with the site, reviewers of work submitted for publication in the site's book series, the site's editor, visitors who decided to contribute content to the site, and the network specialists who established security practices at the university that hosts the site. Even as these groups and individuals form the "community" that makes possible and shapes the site, they do so through distributed labor that does not bring all members of the community into direct contact with one other. It is, however, because of their actions that members of the WAC Clearinghouse activity system give rise to useful contradictions that shape the direction of activity within the system.

For example, when contradictions arose in 1998 between the initial object of creating a comprehensive website for the WAC community and the rewards available to faculty involved in the development of the site, the Clearinghouse was radically restructured. In the face of what Condon later described as an inability to find ways to make work on a website count for purposes of merit evaluations (personal communication, 5 Mar. 1998), the site was relaunched in 2000 as *academic.writing*, a peer-reviewed online journal, and the collection of resources developed for the Clearinghouse was converted into a "related resources" section of the new journal. Members of the project team subsequently gained recognition for their work through peer-reviewed publications, editorial positions, and editorial-board memberships.

Over the next few years, the original vision of the Clearinghouse continued to shape the direction of the journal, to the point where *academic.writing* became home to the digital archives of two print journals (*Language and Learning across the Disciplines* and the *WAC Journal*) and one online journal (*Rhet-Net*) and provided access in digital format to out-of-print books. This gave rise, in turn, to another important contradiction. The dissonance produced by housing journals and book series within a journal, along with changes in the reward structures conditioning the work of the individuals involved with the site, led to the reemergence in 2002 of the WAC Clearinghouse as the container for the scholarly work that had been collected on the site.

The site subsequently became home to the International Network of Writing across the Curriculum Programs, launched four new books series, entered into partnerships with Parlor Press to distribute its digital books in print format, and reached an agreement with the National Council of Teachers of English (NCTE) to provide digital access to NCTE books and journal articles about WAC. A key element of its new instantiation was a reliance on a cooperative approach in which visitors to the site could contribute to the site's development by creating an account and adding information to the site's database. By the beginning of 2011, more than two thousand individuals had created accounts on the site, and the Clearinghouse had become the leading site supporting writing across the curriculum.

The reemergence of the WAC Clearinghouse name, and associated changes to the structure of the site, reshaped the understanding of community shared by the individuals working on the site. Over time, the small group of scholars involved in establishing the WAC Clearinghouse grew to include a large editorial board and staff for *academic.writing* and, later, the members of the editorial boards for affiliated journals; the publications board, reviewers, and editors of the books published on the site; the members of the consultants board for the International Network of Writing across the Curriculum Programs; the editors and members of REx; and the hundreds of Clearinghouse members who have added content to the site. As the number of individuals working on the site grew, the sense of community shared by the group as a whole diminished to the point where the editorial boards and staffs of publications associated with the Clearinghouse began to view themselves less as members of the larger community and more as members of smaller communities built around each publication. With this development in mind, the site was redesigned in 2011 to emphasize, visually and structurally, the interrelationships among the site's various publishing and resource activities (see fig. 18.2).

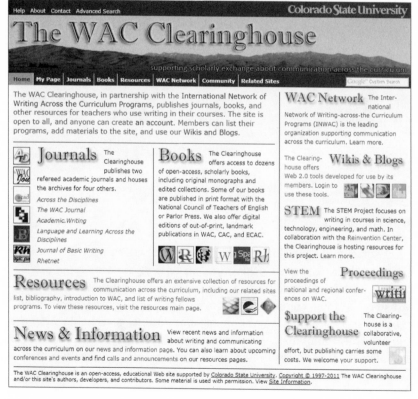

Fig. 18.2. Home page of the WAC Clearinghouse in 2011.

CompPile

CompPile offers another example of an activity system nested within the systems that constitute work in the field of composition studies. The site was envisioned in 2000 by Richard H. Haswell and Glenn Blalock as a searchable database of scholarly work published in composition studies between 1939 and 1999. Their goal was to develop a freely available and comprehensive (as opposed to a proprietary and selective) bibliographic database of work in composition studies. That goal was revised in 2005 to extend coverage to all work published in the field since 1939, and Comp-Pile is now the largest database covering postsecondary composition studies (see fig. 18.3).

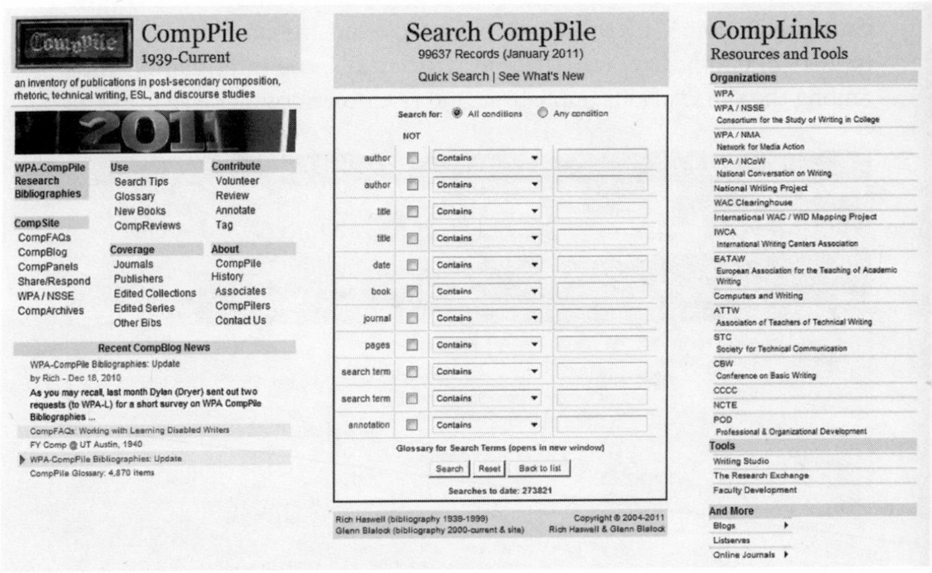

Fig. 18.3. Home page of CompPile.

The origins of CompPile can be traced to Haswell's review in *Assessing Writing* of Bruce Speck's *Grading Student Writing: An Annotated Bibliography.* Haswell lamented the lack of a "single bibliographic source that affords a respectable search for the literature of assessment and evaluation." Haswell advocated the development of an online, searchable database compiled and maintained by volunteers. He argued that, in comparison to disciplines that had already developed such systems, composition studies needed to have "respect, and use, for its own acquired knowledge" (138).

Viewed through the lens of activity analysis, CompPile was meant from its beginning to be both an object and an outcome of a community of scholars whose work would be governed by rules and a division of labor that were new to our field. Since its inception, CompPile's cofounders invited the professional community to contribute to the development and maintenance of the growing bibliographical database and to make it as useful and authoritative as possible. However, the roles of the community of CompPile users, the rules that govern their use, and the value system that determines the division of labor have not changed or expanded as they might have.

For example, of the current eighty-five-thousand-plus records dated 1939 through 1999, Haswell was responsible for locating and creating at least seventy-five thousand of them. During those early years, Haswell focused considerable time, effort, research stipends, and personal expense (travel to libraries and so on) to build the 1939–99 core bibliography. His investment and contributions serve as an important cautionary reminder of the numerous relationships between community building and the division of labor among community members. During these same years, Blalock was responsible for designing, building, implementing, and maintaining the database, its search tools, and the site itself. In other words, especially during the first five years of its development, CompPile was primarily the work of two individuals, a project serving a growing community of users but also a project looking for a community of contributors and participants in the ongoing project.

Although CompPile has become a valuable tool for the community, its implementation, growth, and maintenance have not been wildly successful examples of an activity system in which members of the community have fulfilled all of the available roles in anything nearing an even division of labor. In the activity system within which CompPile has been developed, the rules of the community do not encourage or value community participation in the kinds of work necessary to develop and maintain the project. In fact, until 2005 and to a lesser extent since then, CompPile illustrates the challenges of implementing and sustaining innovative and potentially transformative projects in the academy, as does REx.

REx

Like CompPile and the WAC Clearinghouse, the development of REx, the Research Exchange Index, reflects the need for new tools within the larger field of composition studies (see fig. 18.4). The site provides a response to a traditional publishing model that does not accommodate the needs of a significant number of scholars within composition studies, particularly those who wish to share and gain feedback on research more quickly than—and in many cases without the pressure accompanying—the established model of peer-reviewed publication in journals and monographs. In this sense, REx is a response to a contradiction in the larger activity system of composition studies, even as it can be viewed as an activity system in its own right, with division of labor, rules governing that labor, and tools such as web servers and coding languages that shape the development of the site. In that sense, it both challenges and supports the rules of the larger composition-studies community governing production and publication of scholarly work.[6]

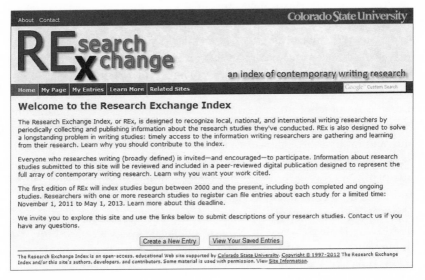

Fig. 18.4. REx home page.

The initial idea for the exchange was formulated in response to a roundtable at the 2006 Conference on College Composition and Communication entitled "Collaborating across Institutions" (Fishman et al.). Focused initially on the future of longitudinal research, members of the roundtable also addressed broader issues of mutual interest to panelists and audience members alike. Mullin, a member of the audience, noted that as program director at the University of Toledo, she had done research on an ad hoc basis, rather than as part of a formal study, "usually to prove a point—and often to save my program or get funding." Mullin pointed out that although the methodology and resulting data had value, "it was not worth my time to write up, or it would have been difficult to situate it in the research as expected for publication." She noted that many members of the Writing Center and WAC communities conducted this kind of ad hoc research frequently and that the field would not only benefit from viewing models of research others had used to solve similar institutional challenges to programs but also possibly be able to aggregate data from similar kinds of studies—if a venue could be found to distribute it.

Subsequent discussions brought the problem into clearer focus, resulting in the development of what would become REx. A community was already formed, a division of labor ensued, and what remained to be considered were the "rules." Initially developed as part of the WAC Clearinghouse website, where it was named the Research Exchange, it became an independent site in 2008. In 2011, it was renamed REx.

REx is envisioned as a site that combines the ethos of a wiki with a democratic accountability to and valuation by a peer group potentially wider than that of an edited journal. Created to gather reports about recent research and research-in-progress, it can be used as a metasource: a site on which data can be aggregated, where researchers can explore methodologies for new studies, and where students can see models of research in action and add to knowledge making.

While emerging from and creating a new community, REx drew on and deepened the partnership between the developers of CompPile and the WAC Clearinghouse. However, as with the other sites discussed here, a core group maintains the impetus for the site, and that group faces significant challenges as it works to create, maintain, and extend the community centered around the site.

Activity, Tools, and Community Revisited

Our analysis of these sites—their development and their use—has focused primarily on their potential as new tools for expanding our current sense of research, as an individual and community activity, and as a product used by and defining communities of knowledge and practice. However, our analysis of these sites has also revealed the challenges of realizing this potential, including especially the challenges of redefining (yet again) our "idea of community"—changing community value systems, community rules, and community understandings of appropriate division of labor in the activity system we might define as "research(ing)."

Tools

In the case of the websites discussed in this chapter, it is especially important to consider the role of tools in these activity systems. These tools include not only the technologies that support communication on the sites as well as knowledge production and dissemination but also language itself, which conditions activity and shapes the division of labor by members of an activity system. Characterized by Leontiev as "the vehicle of a certain method of action, and, moreover, a social method of action," tools can not only be used in the labor associated with an activity system but can also "become a goal toward which action is directed" ("Genesis" 66). In the case of work within composition studies, then, language becomes both a tool and an object of study.

Viewing the creation of the WAC Clearinghouse, CompPile, and REx as the creation of tools allows us to understand them as historically situated projects that produce outcomes that serve as tools in related activity systems. It is possible, as a result, not only to explore the creation of each of these sites as an activity system in and of itself but also to view each site as a collection of tools (e.g., as a bibliographic database, as a set of communication tools, as a set of scholarly publications, as a system for sharing scholarly work).

In a time when the tools used to share information are changing as rapidly as at any time in recorded history, the development of sites such as CompPile, the WAC Clearinghouse, and REx are best viewed as attempts to approximate the needs of members of the community, rather than as polished and potentially enduring projects. It seems likely, as a result, that these sites will continue to adapt and change in coming years. As the rewards systems shaping work in the field of composition studies continue to shift in response to the contradictions felt by members of the field, we are likely to see a greater willingness to recognize the dissemination of work outside the traditional academic publication apparatus. And as these changes in reward structures occur, it is likely that new tools will be developed to support that work. The most likely source of those tools are small groups of scholars who recognize the potential of new technologies and see ways to position their tools as having advantages over existing tools or of repurposing existing tools (or parts of existing tools) to achieve different outcomes.

The value of the activity perspective will become clear when scholars expand their perspective for tool development, recognizing the ways that an outcome of one activity system might be a tool in another system or that a problem in one system becomes the motivation/object for another system. In other words, activity systems can be seen as nested or chained, helping us to identify important relationships among the different parts of different systems. For example, CompPile was initially the outcome of an activity system that used new and established tools: web-based databases, search algorithms, and repurposed scholarly bibliographical strategies. Now CompPile is one tool that researchers can use to achieve outcomes previously difficult or impossible to achieve, the construction of new knowledge about composition or the possibility of a disciplinary glossary. We can say the same kinds of things about the WAC Clearinghouse and REx.

Communities

Although the "idea of community" has been challenged, revisited, and revised for at least twenty-five years, we continue to use the concept in ways that are imprecise and sometimes less than useful, especially as we consider how definitions can limit the ways we act as communities of scholars. Activity theory allows us to move beyond the notion of community fostered by theories based on the concept of discourse community.[7] Tom Deans observes:

> Activity theorists point out that the discourse community is generally imagined as a static, uniform, ahistorical thing or place (Prior 1998). One enters a discourse community, almost as one would enter a building. . . . Such a view calcifies the divide between outside and inside, between social context and individual behavior; it also assumes that context largely determines individual behavior. Using the discourse community as the main unit also masks the struggles and contradictions roiling within a community (Harris 1989). It steers our attention away from the dynamic interactions among various communities, it pays little attention to individual agency, and it offers no means for explaining how individuals or collectives change over time (Russell 1997). (292)

Analysis based on activity theory offers a useful lens for understanding the complex interactions, motives, and contradictions that arise over time as individuals form communities—and as those communities disband. Using activity analysis, the development of the WAC Clearinghouse, CompPile, and REx can be understood as an expression of the will of existing communities, communities whose members are seeking tools to support and share traditional scholarly work, and as a vehicle for emerging communities, whose members are seeking tools to support and share scholarly work in new ways. The motives informing the activity systems that resulted in the three sites can be viewed, in this sense, as arising from within the larger field of composition studies and as such are conditioned by contradictions perceived by members of these communities about their needs to produce and share work, the tools available to do so, and the rules conditioning the use of those tools. It is in the analysis we offer here that we can compare the public face of a community (as enacted in its practices, contexts, and theories) with the values of that community as articulated in the underlying activity system. These emerge as the community evolves through a series of negotiations, expressions of desires, and enactments that lead to the formation of new tools, new rules, new divisions of labor, and new communities.

Given the noted conservativism of the academy, at least when it comes to faculty governance and evaluation, it seems likely that departments of English, departments of writing studies, and independent composition programs will be slow to accept the value of scholarly work that is produced or distributed outside the traditional peer-review, print-based academic publishing structure. As a result, sites such as the Clearinghouse and CompPile, both of which operate to a large degree within that structure, are likely to experience greater success than a site such as REx, which departs from—and might even be understood as challenging—that structure. We view the long-term success of these projects, however, as less important than their role in the development of new tools for producing, distributing, and reviewing scholarly work in the field of composition studies and their role in enabling and supporting the formation of new communities, whose members will continue the innovative and transformative kinds of work that these three sites have pursued.

Notes

1. The websites are http://wac.colostate.edu, http://comppile.org, and http://researchexchange.colostate.edu, respectively.

2. For a more detailed example of the application of activity theory to a technology-supported writing initiative, and in particular for a consideration of the differences between Vygotsky's and Engeström's elaborations of Leontiev's work, see Palmquist, Kiefer, and Salahub.

3. See, for example, the essays in Bazerman and Russell's 2003 collection, *Writing Selves/Writing Societies*. See also Bazerman; Deans; Russell, all listed.

4. The Writing@CSU address is http://writing.colostate.edu.

5. For a more detailed history of the WAC Clearinghouse, see http://wac.colostate.edu/about/history.cfm.

6. For a more detailed history of REx, see http://researchexchange.colostate.edu/about/history.cfm.

7. See, for example, Bartholomae; Bizzel; Harris; Nystrand; Porter (*Audience and Rhetoric*, "Intertextuality"); and Swales. For overviews of discourse community theory, see Deans, "Shifting Locations, Genres, and Motives," and Kennedy, *Theorizing Composition*.

Works Cited

Barab, Sasha A., Michael A. Evans, and Eun-Ok Baek. "Activity Theory as a Lens for Characterizing the Participatory Unit." *Handbook of Research on Educational Communications and Technology.* Ed. David H. Jonassen. Mahwah: Erlbaum. 2004. 199–214. Print.

Bartholomae, David. "Inventing the University." *When a Writer Can't Write.* Ed. Mike Rose. New York: Guilford, 1985. 134–65. Print.

Bazerman, Charles. (2004). "Speech Acts, Genres, and Activity Systems: How Texts Organize Activity and People." *What Writing Does and How It Does It: An Introduction to Analyzing Texts and Textual Practices.* Ed. Charles Bazerman and Paul Prior. Mahwah: Erlbaum, 2004. 309–39. Print.

Bazerman, Charles, and David Russell, eds. "Writing Selves/Writing Societies: Research from Activity Perspectives." *WAC Clearinghouse.* 2003. Web. 12 Jan. 2011. <http://wac.colostate.edu/books/selves_societies/>.

Bizzel, Patricia. "Cognition, Convention, and Certainty: What We Need to Know about Writing." *Pre/Text* 3 (1982): 213–43. Print.

Council of Writing Program Administrators. "Thank You to Rich Haswell and Glenn Blalock for CompPile and CompFAQs." *Council of Writing Program Administrators.* 2006. Web. 12 Jan. 2011. <http://wpacouncil.org/ThnxCompPileCompFAQs>.

Deans, Tom. "Shifting Locations, Genres, and Motives: An Activity Theory Analysis of Service-Learning Writing Pedagogies." *The Location of Composition.* Ed. Christopher J. Keller and Christian R. Weisser. Albany: State U of New York P, 2007. 289–306. Print.

Engeström, Yrjö. "Activity Theory and Individual and Social Transformation." *Perspectives on Activity Theory.* Ed. Reijo Miettinen Engeström, and Raija Leena Punamäki. Cambridge: Cambridge UP, 1999. 19–38. Print.

———. *Learning by Expanding.* Helsinki: Orienta-Konsultit, 1999. Print.

Fishman, Jenn, LeeAnn Carroll, Smokey Wilson, Sally Barr Ebest, Stephen Wilhoit, Karen Paley, Doug Hesse, Andrea Lunsford, and Nancy Sommers. "Collaborating across Institutions: A Roundtable on Future Longitudinal Writing Research." Conference on College Composition and Communication. Palmer House Hilton, Chicago. 25 Mar. 2006. Panel presentation.

Flower, Linda. "Intercultural Knowledge Building: The Literate Action of a Community Think Tank." Bazerman and Russell, *Writing Selves/Society,* 239–79.

Harris, Joseph. "The Idea of Community in the Study of Writing." *College Composition and Communication* 40.1 (1989): 11–22. Print.

Haswell, Richard H. "Grading Student Writing." *Assessing Writing* 6.1 (1999): 133–38. Print.

Kennedy, Mary Lynch, ed. *Theorizing Composition: A Critical Sourcebook of Theory and Scholarship in Contemporary Composition Studies.* Westport: Greenwood, 2006. Print.

Leontiev, Alexei N. *Activity, Consciousness, and Personality.* Trans. Marie J. Hall. Hillsdale: Prentice-Hall, 1978. Print.

———. "The Genesis of Activity." *Journal of Russian and East European Psychology* 43.4 (2005): 58–71. Print.

Nystrand, Martin. *What Writers Know: The Language, Process, and Structure of*

Written Discourse. New York: Academic, 1982. Print.

Palmquist, Mike, Kate Kiefer, and Jill Salahub. "Sustaining (and Growing) a Pedagogical Writing Environment: An Activity Theory Analysis." *Technological Ecologies
and Sustainability: Methods, Modes, and Assessment.* Ed. Dànielle Nicole DeVoss,
Heidi A. McKee, and Richard (Dickie) Selfe. Logan, UT: Computers and Composition Digital Press, Utah State University Press, 2009. Web. 12 Jan. 2011. <http://
ccdigitalpress.org/ebooks-and-projects/tes>.

Porter, James. *Audience and Rhetoric: An Archaeological Composition of the Discourse Community.* Englewood Cliffs: Prentice Hall. 1992. Print.

——. "Intertextuality and the Discourse Community." *Rhetoric Review* 5 (1986):
34–47. Print.

Russell, David R. "Activity Theory and Its Implications for Writing Instruction."
Reconceiving Writing, Rethinking Writing Instruction. Ed. Joseph Petraglia. Hillsdale: Erlbaum, 1995. 51–78. Print.

——. "Activity Theory and Process Approaches: Writing (Power) in School, and
Society." *Post-Process Theory: Beyond the Writing Process Paradigm.* Ed. Thomas
Kent. Carbondale: Southern Illinois UP, 1999. 80–95. Print.

——. "Looking beyond the Interface: Activity Theory and Distributed Learning."
The Routledge Falmer Reader in Psychology of Education. Ed. Harry Daniels and
Anne Edwards. London: Routledge, 2004. 309–25. Print.

——. "Russian Activity Theory." *Theorizing Composition: A Critical Sourcebook of
Theory and Scholarship in Contemporary Composition Studies.* Ed. Mary Lynch
Kennedy. Westport: Greenwood, 1998. 265–68. Print.

Speck, Bruce. *Grading Student Writing: An Annotated Bibliography.* Santa Barbara:
Greenwood, 1998. Print.

Swales, John M. *Genre Analysis: English in Academic and Research Settings.* Cambridge: Cambridge UP, 1990. Print.

Vygotsky, Lev. *Mind in Culture.* Cambridge: Harvard UP, 1978. Print.

——. *Thought and Language.* Trans. Alex Kozulin. Cambridge: MIT P, 1986. Print.

19.

The Ethics of Conducting Writing Research on the Internet: How Heuristics Help

Heidi A. McKee and James E. Porter

With the amount and variety of writing on the Internet, especially on the World Wide Web, it is not surprising that rhetoric/composition researchers are doing more and more Internet-based research. The Internet is, after all, a writing space—and probably *the* principal writing space. From personal and corporate websites to blogs, discussion boards, and multimodal videos, from tweets and wall posts to text messages on mobile devices and chats in virtual worlds, people worldwide are writing online. And where there are writers, there are sure to be writing researchers.

Our view is that research on and with Internet technologies raises distinctive ethical questions, ones that are often quite different from what researchers would encounter doing traditional print-based textual scholarship or conducting person-based, face-to-face research. As more and more rhetoric/composition scholars shift to studying online writing, as the Internet and its supporting technologies (including mobile devices) continue to evolve, as new writing contexts and forms of writing continue to appear, researchers are likely to face significant ethical questions regarding their interactions with online writers and their use of online writing. For example, how does a researcher determine what is "public" versus "private" on the Internet? When should online information be considered as "text" and when as the communications of a "living person" for whom a different set of ethical considerations apply? Should an avatar in a virtual world such as *Second Life* be treated like a fictional character or like a person? When (and how) should researchers seek informed consent? How can researchers ethically and legally conduct research when the Internet spans so many geographical and cultural borders?

Underlying specific questions like these are even more fundamental questions: What are ethical practices for Internet research?[1] In the process of planning, conducting, and writing up research, what criteria and procedures should researchers use to guide their ethical decisions?

This chapter takes up some of these questions, offering a rhetorical, case-based approach for analyzing and, importantly, for *making* ethical decisions for Internet research. As a key component of our research, we interviewed Internet researchers from around the world and from a wide variety of disciplines who are studying diverse aspects of the Internet and Internet communications, including online writing. We do not have the space in this chapter to present this argument or its supporting theory and research in full.[2] But we do aim to provide here a general framework to help writing researchers identify and negotiate some of the sticky ethical issues they may encounter online.[3] We frame these issues as questions, and, as we hope our discussion makes clear, answering these questions is not always easy or, ultimately, the central ethical move. Rather, the process of how a researcher approaches such questions is key.

Bringing Ethical Issues to the Fore: Questions to Consider

Are you studying texts or persons or both?

This is *the* fundamental and first question for Internet researchers, shaping all ensuing ethical and methodological decisions. Some online digital writing clearly does operate according to print analogs—for example, articles at *Newsweek.com*, posts made by an academic blogger communicating with a public audience (e.g., Schrag). Quoting from texts like these is a clear paradigm decision—a researcher needs to consider copyright certainly but not issues of informed consent. In another clear-cut paradigm, some online research clearly falls in the realm of person-based studies, such as conducting in-world interviews with gamers. But much online-writing research raises the difficult question of whether a researcher is studying a text (and thus may quote as if using a book in the library) or online conversations, thus bringing ethical questions of person-based research to the fore. The ethical treatment of published texts and the ethical treatment of persons are at times divergent practices: A study of texts requires following guidelines and expectations for fair use of others' work (e.g., attribution, author or publisher permissions); a study of persons often requires obtaining informed consent and considerations for ethical researcher-participant interactions.

Do you view the Internet as a space or a place?

As with any research site and research question, Internet researchers bring many (often unexamined) premises to their research. Thus, it can be helpful to map your own and others' perspectives of both the Internet in general and particular Internet venues specifically so as to make more explicit the epistemologies shaping your views. Figure 19.1 presents a heuristic for mapping *views* of research. On the left side of the continuum is the ethical position emphasizing the public/published nature of most observable and/or archived communications on the Internet. That position views Internet-based communications as occurring in public *spaces* (at least on non–password-protected sites) and views Internet research as aligned more with public observation, public archive work, or work with published texts.

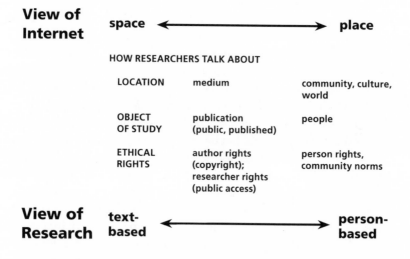

Fig. 19.1. Views of the Internet and views of research. From *The Ethics of Internet Research*, by Heidi A. McKee and James E. Porter. Courtesy of Peter Lang.

On the right-hand side of the continuum in figure 19.1 is the position that views much Internet research as occurring in community *places* where people gather to interact. Thus, this position espouses approaches for person-based research frequently aligned with assumptions of ethnographic and other qualitative research practices and tilting ethical decision making toward the needs, expectations, and wishes of the people whose communications are being studied. We emphasize that figure 19.1

is a heuristic for mapping *views* of research rather than a mapping of individual researchers. With some exceptions, most researchers do not exist exclusively and always in one spot; their views shift and slide depending on the circumstances of specific cases. For example, probably all researchers believe in researcher rights to quote public texts, but the difference would be in how they determine what is "public." When as a researcher are you in a *space* working with public texts, and when are you in a *place* with differing expectations for privacy and use?

What are "public" and "private" online?

Determining what is public and private on the Internet and by whose perspective is difficult, particularly given the wide range of understandings of what constitutes public and private in diverse cultures. In general, in face-to-face research (especially in cultures shaped by Euro-Western traditions), communications in a "public" venue are available for researchers to study provided they are conducting observational research and provided they follow the regulations governing the use of others' intellectual property.[4] So in face-to-face research, studying and quoting placards and banners displayed at a protest march would be acceptable, but hiding an audio recorder underneath a park bench to record conversations without people's knowledge would not be. Yes, the park is public property anyone can use and access, and yes, people should expect that others nearby might overhear their conversations, but because people do not expect their conversations to be recorded, such research practices would be considered unethical. Imagine how you would feel if your heart-to-heart conversation with your partner in a park was recorded, analyzed, and written about? Now move these considerations online. Are posts (be they in text, in still images, in video, or in audio) made to discussion boards, virtual worlds, and social networking sites like placards at a march (completely public and available to be quoted), or are they more like park-bench conversations (somewhat public but carrying expectations of privacy)?

One perspective is that if the writing is online and it can be accessed by anyone with an Internet connection, then it is published and public—end of discussion. For example, Heather Kitchin in "The Tri-Council on Cyberspace" argues that it is perfectly acceptable to collect publicly available writings on the Internet, such as she did from *alt.recovery.AA*, a newsgroup for recovering alcoholics. As she explains more extensively in *Research Ethics and the Internet*, people who post information on the Internet should know that it is public, just the way that people speaking on the radio or television know their information is public.[5]

But, we ask, are all writings on the Internet really like broadcast media? Did the discussants in the newsgroups in the 1980s and early 1990s, for example, envision the powerful search engine capabilities of Google and the like making their posts easily traceable? Do Internet users today feel that their communications are truly public?

With questions like these in mind, a more nuanced perspective on the question of what are public online and private online has been articulated by many researchers.[6] This perspective argues that researchers need to consider online users' expectations of privacy when making decisions about what are public and private online.

When describing their decisions when researching the multifaceted website of *Gaygirls.com*, E. H. Bassett and Kathleen O'Riordan also argue for taking users' expectations into account:

> Although clearly in the public domain, the participants' use of this section [on the Gaygirls.com website] indicated that they perceived it as a semi-private space. They used confessional postings and stratified their audiences by discussing 'other' audiences to whom they would not communicate this information, thus implying that they had specific assumptions about who would use the web site. [. . .] There was an illusory sense of partial privacy because the participants constructed utterances that they stated they would not convey to certain audiences such as their family.

That the privacy felt online may be illusory is at the heart of the matter. James M. Hudson and Amy Bruckman conducted a study of users' expectations in chat rooms, finding out that the majority of people do not want their communications researched, a finding that Shing-Ling Sarina Chen, G. Jon Hall, and Mark D. Johns also discovered when conducting surveys of discussion administrators for online venues. So there's the rub. People post in forums, send text messages, join virtual worlds, and participate in various other social networks, thinking they are communicating in some sort of private space. They may be lulled into thinking that their online writings are, as communications researcher Radhika Gajjala explains, like "conversations in a friend's living room, where their privacy could not be invaded by unwanted researchers" (24). Given that people writing online have these expectations of privacy, but their writings are not *actually* private, should a researcher then respect that expectation of privacy even if it is illusory?

We argue, as do Janne C. H. Bromseth, Gajjala, and others, that considerations of participants' perspectives are central to the process of decision making about this issue. Simply because online writing is publicly accessible does not mean that it is *published* or even *public* for that matter. Published and public are not the same thing on the Internet (or anywhere). Because there are different cultural and community norms and expectations for public and private on the Internet, researchers need to assess, to the best of their ability, what those expectations are through discussion with colleagues and fellow researchers, through careful analysis of the online venue and comparative analysis with other studies, and, if possible, through interaction with participants or through deep immersion in the places and spaces to be studied.

Is informed consent necessary?

In addition to assessing the public/private nature of online venues, researchers need to consider a wide range of variables, including whether informed consent is needed to study and quote online writings.

In general, if online data (whether it is considered text or conversation) is deemed to be public, then no consent is needed to study and quote from the material (although copyright permissions may be needed). If online data is deemed to be private (in some sense of the word), then informed consent may be needed. But there are many other variables that affect issues of informed consent as well, including how identifiable the data is that is reported, the degree of interaction among the researcher and potential research participants, the sensitivity of the topics discussed online, and the vulnerability of the person/authors composing the materials.[7]

What is the degree of interaction of researcher with online participants?

Interaction is one of the determinants used in the United States by institutional review boards (IRBs) to determine if someone is conducting person-based or text-based research (U.S. Department of Health and Human Services). In general, the greater the degree of interaction, the greater the likelihood of needing informed consent. Different levels of interaction bring different ethical issues to the fore. In her multiyear study of the massively multiplayer online game *Lineage*, Constance Steinkuehler had a variety of interactions with participants:

> So everyone in my guild knew I was a researcher, but not everyone in my guild was a [research] participant. I had core participants that I talked with on the phone a lot that I interviewed both formally and informally. I did a lot of interaction with, not all of which was reported as data. Those were my core informants.

Then I had participants who were people that I interviewed who I might talk to maybe only once, and I interviewed them in game. And all those people I got permission from.

And on top of that I had people who posted to forums or people who are in the background of interactions, and what do you do with those people? [. . .] So there was a lot of variation in who I considered participants and needed consent from and who I considered—and I was about to say background noise, but they're not noise—more part of the environment, maybe. Not full blown participants.

Figure 19.2 shows varying types and levels of researcher interaction with participants. Of course, there are exceptions to the correspondences shown in the figure, but in general, the higher the level of interaction between researcher and participant/s, the greater likelihood that informed consent is needed.

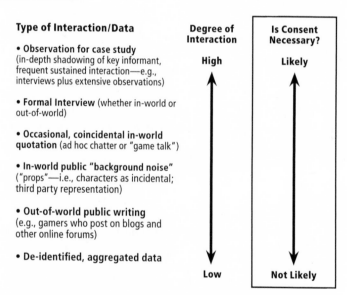

Fig. 19.2. Levels of interaction/data collection and informed consent. From *The Ethics of Internet Research*, by Heidi A. McKee and James E. Porter. Courtesy of Peter Lang.

What is the sensitivity of material being studied?

Some information online is more sensitive than other information, and researchers need to be aware of the potential risks of public exposure. The risks may range from fairly mild embarrassment to more serious consequences from family members, employers, or even governments.

Maybe "Allen" is just one of millions of blog writers online, but when his blog is quoted in research, he now has attention brought to him in a way that would otherwise not happen. And it is not just individuals who can be called out—entire communities can be as well with potentially negative consequences.

For example, in a report for the American Psychological Association, Robert Kraut, Judith Olson, Mahzarin Banaji, Amy Bruckman, Jeffrey Cohen, and Mick Couper note:

> Research may damage communication and community in these forums. [Susan] King (1996) quotes a member of an online support group who wrote to the list that she was not going to participate actively because of a researcher's presence in the group. "When I joined this I thought it would be a *support* group, not a fishbowl for a bunch of guinea pigs. I certainly don't feel at this point that it is a 'safe' environment, as a support group is supposed to be, and I will not open myself up to be dissected by students and scientists. I'm sure I'm not the only person who feels this way." [. . .] When conducting cost-benefit analysis, investigator and IRB alike must anticipate these subtle consequences of their decisions. (15)

For Internet researchers, it is particularly important not to think solely individualistically but also collectively because often as a result of conducting and publishing research, the nature of an online community can be changed, either through the researcher's interactions with participants or through the effect of publicizing the site. Even though an individual may not have his or her posts researched directly, the presence or potential presence of a researcher could have a chilling effect on a community, particularly because of the traceability of online information.

Unless information is reported in aggregate or de-identified (without quotation even), it is completely and easily traceable. This creates a greater potential risk for participants, as David Clark explained in an interview with us:

> People don't seem to take the risks of online research very seriously, and I don't know why that is. [. . .] There's actually more overt risk because with online information I can track down these people. For example, I was reviewing an article for a journal, and it was about breast cancer support groups online, and I was able to pull up full contact information for these people. And I find it astonishing that someone would argue that that's not important. Even if it's something that seems as harmless as Linux [the software discussed by

the online community Clark studied], but who knows? I mean who knows? I don't know what people's priorities are.

What constitutes sensitive information varies widely, thus, just as with considerations of public and private, researchers need to consider issues of sensitivity from the contexts and perspectives of the persons whose online writing they are studying, especially when working with especially vulnerable populations.

What is the vulnerability of the persons/authors being studied?

A number of factors may make individuals who write and communicate online more vulnerable to risks from Internet researchers. Studies have shown that children and teenagers often post a great deal more personal information online because they think that their writing is private simply if their parents cannot read it (Lenhart, Smith, and Macgill; Stern). Researchers whose work focuses on children and youth may need to be more careful and selective about what information they choose to report.

Participants online may also be more vulnerable because of their technical knowledge. For example, if we were conducting a study in the virtual world *Second Life*, we may take into consideration the greater vulnerability of new users to the environment and report data differently when collected at Orientation Island (the default location where all new users first enter the world) versus some other location in *Second Life*. At Orientation Island, newbies are still trying to figure out how to move and communicate in-world and probably have not gotten to the level of technical familiarity to control what information they display to whom.

Participants online may also be more vulnerable because of workplace regulations or national (and international) laws that impact what they may and may not say and do on the Internet. A researcher studying discussion forums for lesbian, gay, bisexual, and transsexual (LGBT) persons, for example, needs to consider issues of censorship and legal and social risks for potentially outing any person who posts to such a forum, an example taking on greater urgency, as some countries have extreme penalties for homosexuality.

A Heuristic for Mapping Research and Assisting Decision Making

So far, we have provided a lot of issues for researchers to consider. Rather than making the process easier, it probably feels like we have made researching online a whole lot harder. What we hope to do now is clarify, but not simplify, the process by providing one example of a visual heuristic useful for researchers as they seek to make ethical decisions throughout the research process.[8]

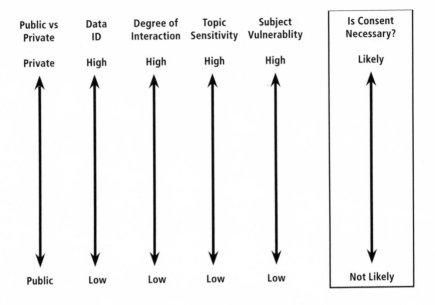

Fig. 19.3. A heuristic for mapping research questions and cases.

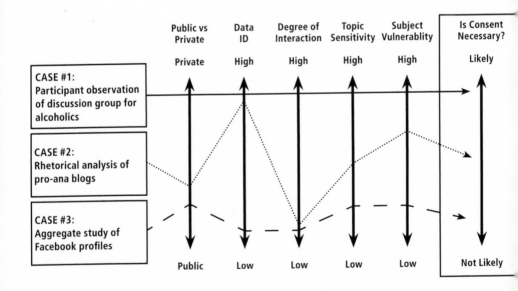

Fig. 19.4. A sample map of research cases.

Figure 19.3 sets the heuristic to address one of the main questions we have focused on in this chapter: Is consent needed from the online writers to quote and study their posts? By mapping specific cases on this grid, as we have done in figure 19.4, researchers (and the readers of research) can consider various factors about a specific case and, important, can conduct a comparative analysis of cases.

Case 1 is a clear paradigm case—a researcher is conducting a participant observation in an online discussion forum for alcoholics that although publicly accessible carries a high degree of privacy expectations, people share information in this forum that they would not be comfortable having others know. The data identification is high because the researcher intends to use direct quotes in write-ups that are traceable with search engines. The topic sensitivity is high—individuals' struggles with alcoholism; the degree of interaction (participant-observation) is high; and the vulnerability of participants is high. Thus, consent is needed so individuals can decide if they wish to have their online posts quoted for others in a broader public to read.

Case 3 is also a clear paradigm case—a researcher studying public profiles on Facebook and reporting data online in aggregate. That is, reporting such things as, of the 200 profiles examined, 146 included a personal photo, and 178 included a birthdate. Case 3 would move to the area of a problematic case if the method of reporting were to change. What if instead of completely de-identified data, researchers conducting this study reported specific, more identifiable information about individuals, including screenshots of profile pages, specific URLs, and the fact that "Sarah" was born in Texas, is 5'6", loves chocolate, attends Texas Tech, and just broke-up with her boyfriend? Such specificity in reporting may change the considerations of whether informed consent is needed, moving case 3 to the problematic realm.

Case 2 is a problematic case, one in which the determination of whether informed consent is needed or not is not as clear. In this rhetorical analysis of pro-anorexia (pro-ana) bloggers, the researcher is reading posts but not interacting in other ways such as by posting comments. In her reading of the posts, she feels that the blogs are primarily public—the individuals are actively seeking broader readership to spread their message. The sensitivity of the topic is fairly high, and the researcher does plan to use direct quotations from the blogs that are easily traceable via search engines. The bloggers' vulnerability is potentially high, particularly because many are teenagers. Some of the factors here would lean toward informed consent not being likely, but others point toward its likelihood, hence this being a problematic case—one that a researcher would need to weigh carefully, consulting with multiple audiences and comparing to other studies of similar contexts.

The flexibility of this heuristic for addressing a wide variety of cases, issues, and questions will be, we hope, useful for Internet researchers, especially writing researchers as they address the challenges of researching online.

Recommendations and Ramifications

In closing, we offer some recommendations for researchers to consider. When preparing to do an Internet research project, and throughout the project, writing researchers should take care to:

- Articulate and critically examine your own and others' perspectives, including disciplinary perspectives, of the Internet as a space versus place.

- Be deeply suspicious of blanket pronouncements such as "If it's public, you may quote it" or "You must always seek consent." The Internet is vastly complex and differentiated. A blog is not a blog is not a blog, and specific circumstances matter.

- Consult with multiple audiences on the important ethical questions in your study.

- Immerse yourself in the specifics of the research context, seeking to understand the expectations and community norms of the online venues from which you seek to collect data.

- Identify and consider various regulations and laws, including issues of intellectual property, and how they may impact the research, the researcher, and the persons and communications/experiences being studied.

- Except where deception is a key part of the study (with debriefing planned), be as transparent and as open about your role as a researcher as possible when studying online communities.

- Be explicit in your research write-up about the ethical issues and decisions you have made.

It is essential that researchers move ethical considerations to the fore in their work because our actions as researchers carry a number of ramifications—for individuals and communities online (as we have focused on here) but also for researchers and research. As the virtual-world researcher Aleks Krotoski explained about her research in *Second Life*:

> From a personal perspective, I didn't want to hurt anybody. I didn't want to muck around with what I consider an important and exciting medium—i.e., the Internet, virtual communities—so I wanted to both maintain my own reputation in that community and also in some ways also maintain a positive working environment so that other researchers in the future could work with virtual communities.

Krotoski's point about the Internet is an important one. The Internet is still so young and in such early stages of development (think film in the 1920s) that our actions as researchers throughout the research process can certainly impact the Internet and how people use it, particularly because the landscape of the Internet is still very much in flux. We are constantly seeing new applications, and new uses emerge that raise new ethical issues that researchers face when studying writers and writing online. As the Internet continues to grow and morph, as new applications emerge that enable new forms of interaction, there will be, inevitably, new ethical issues of the sort that we have not addressed and that we can only dimly imagine at this point. And so what we need as researchers studying writing and writers online is not so much clear-cut *guidelines* but rather clear-cut *processes* that are productive in the real and ever-changing circumstances in which we find ourselves. Ten years from now, who knows what people will be doing online, what communications and media they will be sharing, what sorts of technologies they will be using, and what sorts of interactions they will be having. Amid the ever-changing nature of the Internet (and thus of the writing and writers we study), what is important is having a flexible *process* for ethical decision making, one that can be adapted for the new technologies and new interactions that will eventually emerge.

Notes

1. Although we focus primarily on the World Wide Web, we use the phrase *Internet research* rather than *web research* because Internet research is an interdisciplinary term and field of studies (see the Association of Internet Researchers, for example). Despite the singularity of the term *Internet*, it is important to remember that the Internet is not one entity—there are innumerable Internet tools, texts, and communities to be studied, each raising specific contextual, methodological, and ethical issues for researchers.

2. Our research is based both on published accounts and on interviews with thirty Internet researchers from eleven different countries who work in a variety of disciplines and with a variety of methodologies. Our book *The Ethics of Internet Research: A Rhetorical, Case-Based Process* (2009) provides the most detailed presentation of our work (see also McKee and Porter, "Ethics of Digital Writing Research"; McKee and Porter, "Playing a Good Game").

3. For discussions of Internet research ethics by other writing-studies scholars, see Banks and Eble; Clark; Gurak and Duin; Gurak and Silker; and Sapienza.

4. See McKee and Porter, *Ethics of Internet Research*, chap. 3.

5. See also Denzin; Herring; Walther.

6. See Bromseth, "Ethical and Methodological" and *Genre Trouble*; Bruckman; Buchanan; Elm; Ess; Gajjala.

7. We emphasize that in many contexts, researchers do not, ultimately, have the authority to decide if informed consent is needed because that decision is made by an ethics review board, such as institutional review boards in the United States. Unless a researcher is studying a clear paradigm venue for public, published texts (e.g., studying online magazine articles or government websites), we recommend that all researchers conducting Internet-based studies check with their local review boards prior to commencing research.

8. See McKee and Porter, *Ethics of Internet Research*, for more visual heuristics, as well as discussion of many other issues, including the intersections of legal and ethical issues, cultural differences, representation, and publication.

Works Cited

Banks, Will, and Michelle Eble. "Digital Spaces, Online Environments, and Human Participant Research: Interfacing with Institutional Review Boards." McKee and DeVoss, *Digital Writing Research* 27–47.

Bassett, E. H., and Kathleen O'Riordan. "Ethics of Internet Research: Contesting the Human Subjects Research Model." *Internet Research Ethics*. 2002. Web. 26 Feb. 2012. <http://www.nyu.edu/projects/nissenbaum/ethics_bassett.html>.

Bromseth, Janne C. H. "Ethical and Methodological Challenges in Research on Net-Mediated Communication in a Norwegian Research Context." Thorseth, *Applied Ethics in Internet Research* 67–85.

———. "Genre Trouble and the Body That Mattered: Negotiations of Gender, Sexuality and Identity in a Scandinavian Mailing List Community for Lesbian and Bisexual Women." Diss. Norwegian U of Science and Technology. *Norwegian University of Science and Technology.* 2006. Web. 26 Feb. 2012. <http://ntnu.diva-portal.org/smash/record.jsf?pid=diva2:122317>.

Bruckman, Amy. "Studying the Amateur Artist: A Perspective on Disguising Data Collected in Human Subjects Research on the Internet." *Internet Research Ethics*. 2002. Web. 26 Feb. 2012. <http://www.nyu.edu/projects/nissenbaum/ethics_bruckman.html>.

Buchanan, Elizabeth A., ed. *Readings in Virtual Research Ethics: Issues and Controversies*. Hershey: Information Science, 2004. Print.

Chen, Shing-Ling Sarina, G. Jon Hall, and Mark D. Johns. "Research Paparazzi in Cyberspace: The Voices of the Researched." Johns, Hall, and Chen, *Online Social Research* 157–72.

Clark, David. Personal interview. 23 Mar. 2006.

——. "What If You Meet Face to Face? A Case Study in Virtual/Material Research Ethics." Buchanan, *Readings in Virtual Research Ethics* 246–61.

Denzin, Norman K. "Cybertalk and the Method of Instances." Jones, *Doing Internet Research* 107–25.

Elm, Malin Sveningsson. "How Do Various Notions of Privacy Influence Decisions in Qualitative Internet Research?" Markham and Baym, *Internet Inquiry* 69–87.

Ess, Charles, ed. "Introduction: Internet Research Ethics." *Internet Research Ethics.* 2002. Web. 26 Feb. 2012. <http://www.nyu.edu/projects/nissenbaum/ethics_ess. html>.

Gajjala, Radhika. *Cyberselves: Feminist Ethnographies of South Asian Women.* New York: Altamira, 2004. Print.

Gurak, Laura J., and Ann Hill Duin. "The Impact of the Internet and Digital Technologies on Teaching and Research in Technical Communication." *Technical Communication Quarterly* 13 (2004): 187–98. Print.

Gurak, Laura J., and Christine M. Silker. "Technical Communication Research in Cyberspace." *Research in Technical Communication.* Ed. Gurak and Mary M. Lay. Westport: Praeger, 2002. 229–48. Print.

Herring, Susan. "Linguistic and Critical Analysis of Computer-Mediated Communication: Some Ethical and Scholarly Considerations." *Information Society* 12 (1996): 153–68. Print.

Hudson, James M., and Amy Bruckman. "'Go Away': Participant Objections to Being Studied and the Ethics of Chatroom Research." *Information Society* 20 (2004): 127–39. Print.

Johns, Mark D., G. Jon Hall, and Shing-Ling Chen, eds. *Online Social Research: Methods, Issues, and Ethics.* New York: Lang, 2004. Print.

Jones, Steve, ed. *Doing Internet Research: Critical Issues and Methods for Examining the Net.* Thousand Oaks: Sage, 1999. Print.

Kitchin, Heather A. *Research Ethics and the Internet: Negotiating Canada's Tri-Council Policy Statement.* Black Point: Fernwood, 2007. Print.

——. "The Tri-Council on Cyberspace: Insights, Oversights, and Extrapolations." van den Hoonard, *Walking the Tightrope* 160–74.

Kraut, Robert, Judith Olson, Mahzarin Banaji, Amy Bruckman, Jeffrey Cohen, and Mick Couper. "Psychological Research Online: Opportunities and Challenges." *American Psychological Association.* 30 Sept. 2003. Web. 26 Feb. 2012. <http:// www.apa.org/science/apainternetresearch.pdf>.

Krotoski, Aleks. Skype interview. 23 Oct. 2006.

Lenhart, Amanda, Aaron Smith, and Alexandra Rankin Macgill. "Writing, Technology and Teens: A Pew Research Center Report." *Pew Research Center.* 24 Apr. 2008. Web. 26 Feb. 2012. <http://pewresearch.org/pubs/808/writing-technology-and-teens>.

Markham, Annette N., and Nancy Baym, eds. *Internet Inquiry: Conversations about Method.* Thousand Oaks: Sage, 2009. Print.

McKee, Heidi A., and Dànielle Nicole DeVoss, eds. *Digital Writing Research: Technologies, Methodologies, and Ethical Issues.* Cresskill: Hampton, 2007. Print.

McKee, Heidi A., and James E. Porter. "The Ethics of Digital Writing Research: A Rhetorical Approach." *College Composition and Communication* 59.4 (2008): 711–49. Print.

———. *The Ethics of Internet Research: A Rhetorical, Case-Based Process.* New York: Lang, 2009. Print.

———. "Playing a Good Game: Ethical Issues in Researching MMOGs and Virtual Worlds." *International Journal of Internet Research Ethics* 2.1. 2009. Web. 26 Feb. 2012. <http://ijire.net/issue_2.1/mckee.pdf>.

Sapienza, Filipp. "Ethos and Research Positionality in Studies of Virtual Communities." McKee and DeVoss, *Digital Writing Research* 89–106.

Schrag, Zachary M. "Institutional Review Blog." *Institutional Review Blog.* 2012. Web. 26 Feb. 2012. <http://www.institutionalreviewblog.com>.

Steinkuehler, Constance. Telephone interview. 19 July 2007.

Stern, Susannah R. "Studying Adolescents Online: A Consideration of Ethical Issues. Buchanan, *Readings in Virtual Research Ethics* 274–87.

Thorseth, May, ed. *Applied Ethics in Internet Research.* Trondheim: NTNU UP, 2003. Print.

U.S. Department of Health and Human Services. "Code of Federal Regulations, Title 45 Public Welfare, Part 46, Protection of Human Subjects (45 CFR 46)." *U.S. Department of Health and Human Services.* 23 June 2005. Web. 26 Feb. 2012. <http://www.hhs.gov/ohrp/humansubjects/guidance/45cfr46.html>.

van den Hoonard, Will C., ed. *Walking the Tightrope: Ethical Issues for Qualitative Researchers.* Toronto: U of Toronto P, 2002. Print.

Walther, Joseph B. "Research Ethics in Internet-Enabled Research: Human Subjects Issues and Methodological Myopia." *Internet Research Ethics.* 2002. Web. 26 Feb. 2012. <http://www.nyu.edu/projects/nissenbaum/ethics_walther.html>.

After Words: Postmethodological Musings

Rebecca J. Rickly

The preceding chapters have all addressed pragmatics, problems, and possibilities in writing research and practice. Although these chapters are all very different, they nonetheless enter into the ongoing conversation about research and writing studies. Given the title of the book—*Writing Studies Research in Practice: Methods and Methodologies*—I would like to go beyond a "recap" of what has gone before and suggest how the chapters in this book, folded in with my own experience and research, enter into what I hope is a continuing, vital conversation about what directions writing research studies might be taking in the near future.

In my own journey as a writing researcher, I can recall several significant texts that influenced my emerging understanding of and conversation with research in writing. These texts became channels for information exchange, creating thoroughfares of ideas in our field. I postulate that the reception of this book will be similar to one such text, the edited collection that inspired it: *Methods and Methodology in Composition Research*, edited by Patricia A. Sullivan and Gesa E. Kirsch. This book challenged what I and others in composition and rhetoric had come to know as "rigid," formalized, lock-step methods and gave me a more nuanced understanding (and just as important, language) to articulate what I was doing in my own research. In addition, the chapters encouraged me to reflect on who I was as a researcher, why I chose a particular stance, and what my relationship was to that which (and those whom) I researched.

Starting with Sandra Harding's fundamental distinctions between method ("technique for [or way of proceeding in] gathering of evidence"), methodology ("a theory and analysis of how research does or should proceed"), and epistemology (a theory of knowledge that answers questions about "who can be a 'knower' . . . , what tests beliefs must pass in order to be legitimated knowledge . . . , what kinds of things can be knowledge . . . , and so forth") (3), I was able to see how the methods I chose to answer specific questions were influenced not only by the discipline in which they had originated but also by my underlying epistemological grounding. In addition, this edited collection allowed for—in fact, demanded—the sort of reflection on how we conducted and analyzed research that would later lead to groundbreaking works like Peter Mortensen and Gesa E. Kirsch's *Ethics and Representation in Qualitative Studies of Literacy*, James E. Porter and Patricia Sullivan's *Opening Spaces*, Cindy Johanek's *Composing Research*, and Dànielle Nicole DeVoss and Heidi A. McKee's *Digital Writing Research*. Just as important, the collection led to a productive conversation that went beyond the "us/them" splits of qualitative versus quantitative, encouraging us to use productive tensions to create new and substantial revisions of how we learn, apply, analyze, and represent research in our field.

Like *Methods and Methodologies*, this edited collection brings new and renewed topics to this conversation, providing dialogic fodder for students, writers, researchers, and those who teach. Here are some of the issues I envision springing from this text as we journey (trek?) in our new directions.

New (and "Messy") Contexts/New (and "Messy") Methods

The contexts and problems involved in researching writing are becoming exceedingly multifaceted, wrought with involved (and often tacit) practices, and diverse populations, situated in integrated and varied contexts. How can we possibly conduct meaningful, systematic research in such scenarios? In *After Method: Mess in Social Science Research*, sociologist John Law maintains that "methods, their rules, and even more methods' practices, not only describe but also help to *produce* the reality that they understand" (5). Does this mean that "traditional" methods will produce oversimplified results? Perhaps they will, particularly if we choose to apply them rigidly, not taking into account the complexity of the situation or problem. If the context or problem we wish to understand is "complex, diffuse, and messy," Law asserts, then we need to "find ways of knowing the indistinct and the slippery without trying to grasp and hold them tight" (2, 3). In other words, we need to situate our methods (and our application/analysis) so that they help us understand more complicated research scenarios and questions. This may mean we need to go beyond a traditional understanding of methods/methodologies, to (as Law asserts) "teach ourselves to think, to practice, to relate, and to know in new ways" (2). "Messy" contexts include new technologies (such as instant messaging that Christina Haas, Pamela Takayoshi, and Brandon Carr discuss in the current collection), administrative sites (such as the ones Douglas Hesse and Steve Lamos discuss), reenvisioned archival research (such as Liz Rohan describes), communities and workplaces (such as Mike Palmquist, Joan Mullen, and Glenn Blalock portray), and a thousand other situations that involve people and writing.

In "The Importance of Harmony: An Ecological Metaphor for Writing Research," Kris Fleckenstein, Clay Spinuzzi, Carole Clark Papper, and I argue that "an ecological way of researching writing directs the researcher's gaze to relationships, including the researcher's own active involvement in and contribution to a research ecosystem." In seeing the research process as a harmonious ecosystem, we are made aware of the variable nature of our research contexts. Thus, our methods and techniques for researching these contexts must be modified, as well as the precarious positioning of ourselves as researchers, fusing "the knower, the known, and the context of knowing" (395). We need to continue the conversation of what contexts are appropriate for study, how we might suitably modify methods and techniques in our research, and how we, as researchers, affect the sites we inhabit in our research.

As James E. Porter and Heidi A. McKee point out in this volume, though, complicated questions and contexts come with difficult (and often vague) ethical responsibilities. Are technologized transcripts "human subjects"? How anonymous is a student paper stripped of a name or a blog posted under a pseudonym? Can "harm" actually come from quoting an e-mail exchange? We need to continue to complicate these and other difficult questions as we enter new research sites, recognizing that our ethics as well as our methods need to mirror the complexity—the messiness—of these new sites.

Blurring Our Boundaries—and Our Blinders

Clear boundaries, procedures, and definitions are comforting, but they don't allow for the increasing complexity of our contexts. As such, our terminology and our understanding of it must continue to evolve. As Bob Broad argues in this collection, for instance, the terms *quantitative* and *qualitative* are often posed as polar opposites rather than integrated concepts. Simply noting that one privileges numbers and the other words reinforces this perceived dichotomy. Yet, we know that that statistics can be articulated well—or not. And words can be quantified. I would love to see us forget these somewhat superficial distinctions, then, and concentrate on how to answer a research question effectively, given the context, the scope, the population, and the researcher's stance.

Along these lines, too, writing studies research has borrowed from other fields—most notably, social science, education, anthropology, cognitive psychology, and linguistics—yet, we rarely employ texts from other disciplines in our own research or courses. John W. Creswell, a professor of educational psychology, for instance, has several excellent texts on planning, conducting, analyzing, and representing both qualitative and mixed-methods research. Social scientist Law has written articles and books that challenge our understanding of social-science research. Matthew B. Miles and A. Michael Huberman, as well as Norma K. Denizen and Yvonna S. Lincoln, both provide excellent texts on qualitative research and analysis. Both Robert K. Yin and Peter M. Nardi, from cognitive psychology and business, respectively, have authored seminal texts on case study and survey research. Although we have some exceptional research-methods texts in our field, we would do well to triangulate them with outstanding texts in other fields, entering into a productive, engaging dialogue.

We are more secure, too, reading and citing work produced locally and nationally rather than internationally. As Karen J. Lunsford notes in her chapter in the current volume, the twenty-first century brought with it a global economy and increased technology that necessitate an international (and multidisciplinary) perspective in how we conduct research and understand writing. As such, we need to invite more and varied individuals to the burgeoning conversation, and we need to articulate ways to better understand their unique perspectives. Krista Ratcliffe suggests that we learn to "listen rhetorically" to those who do not share our backgrounds, beliefs, and experiences. In the current collection, Asao B. Inoue introduces the concept of racial methodologies to better understand the ways race functions in and is produced by, our research methods, particularly in terms of writing assessment. These disparate voices need to be acknowledged, listened to, and integrated into our understanding and application of research.

We tend to stay within our comfort zone in terms of acceptable fields to borrow from/learn from as well. Jeffrey T. Grabill (this volume) discusses usability and user-centered methods, which spring from computer science and human-computer interaction studies, and we are not nearly as quick to embrace these or other corporate field methods (which, ironically, have borrowed from the same disciplines we have!). I realize this hesitance comes from the corporate/humanist "split," but I wonder if perhaps this apparent dichotomy could be proven to be less of an opposition and more of a productive tension. Spinuzzi, in "Lost in Translation," follows a design technique known as *prototyping* in four different contexts, noting how the context shapes the application and analysis of the technique. He sees the translation of a design technique as parallel to the translation of a research method applied in different contexts, that is, "picked up and renegotiated to meet the goals of stakeholders in a given problem space" (415). Our field discusses the economics of literacy, and we frequently lament the lack of research on "real world" writing. Perhaps we would do well to emulate/borrow some "real world" research techniques, techniques that are translated to meet the needs of the situation, that are not static but dynamic and rhetorical. By applying them rhetorically in our own discipline, we make them our own.

Representation and Rigor

Several of the authors in this volume and in previous texts have discussed key notions of "rigor," and with the renewed focus on applying mixed/borrowed methods and altering them to be appropriate to the research question and contexts, we need to revisit the notion of "rigor." No longer associated with how a method should be applied (often associated with the discipline from which it originated), the concept of rigor must be translated as well, often rhetorically. If research is persuasion (and while I would argue that research is where we gain knowledge, I will also acknowledge that publications stemming from research are the cultural capital of our field), we need to understand how the choice, application, analysis, and representation of research will make a persuasive argument to our intended audiences.

As methods become contextually bound, however, rigor becomes less clear. Creswell suggests the following ways to encourage rigor in qualitative research:

- employing triangulation

- using member-checking

- creating rich, thick description

- clarifying researcher bias

- presenting balanced, negative, or discrepant information

- spending prolonged/systematic time in the research site

- using peer debriefing

- using an external auditor (196–97)

We might add to this list, depending on our context, questions, and methods. For instance, we might include the use of reflective memos in our analysis. We might choose to overlay a computer analysis of text onto a more theoretical analysis. We might choose to incorporate some of the actual discourse/video/and the like into our representation, allowing for new ways to present our findings more in line with the complexity of our sites.

Another way we might approach rigor is by placing more value on replication. By replicating existing research, we know that the design is workable, and we are looking to see how the application in different contexts might influence the outcome. Replication is particularly useful to new/fledgling researchers, as it offers an opportunity to conduct real research without having to worry about isolating a question or choosing an appropriate method or methods. If, in fact, we learn to write at least in part via imitation, why not learn to research in the same way?

Ultimately, I would like to see our field become a little more comfortable with what Law refers to as the "messiness" of research. Too often, we see published neat, clean, easy-looking research results, with no idea that the research behind it was chaotic, unmanageable, and nearly catastrophic! And although not all research could be considered "messy," I nonetheless would like to see us talk more publically about what we learned from failed research attempts and how we came to understand a situation (or even a research method!) better through initial misunderstanding. While, ideally, research should be planned out thoroughly, designed carefully, applied meticulously, analyzed with great detail, and represented appropriately for the venue, we know that the research process is a lot like the writing process. Sometimes it is tangential, muddled, recursive, and takes us in directions we had no idea we were going to end up in. That does not mean we wallow in the mess—at least, not for too long—but instead it means we rethink our plan and continue with renewed focus and care. We need to recognize that sometimes things do not go according to plan, and we need to start approaching the research process like we do the writing process: more reflectively and more holistically and with the understanding that maxims and rules may need to be altered to best answer a research question given specific individuals, problems, and contexts.

Renewed Attention to Preparation of Researchers

Finally, one of the continuing conversations I see us having for quite some time is how to best prepare researchers. Virtually every year, several notable figures point to the lack of quality research in writing studies.

Richard H. Haswell went so far as to suggest that NCTE has declared war on replicable empirical research. What might be the underlying causes of this dearth of quantified scholarship? There are several I might posit: Research takes time to plan, conduct, analyze, and write up. For those in a graduate program or on the tenure clock, time is in short supply, and often research projects go by the wayside while other more time-efficient projects consume all of the possible research time.

Conducting research is like speaking a second language: If you don't use it, you lose it. If we are not continually conducting research, we can get rusty and be less likely to want to "jump in." And if you have never had the time to practice but only read about research, it is unlikely that you will be comfortable foraying out on your own trying it out once you are out of your graduate program.

Face it: Research can be intimidating. In their replication of the "Ma and Pa Kettle Do Research" article, Andrea A. Lunsford and Karen J. Lunsford note that one of the largest stumbling blocks to being able to finish their study was the often confusing and complex process of institutional review boards (IRBs) at various institutions. IRBs can be intimidating, just as the processes (and constraints) associated with various methods and methodologies can be daunting, and if the researcher is not in the midst of a supportive research community, it can be a lonely, disheartening experience . . . enough to discourage just about anyone from conducting research.

What can we do about these obstacles? We need to recognize that research takes time and to try to build it into our graduate curricula and our professional lives. That may mean applications for grants/released time, better funding models, or simply an understanding tenure committee. We also need to make sure that graduate students come to the profession having had hands-on experience planning, conducting, analyzing, and representing research and to encourage them to continue these practices once they graduate.

Ultimately, we need to revisit what is being covered in graduate programs. Several colleagues and I have undertaken a longitudinal research project looking at research-methods course requirements in PhD programs in composition/rhetoric and technical communication/professional writing. We are also looking at the courses themselves to see what kind of readings, assignments, and actual practice students are exposed to. In addition, we are surveying graduate students and new faculty who are three years or less in their first tenure-track job to see what type of research-methods coursework they took as well as how confident they feel they are to plan, conduct, analyze, and represent research.

From this research, we hope to comment on what seems to be working in various programs; we also hope to suggest ways we might better prepare faculty to be confident in their ability to conduct research and to be productive in conducting it. We are finding that many students only read and critique research in coursework, and their first (and often only) hands-on experience is with their dissertation. And while many students express confidence in conducting qualitative inquiry, few students or faculty have experience with or confidence in designing an experiment or a study employing statistics of any kind. We need to do better if we want to produce rhetorically persuasive research, particularly research that is disseminated and valued outside our field.

May we converse and research for a long time to come.

Works Cited

Creswell, John W. *Research Design: Qualitative, Quantitative, and Mixed Methods Approaches.* 3rd ed. Thousand Oaks: Sage, 2009. Print.

Fleckenstein, Kris, Clay Spinuzzi, Carole Clark Papper, and Rebecca Rickly. "The Importance of Harmony: An Ecological Metaphor for Writing Research." *College Composition and Communication* 60.2 (2008): 388–419. Print.

Harding, Sandra. *"Is There a Feminist Method?" Feminism and Methodology.* New York: Oxford UP, 1998. Print.

Haswell, Richard H. "NCTE/CCCC's Recent War on Scholarship." *Written Communication* 22.2 (2005): 198–223. Print.

Kirsch, Gesa E., and Patricia A. Sullivan, eds. *Methods and Methodologies in Composition Research.* Carbondale: Southern Illinois UP, 1992.

Law, John. *After Method: Mess in Social Science Research.* London: Routledge, 2004. Print.

Lunsford, Andrea A., and Karen J. Lunsford. "'Mistakes Are a Part of Life': A National Comparative Study." *College Composition and Communication* 59.4 (2008): 781–806. Print.

Ratcliffe, Krista. *Rhetorical Listening: Identification, Gender, and Whiteness.* Carbondale: Southern Illinois UP, 2005. Print.

Spinuzzi, Clay. "Lost in Translation: Shifting Claims in the Migration of a Research Technique." *Technical Communication Quarterly* 14.4 (2005): 411–46. Print.

Contributors
Index

Contributors

Kristine L. Blair is a professor in and the chair of the English department at Bowling Green State University, where she teaches in the rhetoric and writing doctoral program. Since 2002, she has served as editor of *Computers and Composition Online*, and in 2007, she received the technology innovator award from the Conference on College Composition and Communication's committee on computers and composition. Her most recent project is the coedited *Webbing Cyberfeminist Practice: Communities, Pedagogies, and Social Action* (2008). She currently directs Digital Mirror, a computer camp for girls in grades 6 through 8.

Glenn Blalock is an associate professor of English at Our Lady of the Lake College, Baton Rouge, Louisiana, and directs the new Engaged Learning through Writing initiative. With Rich Haswell, he is the cofounder of CompPile and CompFAQs.

Bob Broad is a professor of English at Illinois State University. He teaches graduate courses in writing assessment, composition pedagogy, and research methods, as well as undergraduate courses in composition, pedagogy, and English studies. Broad wrote *What We Really Value: Beyond Rubrics in Teaching and Assessing Writing* (2003), and his articles and book reviews have appeared in *Research in the Teaching of English, Assessing Writing*, the *Journal of Writing Assessment, Teaching English in the Two-Year College, Works and Days*, and *African American Review*. Broad contributed a chapter to Ericsson and Haswell's collection on computerized writing assessment, *The Machine Scoring of Student Essays: Truth and Consequences* (2006), and he coauthored *Organic Writing Assessment: Dynamic Criteria Mapping in Action* (2009).

A. Suresh Canagarajah is the Erle Sparks Professor and the director of the migration studies project at Pennsylvania State University. He teaches world Englishes, ethnographic methods, and postcolonial studies in the departments of English and applied linguistics. He also has taught at the

University of Jaffna, Sri Lanka, and the City University of New York. His book *Resisting Linguistic Imperialism in English Teaching* (1999) won the Modern Language Association's Mina Shaughnessy Award. His subsequent publication *Geopolitics of Academic Writing* (2002) won the Gary Olson Award for the best book in social and rhetorical theory. His study of world Englishes in composition won the 2007 Braddock Award for the best article in the *College Composition and Communication* journal. He is currently analyzing interview transcripts and survey data from South Asian immigrants in Canada, the United States, and the United Kingdom to consider questions of identity, community, and heritage languages in diaspora communities.

Brandon Carr earned his master's in English literature from the University of Florida and is continuing his graduate studies in comparative literature at the University of Illinois at Urbana-Champaign. His research examines relationships between twentieth-century Russian and French philosophies of language. He writes about Marxism, anthropology, numismatics, and the history of writing.

Jenn Fishman teaches rhetoric and composition at Marquette University, where her abiding interests in performance and pedagogy inform both her historical scholarship and her contemporary writing research, including her work on REx, the Research Exchange Index, and the Stanford Study of Writing. Her scholarship appears in *College Composition and Communication, Composition Forum, Composition Studies*, and *Stories of Mentoring*, and she is guest editor of the inaugural issue of *CCC Online.* Her next projects include a two-year study of writing at Kenyon College and a historical study of the role eighteenth-century British public theater played in the development of modern rhetorical education.

Kristie Fleckenstein is a professor of English at Florida State University, where she teaches undergraduate and graduate courses in rhetorical theory, visual rhetoric, and composition studies. Her research focuses on the intersections of embodiment, imagery, and literacies. She is the author of *Embodied Literacies: Imageword and a Poetics of Teaching* (winner of the 2005 Conference on College Composition and Communication best book award) and of *Vision, Rhetoric, and Social Action in the Composition Classroom* (winner of the 2010 W. Ross Winterowd Award for best book in composition theory). Her current book project examines the impact of photography on nineteenth-century rhetorical practices.

Jeffrey T. Grabill is a professor of rhetoric and professional writing and a codirector of the Writing in Digital Environments (WIDE) Research

Center at Michigan State University. He is interested in the knowledge work of citizens, users, workers, and students within organizational contexts. Grabill has published two books on community literacy and agency, as well as articles in journals such as *College Composition and Communication, Technical Communication Quarterly, Computers and Composition,* and *English Education.*

Christina Haas is a professor of writing studies at the University of Minnesota. Her recent publications include studies of writing in digital spaces, explorations of young people's writing with social media, and analyses of methodologies for the study of writing. She also edits the international research quarterly *Written Communication* and received the 2011 NCTE award for best edited collection in scientific and technical communication for *Written Communication*'s special issue on writing and medicine.

Richard H. Haswell is Haas Professor Emeritus, Texas A&M University–Corpus Christi. He has authored more than twenty quantitative studies of composition. With Janis Haswell, he is coauthor of *Authoring: An Essay for the English Profession on Potentiality and Singularity* (2010) and, with Glenn Blalock, coauthor of *CompPile,* an ongoing and online bibliography of scholarship in rhetoric and composition now in its twelfth year and with over one hundred thousand records.

Gail E. Hawisher is University Distinguished Teacher/Scholar and Professor Emeritus of English at the University of Illinois at Urbana-Champaign, where she is founding director of the Center for Writing Studies and the University of Illinois Writing Project. Her work probes the many connections between literate activity and digital media as reflected in her recent books with Cynthia Selfe: *Literate Lives in the Information Age* (2004), *Gaming Lives in the 21st Century* (2007), and their *Transnational Literate Lives in Digital Times* coauthored with Patrick W. Berry. Along with Selfe, she is founding and executive editor of Computers and Composition Digital Press (CCDP), a new imprint from Utah State University Press.

Douglas Hesse is a professor at and the founding executive director of the writing program at the University of Denver. He is a past chair of Conference on College Composition and Communication, past president of WPA, past editor of *WPA: Writing Program Administration,* and past chair on the MLA Division on Teaching. At Illinois State University, he served as director of the University Honors Program, director of the Center for the Advancement of Teaching, and director of writing. Hesse is a coauthor of four books, most recently *Creating Nonfiction* (with Becky Bradway), and of fifty articles, in journals ranging from *College Composition and Communication* to *JAC,* and of book chapters in the areas of creative nonfiction, writing program administration and research, and rhetoric and narrative.

Asao B. Inoue is an associate professor of rhetoric and composition at California State University, Fresno, where he also is the special assistant to the provost for writing across the curriculum. His areas of research are writing assessment, validity studies, and racism. He has published articles in various edited collections as well as in *Assessing Writing,* the *Journal of Writing Assessment,* and *Composition Forum.* Currently, he is the book review editor for *Composition Studies* and is working on a monograph that theorizes writing assessment as a technology.

Debra Journet is a professor of English at the University of Louisville. Her recent research centers on the use of narrative as a rhetorical and epistemological resource in a variety of venues, including composition studies, digital media, and evolutionary biology. Her work has appeared in such journals as *Written Communication, Journal of Business and Technical Communication, Social Epistemology,* and *Narrative*; a coedited collection of essays, *Narrative Acts: Rhetoric, Race and Identity, Knowledge* was published in 2011.

Gesa E. Kirsch is a professor of English at Bentley University in Waltham, Massachusetts. Her research and teaching interests include feminism and composition, ethics and representation, qualitative research methods, archival research and methodology, and environmental rhetoric. She has authored and edited numerous books, including *Methods and Methodology in Composition Research, Ethical Dilemmas in Feminist Research: The Politics of Location, Interpretation, and Publication,* and *Beyond the Archives: Research as a Lived Process.* Most recently, she coauthored with Jacqueline Jones Royster *Feminist Rhetorical Practices: New Horizons for Rhetoric, Composition, and Literacy Studies.*

Steve Lamos is an assistant professor in the Program for Writing and Rhetoric and in the English department at the University of Colorado Boulder. He has recently published *Interests and Opportunities: Race, Racism, and University Writing Instruction in the Post-Civil Rights Era* (2011), a book examining the influence of racism on the institutional structures and functions of writing programs at predominantly white universities. He has also published work in *College Composition and Communication, College English, Writing Program Administration,* and the *Journal of Basic Writing.*

Karen J. Lunsford is an associate professor of writing at the University of California, Santa Barbara. She is one of the founders of the international Writing Research Across Borders conferences, and she is a coeditor of a forthcoming international research collection, *Advances in Writing Research*. Her articles can be found in *Kairos, Written Communication, Across the Disciplines*, and *College Composition and Communication*.

Heidi A. McKee is an associate professor in the department of English and an affiliate faculty member of the Armstrong Center for Interactive Media Studies at Miami University. Her teaching and research interests include digital literacies, multimodal and digital rhetorics, qualitative research methodologies, and ethical research practices. With Dànielle Nicole De-Voss, she coedited *Digital Writing Research: Technologies, Methodologies, and Ethical Issues* (2007); winner of the Computers and Composition distinguished book award for best book in the field). With DeVoss and Dickie Selfe, she coedited *Technological Ecologies & Sustainability* (2009). With James Porter, she researched and wrote *The Ethics of Internet Research: A Rhetorical, Case-Based Process* (2009). Currently, she and DeVoss are coediting *Digital Writing Assessment and Evaluation*.

Joan Mullin has initiated and directed writing-across-the-curriculum programs/writing centers at the University of Toledo and the University of Texas at Austin and is currently chair of the department of English studies at Illinois State University. Mullin publishes in writing center, WAC, and disciplinary journals across the curriculum. Her coauthored book *ARTiculating: Teaching Writing in a Visual World* initiated her research interest in visual literacy across the curriculum, and her latest coedited book, *Who Owns This Text*, examines disciplinary definitions of ownership and plagiarism and their effect on students. One of her chapters in the collection, "Appropriation, Homage, and Pastiche: Using Artistic Tradition to Reconsider and Redefine Plagiarism," also demonstrates her continued collaborative examination of international approaches to the teaching of writing. She serves on editorial boards and committees nationally and internationally and as a consultant evaluator for the Council of Writing Program Administrators.

Lee Nickoson is an associate professor of English and a member of the Rhetoric and Writing Program faculty at Bowling Green State University. Her work appears in *Teaching Audience: Theory and Practice, Practice in Context: Situating the Work of Writing Teachers, Computers & Composition*, and *Composition Studies*. Nickoson is also a coeditor of *Feminism and Composition: A Critical Sourcebook*. Her research interests include writing assessment, composition pedagogy, and feminist approaches to the study and teaching of writing.

Mike Palmquist is the associate vice provost for learning and teaching, a professor of English, and a University Distinguished Teaching Scholar at

Colorado State University, where he directs the university's Institute for Learning and Teaching. His scholarly interests include writing across the curriculum, the effects of computer and network technologies on writing instruction, and new approaches to scholarly publishing. His work has appeared in journals including *College English, Computers and Composition, Written Communication, Writing Program Administration, IEEE Transactions on Professional Communication, Kairos,* and *Social Forces,* as well as in edited collections. He is the author or coauthor of five books, including *Transitions: Teaching Writing in Computer-Supported and Traditional Classrooms* (coauthored with Kate Kiefer, Jake Hartvigsen, and Barbara Godlew) and the textbooks *The Bedford Researcher* and *Joining the Conversation.*

James E. Porter is a professor in English and in the Armstrong Institute for Interactive Media Studies at Miami University. He has published widely on rhetoric theory, digital media, research methodology and ethics, and business/technical communication. His books include *Audience and Rhetoric* (1992); *Opening Spaces: Writing Technologies and Critical Research Practices,* with Patricia Sullivan (1997), which won the NCTE award for best book in technical and scientific communication; *Rhetorical Ethics and Internetworked Writing* (1998), which won the Computers and Composition Award for distinguished book; and *The Ethics of Internet Research,* with Heidi A. McKee (2009).

Rebecca J. Rickly is an associate professor at Texas Tech University, where she teaches undergraduate and graduate courses in rhetoric, research, and writing. Her work revolves around rhetoric but includes such diverse applications as technology, feminisms, methods and methodologies, literacy study, and administration. She has served on the Conference on College Composition and Communication committee on research, computers, and composition and on NCTE's assembly on computers in English, and she has chaired NCTE's instructional technology committee. Her publications include *The Online Writing Classroom* (with Susanmarie Harrington and Michael Day) and *Performing Feminist Administration* (with Krista Ratcliffe), and her work has appeared in several edited collections, as well as *College Composition and Communication, Computers and Composition, CMC Magazine,* the *ACE Journal,* and *Kairos.*

Liz Rohan is an associate professor of composition and rhetoric at the University of Michigan–Dearborn. She has published several articles in journals such as *Rhetoric Review, Pedagogy,* and *Composition Studies.* Most recently, she coedited (with Gesa E. Kirsch) a collection of essays about researchers and writers who use archives, *Beyond the Archives: Research as a Lived Process.*

Cynthia L. Selfe is Humanities Distinguished Professor in the Department of English at the Ohio State University. With Gail E. Hawisher, she was coeditor of *Computers and Composition: An International Journal* through 2011, and she is the cofounder and executive editor of Computers and Composition Digital Press. In 1996, Selfe was recognized as an EDUCOM Medal award winner for innovative computer use in higher education— the first woman and the first English teacher ever to receive this award. Selfe has served as the chair of the Conference on College Composition and Communication and the chair of the college section of the National Council of Teachers of English.

Mary P. Sheridan is a professor of English at the University of Louisville, where she teaches classes at the intersection of community literacy, digital media, and gender. She has published in a variety of journals and edited collections, and her recent books include *Production Literacies: Learning and Innovation in the Digital Media Age* (2010, with Jennifer Rowsell) and *Girls, Feminism, and Grassroots Literacies: Activism in the GirlZone* (2008), winner of the civic scholarship award from *Reflections* and of the Winifred Bryan Horner outstanding book award from the Coalition of Women Scholars in Rhetoric and Composition.

Pamela Takayoshi is an associate professor in the Department of English at Kent State University. Her work has appeared in *College Composition and Communication, Computers and Composition, Research in the Teaching of English,* and numerous edited collections. With Katrina Powell, she recently coedited *Practicing Research in Writing Studies: Reflexive and Ethically Responsible Research.*

Index